Just Cruising

Duncan, Colin, Jamie, Liza and Andy

Just Cruising

Europe to Australia

by
Liza Copeland

1993
Romany Enterprises

Canadian Cataloguing in Publication Data

Copeland, Liza, 1946-
  Just Cruising

ISBN 0-9697690-0-8

  1. Copeland, Liza, 1946- —Journeys. 2.
Bagheera (Yacht). 3. Voyages around the world—
1981- 4.Yachts and yachting. 5. Children—
Travel. 1. Title
G440.C664A3 1993   910.4'1   C93-091891-6

Romany Enterprises
3943 W. Broadway
Vancouver, B.C.
CANADA V6R 2C2
Tel: (604) 228-8712
Fax: (604) 685-2272

Typeset by Vancouver Desktop Publishing Centre, Vancouver, BC
Printed in Canada by Hignell Printing Ltd., Winnipeg, Manitoba

To
Andy, Duncan, Colin and Jamie
my family and wonderful cruising companions

Contents

MAPS

AUTHOR'S NOTE

Metric measurements have been used throughout this book with the following exceptions:

Yacht lengths are in feet as this is common practice.
   3.28 feet = 1 metre

Distances at sea are measured in nautical miles.
   1 nautical mile = 1.85 kilometres = (1.15 statute miles)

This unit has been used traditionally for ease of navigation, because:
   1 minute of latitude = 1 nautical mile,
   1 degree of latitude = 60 nautical miles.

A knot = one nautical mile per hour.

Weights of fish are generally discussed in pounds (and it certainly sounds more impressive!)
   2.2 pounds = 1 kilogram

It might be useful for you to know also that:
   4.55 litres = 1 imperial gallon
   3.78 litres = 1 us gallon

All **prices** are quoted in us dollars

Acknowledgements

My gratitude goes to my friends, both in Vancouver and around the world, who have been so encouraging and supportive.

Special thanks go to Nancy Garrett, my widely travelled next door neighbour, for her unwavering enthusiasm and suggestions, to Trevor Jenkins and Richard Beattie who also spent many hours critiquing my manuscript, to Jane Denison for her recommendations and computer skills, to June Mauthe for her organisational consistency and to Hugh Garling for lending me several useful books.

My stepdaughter Alison Kinsey has my appreciation for her help in choosing the photographs, also Lisa Roote, Carl Schumacher, Des Kearns and Dave Seller for their contributions of photos. I am most grateful to Lewis Perinbam and Dave Miller for their generous words.

Thanks go also to my proof readers Brenda de Roos, Caroline Baker, Pam White, Jean Lee, Mik Madsen, D'Ann Madsen, Chris Hunt, Lesley Christi, Liz Campbell, Althea Rasmussen, Bev Kolsen and Graham Kedgley, for their time and diligence.

In particular I would like to thank my children Duncan, Colin and Jamie for not only being wonderfully stimulating cruising companions, but for helping to refresh my memory and being so tolerant during my long hours at the computer. Finally my heartfelt thanks go to my husband Andy, not only for his diligent editing but also for his competence in coping with any situation that arose during our travels, and for his determination to keep moving!

Foreword

When I think of Liza and Andy I think immediately of the water and the fact that sailing has been so much a part of their lives. I met them for the first time in the mid-70s, racing on Vancouver's English Bay, and found them to be formidable competitors both in their *Bagheera* series of racer/cruisers and later in the Dragon one-design class. Between the two of them they have been involved over the years in just about every facet of the marine field including building a boat yard, operating a chandlery store, running charter yachts, organising group charters and building up a successful yacht brokerage company. The pleasure they derive from just being on the water is self-evident from their ongoing enthusiasm for sailing and the energy they put into beating the competition!

Liza and Andy are the epitome of all-round sailors but almost more important is their zest for life. I don't know two people who try to squeeze more out of a day, whether it's hosting a great party for all their many friends or fulfilling the desire to explore new horizons. By combining their considerable sailing skills with a thirst for adventure, the Copelands have succeeded in doing what most of us just dream about: completing an incredible voyage of discovery lasting six years and covering over 50,000 sea miles.

The culmination of their adventures is the sharing of this odyssey with those of you unable to set sail on your own circumnavigation. So sit back and let Liza take you with her family on a magical journey of exploration, with her very competent hands at the helm.

Dave Miller
Olympic Bronze Medallist 1972 – Soling Class
Manager, North Sails Vancouver

Bagheera

Prologue

As our lives become increasingly frenetic in this modern technological world, many of us look for ways of escape. Our dream was of sailing across tropical oceans and of visiting exotic lands. For years this wish lay dormant; realization was beyond our reach.

This is how our dream not only came true but also far exceeded our expectations. In all we sailed for six years, completed a circumnavigation and visited a total of eighty-two countries and colonies.

Just Cruising is about the first half of our trip: of our preparations before leaving England, exploring modern and ancient cultures in the Mediterranean, crossing the Atlantic in a race with two hundred others, and of vibrant Caribbean Islands, Venezuela and Panama. It tells about personal experiences with the wildlife of Galapagos, trips to remote archipelagos in the South Pacific, and of being a very small Canadian 'Tall Ship' in the Australian Bicentennial celebrations.

As well as visiting with unique cultures, tasting their foods, dancing to their music and being stunned by the beauty of their lands, we learnt about the down-to-earth realities of the lifestyle. We share the early decisions, planning our route, leaving the security of home, the organisation of the boat, the joys and problems of travelling with a young family, and the odd disaster!

The excitement and challenge of travelling the oceans and continents of our world is our focus. Far from finding it a hardship, living in confined quarters and on a limited budget, our boat *Bagheera* was a comfortable home and the voyage an unforgettable highlight in our lives. Our story, we hope, will be an inspiration to help others also live their dreams.

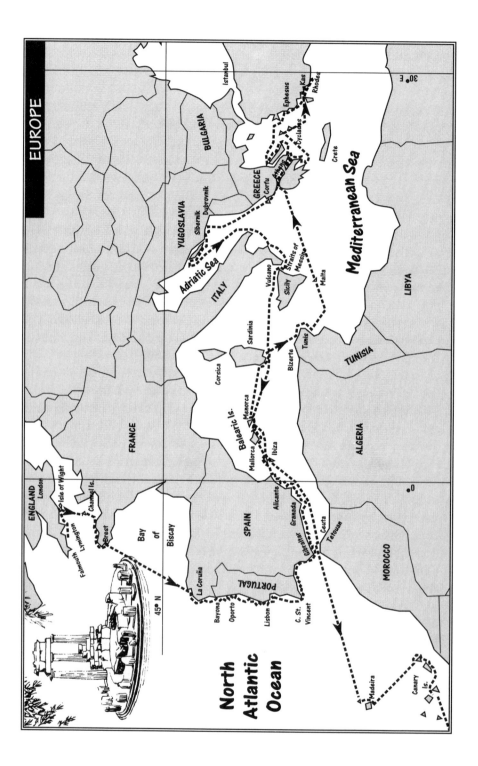

EUROPE

North Atlantic Ocean

ENGLAND
London
Isle of Wight
Falmouth
Lymington
Channel Is.
Brest

Bay of Biscay

45° N

FRANCE

La Coruña
Bayona
Oporto
Lisbon
PORTUGAL
C. St. Vincent

SPAIN
Alicante
Granada
Gibraltar
Ceuta
Tetouan

MOROCCO

Madeira

Canary Is.

0

ALGERIA

Balearic Is.
Menorca
Mallorca
Ibiza

Corsica

Sardinia

ITALY

Vulcano
Sicily
Straits of Messina

Bizerte
Tunis
TUNISIA

Malta

LIBYA

Mediterranean Sea

YUGOSLAVIA
Sibenik
Dubrovnik

Adriatic Sea

BULGARIA

Istanbul

GREECE
Corfu
Athens

Cyclades

Ephesus
Kas
Rhodes

Crete

30° E

The European Atlantic Coast

1. Decision Time and Shakedown Cruise

England

T he weather during the fall of 1984 in Vancouver, western Canada, was distinctly dismal, with constant rain, biting winds and gloomy days. So when my husband Andy announced, "I'm fed up with the rat race, let's go away cruising", it was easy to succumb to thoughts of tropical sun, with blue skies, turquoise seas, and white sands bordered by swaying palms.

Warmth and enthusiasm surged through my veins but the chill of reality quickly followed. Like many others Andy and I had frequently entertained the dream of blue water cruising to distant horizons, but making the decision to actually go was sobering. It was fine to charter a yacht and go sailing in the Caribbean for a couple of weeks but could I really survive going offshore, living with my husband and family twenty-four hours a day in such a tiny space, with few amenities and no escape?

Our children had yet to mature and become self-sufficient. Jamie, at one year, was at that hectic age when cognitive sense had yet to catch up with physical mobility. Duncan was eight and Colin just six and although they had always adapted well to the boat on summer holidays, these were in the lake-like Straits of Georgia. How would they fare, and would they be safe in the large uncomfortable ocean swell? Just thinking about cooking and coping with the needs of a family in a hot, airless cabin was making me feel queasy.

Then there was living in such close quarters. Even though Andy and I had spent considerable time on yachts together, we had decided four years previously that the only prudent answer for us to race harmoniously in the same fleet was in 'his and her' boats, not exactly a realistic option now.

As many people pointed out, sometimes positively but more often negatively, this would be a major change in our lifestyle. What would Andy do with his business and what would we do with our home? How would we manage financially? Was it responsible to haul the children away from their established familiar community, in particular to take them out of school and visit unhealthy countries without proper medical facilities? These were just a few of the concerns. It was only because we had both sailed for years locally, as well as offshore in England and the Caribbean, that our sailing competence was not a major topic as well.

The issues were daunting, but the more we analyzed our lives the more evident it became that if we were ever going to cruise extensively this was the time to do it. In particular, we felt that the children would be more adaptable and receptive to this major change whilst they were young. Now that they are teenagers I think we were right!

One by one we managed to plough through the major decisions, although they seemed to consume our lives. Andy would sell his business. We would keep our house and tailor our cruising budget to the rent we hoped to receive. We were relieved to find that the Province of British Columbia had an excellent education correspondence programme, and we consulted our sailing doctor friends about the medical supplies required.

High on the decision list was, of course, where to go, for how long and in what boat?

An obvious route was to follow in the footsteps of many other British Columbian yachtsmen and depart from Vancouver for the magical South Pacific. However, this meant 'jumping right into the deep end' with an immediate trip offshore of 2300 nautical miles to Hawaii then a similar trip to Tahiti. I get seasick and although I have learnt to cope for myself, fourteen days constantly at sea with three young children was hardly my idea of a relaxed shakedown cruise.

Instead we considered the popular Caribbean with its many islands, bordered by Central and South America, but as Andy and I had spent many years running charter boats between Florida and Trinidad it didn't offer the excitement and challenge of new horizons.

An alternative plan was to sail around the Mediterranean. This was appealing; we were attracted by the great diversity of cultures and cuisine and both had some interesting memories from our youth. The Mediterranean also suited our family needs, for here we would only need to do short day sails, definitely the easiest way to sail with young children. We hoped that after a year they would have adapted to living on board and be practised seamen ready for a Trans-Atlantic crossing. We could then include some visits to Caribbean favourites before sailing up to Florida where we would put the boat up for sale.

We finally decided we could manage two years. Although this seemed a long period to leave family, friends and our home community we felt one year was just too short to buy and commission a boat, acclimatise to living on board full-time and travel this route. How did we end up sailing around the world for six years? That was due to fate and the magnetism of the yachting community, as you will find out.

Andy had a yacht brokerage business so we looked at a myriad of boats, but always came back to the French-built Beneteau First 38s. Andy's concern was that it wouldn't be big enough for a family of five, for the storage required, and for everyone to have their own comfortable area.

We had reached the time to make a decision when Andy arranged that we should look at one last boat, a 44 footer that he thought might be perfect. It was pouring with rain as we ran down the dock in Seattle one cold November weekend, and while Andy battled the elements to check out the deck, I nipped below.

"Well the rig and deck layout looks great," he enthused minutes later, "With all the lines coming back to a roomy cockpit. How about down here?"

"It's terrific, but I think the Beneteau still ranks at the top. It's quite similar in layout, with the two aft double cabins which would be great for the children. The galley is about the same size with two burner stove and oven, but the fridge is smaller, the sinks are rather shallow for sea and there is no place for a dish drainer. Also, it doesn't have the great feature of the locker doors stopping at the horizontal and making more working space. The main cabin is also very comfortable, but doesn't have the bottle locker and shelves for glasses built into the table, and there isn't as much woodwork; in particular, it hasn't the lovely teak arch. The head is roomy and has a good shower but there is no counter which will be a pain with my contacts. And throughout there isn't nearly as much storage space . . ."

Andy seemed rather deflated as we walked back along the dock so, as we passed a Beneteau 38 that was for sale by the same company, I suggested we might go on board for an immediate comparison. The warmth enveloped us as we went below; everything about the layout seemed just right, and with the gleaming brass lamp, designer cushions and Persian carpet, this was definitely a home.

We had to look no further. The Beneteau First 38s with its length of 40 feet overall, beam of 12 foot 9 inches, sloop rig with mast height of 55 feet and draft of 7 foot, was built to sail the oceans. It was easy for the two of us to handle, had a roomy interior with great storage, and was best for our budget besides. The next day Andy ordered our new boat for pick-up at the factory in St. Gilles de Riez on the Bay of Biscay in France.

Five months later, in April 1985, Mike Lando, an old friend and racing crew, joined Andy to sail our new boat from France to England. From all accounts the three week trip was a great success with frequent platters of the shellfish 'fruits de mer' consumed with many a bottle of local wine.

In June, when the school year had ended in Vancouver, the boys and I flew to England to join Andy and Mike in Lymington, a yachting mecca on the south coast.

"Hi Liza, hi boys. Welcome to England and your new *Bagheera*."

The boys were delighted to hear Mike's familiar voice.

"How do you feel, Liza?" Mike enquired.

"Oh fine. Well, actually, pretty exhausted," I replied.

Memories of the last month came flooding to the fore, finishing a teaching certificate that I had started before our travel discussions, renting and packing up the house, going away parties, emotional farewells—I was more than ready to relax.

"You look it, so I thought I should warn you that Andy is just itching to get going."

"Oh, no!" I exclaimed.

Not only did I want to unwind but I really did need a few days to tackle the massive job of stowing the items we had sent in advance as well as purchasing the many basics we required.

It was not an auspicious start. Andy was indeed 'chomping at the bit' to leave. He had been in Lymington for two months commissioning the boat. All the modifications had been completed and the new equipment was in good working order.

We both had our 'issues'. Andy was horrified that I had brought thirteen pieces of luggage, despite seven being school books and the rest just duffle bags, whilst I couldn't believe that he had filled every nook and cranny with boat spare parts. He wanted the boys to sleep in one cabin whilst I had found a similar cabin claustrophobic for just the two of us. He also wanted us to sleep aft, where there was a good motion for sea, whilst I wanted to sleep in the big airy cabin forward. I was particularly disgruntled that my brand new home needed a massive spring cleaning from top to toe. I had just done that to our home in Vancouver . . .

The next evening we went to the Royal Lymington Yacht Club where I met several new acquaintances of Andy and Mike's. Everyone was so welcoming, so positive about our trip; the evening served well in dissipating some of my initial annoyance and resentment.

By the third day everything miraculously had its place, in theory anyway, and I had purchased lifejackets and foul weather gear, galley equipment and bins for toys. Andy had agreed to sleep in the forward berth, Duncan was to have the new upper berth in the port double cabin and he and Colin had arranged their toys, books and tapes so they were securely stowed for sea. Jamie was to sleep in the starboard aft cabin, as he still had an afternoon nap and went to bed early. We also established that this would be the guest cabin when the need arose, and it did frequently, so I endeavoured to keep the hanging locker empty—although this became harder as time went on!

We were ready to head out on the high seas but made our first trip a short one, over to Yarmouth in the Isle of Wight, to see Andy's mother and sister. They had driven from Seaview, where Andy had grown up.

Our spirits were high as we weaved our way out of Lymington, squeezing past the car ferry which totally dominated the narrow channel, then motoring by the hundreds of yachts bobbing on their moorings. This was the first leg of our odyssey; the planning had governed our lives for the last eight months, but here we were at last, setting forth as a family on our travels. Our dream was actually coming true but what had happened to the organisation? Where was the champagne to celebrate?!

Once outside the harbour, we headed *Bagheera* into wind to pull up the mainsail. Duncan, having taken a dinghy sailing course in Vancouver the previous summer, was full of enthusiasm.

"Can I haul up the main halyard, Daddy?"

"Great idea."

Duncan hauled away at the mast, fast at first, then slowing down with the weight of the sail. He just didn't have enough body weight for the last few feet.

"Don't worry," called Andy. "I'll winch up the rest from the cockpit."

Andy's mother was waiting on shore, thankful that we had arrived safe and sound. I realized, with a pang, the anxiety she would be experiencing during our longer trips down the Atlantic European coast, let alone during our Transatlantic crossing. Once on board, however, she was full of her usual pith.

"And how can you afford it?" she challenged.

"We can't," said Andy.

"Just as I thought," she replied and never mentioned the subject again!

Andy and I had been looking forward to re-acquainting ourselves with the south coast of England and possibly visiting the Scilly Isles; unfortunately the weather was not to oblige. The English truly had a reason to grumble that year. It blew and rained and blew again. How lovely it is to have a breeze through the boat in the tropics but half a gale at those low temperatures certainly added to the chill factor, and made us wetter than ever in the dinghy.

Ashore we soon learnt why high streets in the West Country are not on the sea front, for once sheltered from the wind, temperatures appeared quite balmy. The timbered houses, thatched roofs and colourful gardens were quite lovely. Indulging in an English tea, with scones piled high with thick Devonshire cream and strawberry jam, soon became a ritual at the end of the day.

"Mummy, can we go off in the dinghy after lunch?" Duncan asked one morning.

"Where do you want to go?" I asked.

"Just us kids going ashore, like we do at home." he replied.

At home, in British Columbia, where the winds are generally light, this would have been a routine request with a positive response, but almost immediately we had found cruising with the family in England very different. The strong winds made it uncomfortable in the cockpit and wet, and anchoring was mostly in estuaries, where currents were far too strong for the children to row against if the outboard engine failed.

This meant that neither the children nor ourselves had the expected time out from each other, and we all suffered! Fortunately there was room for the boys to have several toys on board; we also played the new games we had been given—soon finding out which were the best for the varying developmental levels of the children and the tolerance levels of their parents. Fortunately two year old Jamie was always delighted to be our partner, or "brrrm,brrrmmmm", with his collection of cars and trucks, to his heart's content.

Heading west, we called in at Lulworth Cove, where the chalk cliffs suddenly end and two arms of Purbeck and Portland limestone form a lake-like body of water. Ashore we all scrambled through the arches and caves, and were buffeted like kites along the cliffs in the blustery winds.

We anchored with the warships in Plymouth for the night before stopping in Exmouth. The sands were all I remembered from my childhood and my memories were renewed further by seeing my old Nanny. Sadly she was in a nursing home, but her mind was vividly alive as she recalled incidents of my youth, first in Exmouth, then in London and of our summers spent at the cottage at Hillhead, between Portsmouth and Southampton.

There was great excitement that evening when a grey mullet attached itself to our fishing line.

"Wonderful," said Andy with a satisfied grin, holding up our unexpected dinner. "The first of many fish in the years to come."

He cooked a mouth watering meal while I enjoyed a quiz game with the boys. It is the custom in our family for Andy to cook if we have fish, as he is the seafood enthusiast. If only I could get the family to eat fish every night . . . although later we learnt that this particular species is generally found off sewage outlets!

Torquay became a famous seaside resort in Victorian times because of its panoramic setting and mild climate. Even palm trees line the boulevards; they must be a very hardy variety. Tourist places don't appeal to Andy and I, but the children needed to run off some energy and they had no such negative thoughts. They loved the carnival rides and a parachute trampoline and Colin was mesmerized by the shops. The more sparkly and full of tourist knick-knacks they were, the more he was fascinated, and when we managed to get him out of one shop he nipped quickly into the next. If you have been to Torquay you will know this could have turned into being a rather lengthy afternoon.

Colin had obviously focused on different visual effects to ourselves as from this time on he began constructing. With a variety of coloured paper, pens, glue and scissors at hand, he would spend hours making colourful, detailed, artistic forms that frequently portrayed animals, birds and plants. Unfortunately they were impossible to keep, but this did not deter his enthusiasm. It was an excellent boat activity and his skills developed in sophistication, and into different mediums, with our travels.

Meanwhile Duncan was becoming an avid fisherman and in Salcombe, at his request, we bought a shrimping net. That night he scooped up a mealful of shrimps for our dinner. After they were steamed he peered in the pot, just as Andy and I had as children, to count the number of pink prawns and brown shrimps. There certainly was a fair division of the spoils that night.

Our visit to Plymouth coincided with an air display by the Royal Air Force aerobatic team, the Red Arrows.

"I want to be a pilot," cried Duncan, who was captivated.

"But Daddy, how do they fly so close together? Aren't they going to touch each other?" Colin asked with concern.

Andy carefully explained the formations and strategies to the boys, as he had been in the Royal Navy's 806 Squadron Ace of Diamonds Aerobatic team and had participated in many similar events.

Vancouver friends, Trevor and Mary Jenkins, came to visit in Falmouth, and at their suggestion we motored up the River Fal. It was one of the few sunny days that summer; we all relaxed in the cockpit, lapping up the warmth and enjoying a cold beer. We anchored by Smugglers' Cottage of Tolverne, a thatched roofed five hundred year old building, with pink roses trailing up the steep steps from the sea. At last I felt I was beginning to unwind.

The next day took us to Pendennis Castle.

"These buildings have stood here, guarding the entrance of the harbour since 1540," Trevor told the boys. "That's four hundred and forty-five years ago. It was built by Henry VIII and then changed by Elizabeth I."

"Four hundred and forty-five years ago," said Colin impressed. "That's a very long time!"

It was the first of many castles we would be seeing down the European coast.

We entered the Helford River in swirling, grey mist. Daphne du Maurier has always been a favourite author of mine and I could easily imagine the eerie ruins of the mansion of Manderley, from her novel 'Rebecca', in the dense woods that rose steeply from the rocky shore. Later, by dinghy, we explored some of the beautiful creeks that wound inland from the estuary. I almost expected to come upon a lurking brigantine, such as the Frenchman's in her 'Frenchman's Creek', as we ducked through the overhanging branches.

That night, enjoying dinner ashore in the Helford passage, we told the boys of the old smugglers of Cornwall. They were enthralled by stories of secret passages from cellar to cove, and farmhouse to cave.

As we made our way down the narrow road, which leads to an Inn and the cluster of cottages which form the village of Helford, Colin pointed out the wild flowers. He had been given a flower press, and wanted to start collecting. He picked some yellow flowers that we identified as Slender Mullein, in the Verbascum family, from our field guide.

"It says they are found wild only in this region of England," Andy read out. Colin was thrilled.

It was blowing hard on the trip to Fowey and I was glad of my new foul-weather suit and boots.

"Mummy, can we bounce on your forward berth?" called Duncan, his face peering up through the companionway.

We were pounding into wind so the waves seemed biggest in our forward cabin. A favourite activity of the boys was to be tossed around up there. I was pleased to see them so happy, and above all not feeling seasick.

As the drizzle increased to a steady downpour I also went below; no point in us all getting soaking wet! The boys cuddled close as I recounted stories of the old days when 'Fowey Gallants' had raided the coasts of France throughout the Hundred Years War.

A lull enabled us to go ashore, but after wandering the steep narrow streets in the persistent drizzle we decided to head for the Yacht Club, hoping to find a hot bath or shower.

One of the benefits of travelling by boat is the hospitality one receives from sailing clubs the world over. Here, as usual, they were most welcoming. We were soon warm but they had been most apologetic about their 'new fangled' shower; their former iron bathtub was big enough for the entire family.

Earlier in the year Steve and Andrea Bayly, our next door neighbours in Vancouver, had decided to buy a Beneteau also and head off with us. Andy had helped them order their boat and equipment, and thought a trip on our boat, where he could explain our installations, would be useful before Steve headed off to France. Steve decided to meet us in Plymouth, but he didn't arrive as planned.

As we waited the next morning Duncan suggested we look up Plymouth in The Children's Encyclopedia, a reference book my father had given to the boys just before he had died, three years before.

"Wow, there's a whole lot on Plymouth," Duncan told us.

It was easy to see that Plymouth was ideal for a seaport. It lies between the mouths of the Tamar and Plym, which flow into the broad estuary of Plymouth Sound, and we found that it has been used as a port since the thirteenth century. Many ships sailed from here against the French during the Hundred Years War. Later it saw the departure of the great Elizabethan sailors, Hawkins, Raleigh and Frobisher. Its most famous seaman of all, however, was Sir Francis Drake, who played his famous game of bowls before setting out to destroy the Spanish Armada in 1588. Despite his vow to complete the game and still win the battle, it has been suggested that he had probably recognized that the wind and tide were not favourable for the fleet to depart anyway. Next, in 1620, the Pilgrim fathers sailed from Plymouth to America in the Mayflower, and in 1772 James Cook left on his three year circumnavigation of the world. In recent times, 1966, Sir Francis Chichester left there to sail around the world single-handed.

"Hi *Bagheera, Baagheeeeeraaa.*"

We all rushed up on deck. Steve had found us. He had been delayed due to the train schedule. In true Andy style, we left immediately for the River Yealm, but had to motor all the way.

Yealm is a charming west country village and obviously a favourite family venue. Children were taking lessons in sailing dinghies and having a lot of fun, judging from the chatter. I wished we could have stayed longer so ours could participate, but they did enjoy being able to go off on their own for a spin, or a zot as they called it, in our inflatable—freedom at last!

Dartmouth is an attractive old medieval town with picturesque green, gold and brown fields rolling up the hills behind. We were taken back in time as we walked up the Butterwalk, a row of 17th century houses on granite pillars with their carved precariously overhanging stories. As we sampled one of the many pubs Duncan was amazed to find a stone sign saying it was built in 1380. He was used to everything being so new in Canada.

We returned to Lymington overnight, our first long trip as a family in the boat although it wasn't much of a test. With no wind we had to motor the entire way; but generally we had been pleased with our shakedown cruise. The furling gear on the 150% genoa, the forward sail, worked well, and the furling line was easy to pull by hand, in any conditions, from the cockpit. Duncan had become an ace at hauling up the mainsail in seconds flat. We had also been given plenty of opportunities to practise reefing the main. The wind, speed and depth instruments were all working correctly and the autohelm was magic, steering an accurate course and giving us so much extra time to interact with the children, complete sail trim and navigate. We had a good 30 mile range with our vhf radio and the engine, a 50 horse power Perkins 4-108, gave us excellent speed (over 7 knots) when required, but was economical at low revs. The refrigerator worked well, not that there had been too much external heat to contend with. Above all we were very comfortable living on board.

We had easily established safety rules. All the boys wore lifejackets at sea. In fact Jamie wore his most of the time, when on deck or the dock. No-one went out of the cockpit, except when Andy or I had to complete some specific activity on the foredeck, such as reef the mainsail or clip on the spinnaker pole to hold out the genoa, and then someone had to watch from the cockpit. We always wore a safety harness when going forward, unless the weather was calm, and had a stainless steel wire along both side decks to clip to, thus having a free run fore and aft and full use of both hands. We also wore our lifeharnesses on night watches as we were alone.

When the temperatures increased we relaxed our rule on lifejackets for Duncan and Colin, who were good swimmers. Instead they wore a life harness when on deck by themselves or when it was very rough. In Lymington Andy had fastened netting around the boat between the lifelines and the toe-rail. We had found this successful previously for preventing the children from slipping overboard and calming my fears that they might!

It was the beginning of an unbelievable August. Later we learnt there were only three days that month when the winds did not reach gale force in the Solent. Vancouver friends, David and Jane Heukelom, and five year old Jason joined us for a few exceedingly blustery days. Being racers we decided to watch the beginning of the Channel Race, part of the Admirals Cup yachting series. In that wind it was an exciting, noisy start but after only a few minutes boats came limping home with breakages—forestays, shrouds and even a couple of masts.

We roared over to Beaulieu looking for a sheltered anchorage in the Beaulieu River. We were towing our inflatable dinghy and as we entered the river it started surging up our stern on the waves. Our concentration was on manoeuvring *Bagheera* in the narrow channel, which was tricky in the strong cross winds.

"Oh, my God," called Dave suddenly. "The dinghy is flipping right over."

We were aghast at the strength of the wind as we had the heavy eight horsepower engine on the dinghy transom. It was not a propitious beginning for a new outboard and it was tricky righting the dinghy itself. We gave the outboard a fresh water flush on shore; it appeared to have suffered no ill effects, but a lesson had been learnt.

We had planned to spend a couple of weeks with Andy's family in Seaview, on the Isle of Wight. *Bagheera* 'flew' across the Solent with no mainsail and only about one sixteenth of the genoa unfurled, doing about nine knots, in winds gusting Force 10 (50 knots). When the rain came belting down Andy turned towards me.

"Blow this," he yelled, trying to be heard over the whine of the wind in the rigging. "Let's see if Lyn can pick us up in Cowes?"

There we saw the damage sustained to several more race participants, and it confirmed our decision to go in early. In fact the weather was so continuously unpleasant we opted out and moved ashore! It was our only choice if we were to see much of relatives and friends, as the anchorage became untenable off the shallow foreshore of Seaview. We had to leave *Bagheera* secured to a mooring buoy in Bembridge, several miles away.

We put this time to good use, however. Andy built extra dividers for the school books and more lockers in our forward cabin. I had some cotton cushion covers made for the main cabin seats. Not only did the Laura Ashley fabric brighten the boat and make it more homely, it was softer and cooler for the heat of the Mediterranean and tropics. Fastened by velcro the covers could easily be washed. We found a brass lamp, mounted pictures on the bulkhead and bought a small Persian rug, that conveniently collected all the dirt at the foot of the companionway steps, and protected the teak and holly varnished floor. I made brightly coloured cushions for the sleeping cabins to give comfort, and hopefully contentment, at sea, and hanging bags for bathing suits and treasures.

Seaview, with dinghy racing and parties, was fun and we had a beautiful day for the beach sports at the Regatta. But when we all returned to the boat on August 22 it really did seem like home, and we couldn't wait to head south for warmer climes.

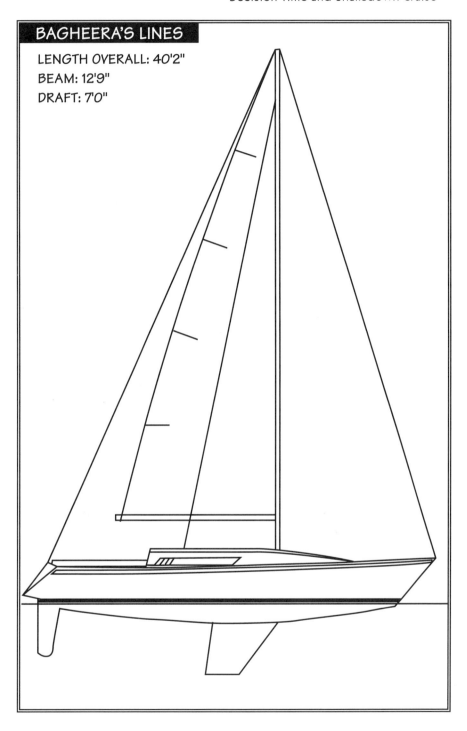

BAGHEERA'S LINES

LENGTH OVERALL: 40'2"
BEAM: 12'9"
DRAFT: 7'0"

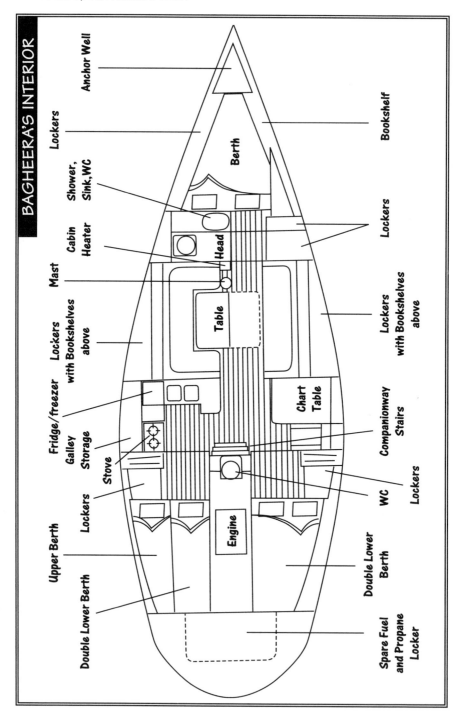

BAGHEERA'S INTERIOR

Anchor Well

Lockers

Bookshelf

Berth

Shower, Sink, WC

Cabin Heater

Head

Mast

Lockers with Bookshelves above

Lockers

Lockers with Bookshelves above

Table

Fridge/freezer

Galley Storage

Stove

Chart Table

Companionway Stairs

Upper Berth

Lockers

WC

Lockers

Double Lower Berth

Engine

Double Lower Berth

Spare Fuel and Propane Locker

2. The Channel Islands, France, Bay of Biscay, and Spain

La Coruña, Lage, Bayona

It was the first of many farewells to newly made friends as we waved our goodbyes in Lymington on the afternoon of August 25, 1985, after a quick haulout to replace the weed guard for the log (speed) impeller. It was another dismal, damp, grey day, with the 25-30 knot south-westerly winds chilling our bones. We anticipated an uncomfortable passage to Guernsey which, with a distance of about 100 nautical miles, would be an overnight trip. "Don't worry," Simon reassured us, "once past the Needles it will be a mill-pond."

We had met Simon and Jenny Collyer on one of the Lymington evening races—'bumped' into each other you could say. Simon, who worked in a family nursery business and his solicitor wife, Jenny, were also avid racers. We had become firm friends and they were to join us twice later in our travels.

Duncan wrote in his log for August 26th: "Arrived in Guernsey in the Channel Islands after a very rough ride."

There was indeed a confused, disturbed sea all the way. The waves buffeted the bow, causing soaking, salty spray and making the hull jerk and shudder unpredictably, throwing us off balance. In addition it was COLD with a persistent drizzle that, despite new oilskins and absorbent neck towels, inevitably penetrated. It trickled down our backs as it seeped in, saturating our clothing.

As I shivered on my night watch, huddled against the cabin on the lee side, I mourned the fact that this was a far cry from the balmy, starry nights of our dreams. As I hung over the side clinging tightly to the life lines, I was particularly annoyed with myself that I hadn't even thought to take a seasick pill. I was not to make that mistake again, and you can imagine how many pills that was in six years! However, the conditions had really tested the boat and we were pleased to find no leaks or breakages.

On watch the trip was uneventful but busy. We were accompanied by Mark, the son of a friend of Andy's, who was at the start of a backpacking trip around the world, having just completed his degree. It seemed fitting that we were setting off on our travels together. Mark was not a seasoned sailor, but was quick to understand instructions and a very willing helper. We had explained the three hour watch routine and basic rules of navigation on the high seas before setting off. Now that the sails were set, we briefly went through the basic ropes, called sheets when used to haul sails in, and halyards when pulling them up. In particular we focused on the lines we might ask him to use if we needed to reef the mainsail. Reducing sail was easy with the genoa, for hauling a line in the cockpit on the starboard side instantly furled the sail up at the bow; the line was secured when the sail was the appropriate size for the wind strength. We generally reefed the mainsail when the wind topped about 20 knots, although the state of the sea and point of sail, whether the wind was ahead or behind us, also influenced our decision.

The boys were 'full of beans', their attention riveted on the disappearing Isle of Wight, and they stayed on deck until the last point had finally faded into the cloud. They felt truly at sea now and happily retired to their berths. I was surprised, but thankful, when they had all wanted cereal for supper. Not only is it easy to prepare (but with the motion I did not want to stay below longer than I had to) but it is nutritious, being food and a drink in one, and rests well in the stomach. As I wedged Jamie in his berth securely, bolstering him with the new cushions, he was chatting enthusiastically. Almost instantly he was in slumberland, dreaming, I'm sure, about the fish and whales that were his last words.

At 10:00 PM Andy noted in the log 'approaching the English Channel shipping lanes. Nine ships in sight'. At 4:00 AM we started the engine to motor sail through the Alderney tide Race and at 7:20 AM Guernsey was sighted.

As we rafted up with one of the many groups of yachts in St. Peter Port the grey sky was starting to clear. By the time I had brunch on the cockpit table we were all in bathing suits basking in the sunshine, lapping up the warmth after our recent chill.

How quickly we forgot the discomforts of the night before whilst exploring the delights of Guernsey, with a relaxing afternoon building sandcastles at Baie des Roches. We made a quick stop at the Yacht club on our return. Andy and I recalled that after our last visit we had experienced similar weather for the passage back to Britain. With the winds aft of the beam, we had had an amazing 'sleigh ride' to Cowes on the 66 foot *American Eagle*. The needle of our boat speed instrument had been almost constantly at the top of the dial.

When we headed off next morning old friends from Seaview called out, "Race you to Treguier?"

We hadn't planned to stop there but a radio chat soon convinced us. The light breeze and flat seas were so different from the morning before, and we looked forward to a pleasant, undemanding sail. But it was not to be for long for soon we had the opposite of the previous trip, and sails were hanging limply as the wind died altogether. The race was abandoned and we motored the rest of the way, lounging in the cockpit and enjoying the shafts of sunshine that penetrated through the haze.

Treguier, an attractive, old Brittany town on the northern French coast, stands high above the banks of the Jaudy River with streets of ancient, half-timbered houses trailing down to the waterfront. Above soars a striking Medieval cathedral.

"Did you know that the spire is pierced with holes?" an old wizened local asked the boys.

"No I didn't," said Duncan. "But why?"

"So the wind doesn't blow it down in the winter gales and I'll tell you something else. The cathedral is dedicated to St. Tugdual because he delivered all the people around here from a fierce dragon!"

"I've just got a new book on dragons," said Colin. "I wonder if he's in it."

That evening we wandered into town, savouring the thought of our first delicious French repast, only to find all the restaurants had completed their last serving. We had managed to forget the one hour time change, and been unaware of the earlier eating hours of the small French towns.

Down on the dock there was considerable social activity and dinner was forgotten. Andy met some men who were also ex-Royal Navy, and they were soon into nightfighters, aircraft carriers and mutual friends. I was being asked the inevitable question of whether I had sailed before. I explained that I had owned a Cadet dinghy and raced since I was nine. I had also had the good fortune of being taught by a knowledgeable, retired gentleman, who had made sailing magic for us children during my summers on the Solent, at Hillhead.

"Was his name Captain Jamain, by any chance?" was the unexpected response.

It was the first of many coincidences in our cruising travels and part of what makes the comraderie of the yachting fraternity so special.

Temperatures were improving and the next day we motored up the river to Morlaix in hot sunshine. Duncan had caught a mackerel en route so we were all set for dinner that night.

Morlaix is the main town of northern Finisterre, its position making it a major trading harbour since the middle ages. Coming up river we were impressed by the high railway viaduct built in 1864, its wide arches straddling the valley. After transitting the lock we tied at the quayside.

We had planned a night in Morlaix and enjoyed the town with its old granite merchants' homes. Duncan had success in catching eels and after dark the boys were mesmerised by the bats that fluttered eerily under the viaduct arches.

Next morning, as I climbed out of bed to make tea, the boat didn't feel right. It was too rigid, not giving with my movements as I made my way to the galley and I realized we were heeling slightly to port. I threw on jeans and a sweater, the reality of the situation dawning through my sleepy haze. My fears were warranted for we were hard aground, the water way below our waterline stripe; but we were firmly supported by the stone harbour wall on our port side.

We quickly deduced that something must have happened to the lock. It had, but we couldn't find out what, no doubt due to our French being more proficient in respect to culinary delights than the working of locks. We finally gathered that it should be working again on the weekend.

It meant a few days in Morlaix but we found some good restaurants with the help of our neighbour's Michelin Food Guide, and I was able to sort through and organize the pertinent school books. The boys were full of enthusiasm.

"Is this my science book? Are we going to do these experiments on the boat? Look, I've got my own geometry set. Can I go and read this book of stories? They look fun!"

Duncan was particularly interested as he had been in a French Immersion school previously and was not used to the texts in the English programme. We worked out how to organise the books on the shelves. One term's worth fitted in the front section and the rest of the years work-books went behind. I was amazed that they had managed to fit in such a small space, as the large boxes of school supplies had been full to the brim. That afternoon we purchased a basket for pencil cases, rulers, stapler, paper clips, coloured pens and pencils etc, which lived further along the shelf so was easily accessible. This arrangement worked well for the entire six years and, unlike at home, we never seemed to run out of supplies.

School in British Columbia always starts on the Tuesday after the Labour Day weekend, the first weekend of September. Time was drawing close.

The delay was making us late for our previously planned rendezvous with Steve and Andrea Bayly, our next-door neighbours in Vancouver. Steve and Mike Lando had flown to France from England, and Andrea had joined them straight from Canada. Together they had commissioned the Beneteau 375 and cruised north to Brest to meet us. We intended to cross the infamous Bay of Biscay in unison. They had called their yacht *Severance*, as the severance pay Steve had received from his last job had substantially eased the way for them to go cruising.

"I do hope they don't go without us," Colin began, when from above chorused a loud,

"Hi, Bagheeras!"

We rushed up the companion way, peered up the wall and there they all were. They had indeed been concerned by our delay and had rented a car to tour the wild Brittany coast to find us. It was a great surprise.

After we had caught up with our news Andrea broached the subject of stowage.

"I just have to see where you manage to put everything, Liza. I seem to have run out of space already," she admitted, perturbed. The layout of their boat was rather different from ours but Andrea gleaned some ideas, in particular—unlike one's house—just how much could be crammed into one small locker. In time we all became experts. It was unbelievable how many treasures we managed to secrete out of sight during our travels to avoid complaint from our captain; although the higher waterline rather gave the game away!

Mark left to continue his trip overland. After a brief visit to Aberwrach we had an exhilarating sail around Ushant in thirty knots of wind. Andy had promised a new weather pattern "around the corner" and remarkably there was a complete line across the sky, grey to blue. It was the start of two and a half months with temperatures well in the 20 degrees Celsius.

Brest's magnificent harbour has sheltered warships and merchantmen since Roman times, more than 2000 years ago; although little remains of the old town, as Brest was almost totally destroyed at the end of World War II.

As we approached the docks we sighted *Severance*. "Look at all the flags she's flying," called out Duncan, "I wonder if they mean anything."

We pulled in ahead of the Bayly's and, after we had tied up, Duncan rushed below to decipher them from the flag chart on the bulkhead.

"It says, 'Hi, five Copelands!'" he called up excitedly.

Steve and Andrea showed us around and introduced us to the Yacht club. The facilities were excellent, although in typical French fashion one never knew who would be wandering around the ladies showers. Initially I thought I must have picked the wrong door!

It was time to start school. I had completed a teaching certificate the year before we left, primarily because it was a requirement if I wanted to work as an educational psychologist in the school system. After our decision to go cruising I had a new focus and found it useful, although not actually necessary, to be familiar with the curriculum and current philosophies and to have realistic expectations for the boys.

The British Columbia Correspondence Programme is well established because many children in the Province are unable to attend regular school due to an economy traditionally focused on primary industries in remote areas such as fishing, logging and mining. I found the programme well structured for a daily routine, and innovative and creative within the subjects themselves. Thirty papers a year have to be completed, each with assignments in language arts—reading, language, spelling and writing—and in math, with additional papers in science, social studies and art. There were six assignments to a paper which removed us from the pressure of a Monday to Friday schedule, which is obviously not appropriate for this lifestyle. During the six years our routine was school every day, unless something else was planned. Although at times I felt we had a perfectly valid educational excuse to skip school almost every day, this system did work well. Of course we observed the regular holidays, the Canadian system of having nearly three months in the summer being most appreciated!

We were now monitoring the weather pictures daily, as the Bay of Biscay has an awesome reputation for disagreeable conditions. Many a ship has foundered in its violent storms whilst crossing this 200 nautical mile stretch, and we wanted to make sure we had an ample good weather 'window' for our crossing. Finally the weather picture looked ideal and it was time for a last shop, a final play on the white sands digging for cockles and catching shrimp and whitebait, and particularly a last feast on 'fruits de mer'. Mike, Andy and I devoured with relish crab, oysters, cockles, clams, winkles, mussels, prawns and lobster, decoratively piled high on a one-metre oval platter.

On September 6, (regretting a little that we had indulged in such a quantity of raw seafood the night before!) we set off across the Bay of Biscay with Mike also on board. The winds filled in from the west and then clocked around to the north. It was perfect for a spinnaker run and the log reads: "Dolphins galore, spinnaker up, sun shining, all copacetic."

"Mummy, Daddy, can't we go up on the bow?" the boys pleaded with us, as dolphins always love frolicking in the bow wave.

The conditions were still mild, and with the netting around the lifelines we felt it was safe.

"Okay," said Andy, "but keep close to me and hold on to the wooden grab rails tightly."

The dolphins seemed as delighted as the boys and gave us a wonderful show of diving and jumping. They were often in pairs and always in perfect synchronisation. Half an hour later they left, and not too soon for the wind was definitely building.

By the afternoon it had increased to 25 knots, gusting 30 on occasion, and had clocked round further to the east. It gave us a fast reach as the wind was now on the beam. It was an easy ride with 'Otto van Hellum", as we had named the automatic pilot, and we completed the 240 nautical mile trip to La Coruña, northern Spain, in two days.

It was our longest trip to date, but the boys weren't bored for a moment. I had bought many children's books in England and Duncan had 'taken-off'. He was pleased to have such long uninterrupted periods to pursue his new interest, and was totally absorbed, curled up snugly in his duvet on his berth. I was delighted but had to laugh when we couldn't even get his attention to come for dinner; it was just like being glued to the TV!

Colin was busy with coloured paper and glue, making minute animals and unique, brightly coloured homes for them to live in. He and Jamie also spent hours listening to tapes; Colin now enjoyed the story book tapes, where he read the words in the corresponding book to the voice. Most of their time was spent on deck, however, fishing, searching for more dolphins and eating meals, for the air stimulated all our appetites. In particular they checked on Steve and Andrea, making sure they were still in sight, and had many suggestions for our frequent radio conversations.

Andy, Mike and I rotated on our usual three hour watch system, giving each of us six hours off to sleep and a change of watch for cooking duties. It worked well and the whole crew were full of energy on arrival.

We saw little other traffic until we were approaching La Coruña on our third day at dawn. Andy notes in the log, "Fishing fleet to starboard and ahead." In the next hour more fishing vessels were mentioned and at 8:00 AM Mike wrote, "Dodging ships!"

La Coruña is on a small peninsula. We anchored in the port and went ashore by dinghy. Senor Roberts at the Real Club was extremely welcoming.

"Did you have a good passage, the weather has been good for the last two days, yes? If you need to clear customs, I can do it for you, and change money too."

Clearing into a country can sometimes be quite a time consuming and frustrating chore as you try to find where the officials have their offices and in which order they wish you to visit them. Senor Roberts knew all the ropes and gave us a lot of other information besides, in English.

The road up from the docks gave a lovely perspective of the city. It is lined by a park on one side and many windowed galleries on the other. We lapped up the Spanish atmosphere finding the language so different from French on one's ear. Wonderful aromas of the Spanish tapas, savory snacks, emanated from the restaurants making our mouths water. We joined in with the traditional evening amble and were impressed how immaculately the Spanish families were attired. The old quarter was alive at night, particularly in the Plaza de Maria Pita with its colourful pavement cafes, and around the imposing three domed, ornate town hall.

Next day Mike and I set forth on 'mission coffee-pot'. The locker in the galley had not been closed securely during the passage, and the glass on the plunger coffee pot was broken. Andy stayed behind to change the engine oil, his least favourite activity—after blocked heads!

We had become adept at communicating in French dredged up from our school days and hardly in grammatical fashion, but we could all get by with the odd English word thrown in. Neither Mike nor I had any background in Spanish and we soon found none of the shopkeepers here spoke any English. Our limited "si, no and gracias", enhanced by pointing and gesturing, wasn't getting us very far with the purchase of any kind of coffee pot, let alone a specific type. After one particularly verbose, good-natured woman had rattled off directions for at least five minutes—we had the impression it takes a long time to say anything in Spanish—Mike and I collapsed in frustrated laughter and agreed to give up.

We returned to *Bagheera* laden with delicious Spanish goodies, in particular the paprika sausage, 'chorizo', at Andy's request, but having to admit failure regarding the coffee pot. Andy kidded us that he would find one in ten minutes and infuriatingly did so that afternoon. However he grew up in Spain and Portugal and, although somewhat rusty, his Spanish was quite impressive in producing coffee pots—but we did take our old one for visual reinforcement this time!

Early next morning Colin and I made a quick trip ashore to buy fresh rolls. They were still steaming from the oven and we were soon both diving into the bag. Suddenly Colin was jumping and pointing.

"Just look at the lights," he cried.

It was the reflection of the sun off thousands of windows, the pinpoints of brilliance causing La Coruña to be given the name the Crystal City.

We left under power for the 30 nautical mile trip to the village of Lage as there was dense fog and not a ripple of wind on the water. Colin had just discovered Roald Dahl and I read 'Charlie and the Chocolate Factory' to him for a major portion of the trip. We had tried some school but all felt queasy in the swell. It was fine to sit in the cockpit and read, or lie on one's berth, but another matter to sit at the table, focus on school books, keep them still and attempt writing or math.

Lage is an active fishing harbour full of brightly painted local boats and we started a daily ritual of going to see them unload their catch and negotiate for our supper. There was always a great variety of fish to choose from, probably red mullet and bass were our favourites but the sardines and horse mackerel were also quite delicious. The shops were far removed from those in sophisticated La Coruña. Most sold 'every-thing and anything'. On leaving I always felt that if only one had explored further into the dusty rafters there would have been some wonderful treasures to be found.

The next few days were beautiful with the temperature at a constant 25 degrees celsius. It was perfect for the endless hours spent on the long sandy beach with Steve and Andrea and French Canadians Michel, Claudette and four year old Caroline who had arrived on their yacht *Modus Vivendi*. For the next month we continued to cruise together. The three Beneteaus were all similar in size; *Modus Vivendi* an Idylle 11.5, *Severance* a First 375 and *Bagheera* a First 38s.

From Lage we rounded Cape Finistere. It was gusting 45 knots, another full gale, but the wind was almost behind us and the temperatures were still warm. We all stayed on deck, the boys mesmerized by the turbulent seas.

We decided after this rough trip that in these conditions the boys should wear lifelines as well as their lifejackets, so Andy made some up with webbing and clips he had on board. We gave the older two boys longer lines so that they could manoeuvre around the cockpit from a central hook to steer, push the buttons of the autohelm, look at the instruments etc, that were all in the stern. But we made Jamie's line short because years ago I heard of a young girl who had fallen overboard and was strangled by her lifeline. The tragedy of the story had always stayed with me, so Jamie had a short line and sat right next to the padeye hook where he was clipped on.

We celebrated Colin's seventh birthday in Muros. It was the first of many relaxed birthday parties, with friends of the moment. Duncan made and strung up a colourful 'Happy Birthday' sign—a few decorations go a long way on a boat—and we all made and decorated a chocolate cake. It seemed far removed from the moments of panic I had experienced at home when I had felt far from ready when the hordes of friends invaded. Water games on the beach were easy entertainment and some local children joined in, somewhat confused by our soccer rules, or lack of them, but having a great time nevertheless.

Our family birthday tradition is to give the other children a small gift and we had found for two year old Jamie a typical plastic toy telephone. He was thrilled and said into the receiver, "*Severance, Severance*, this is *Bagheera, Bagheera*."

Poor Jamie was most surprised when we all burst out laughing. How quickly he had become a boat kid where his only telephone experience was listening to us using the radio.

Andrea returned to Vancouver for her sister's wedding and Mike went back aboard Severance to help Steve. As we pressed on to Bayona the winds increased and the seas continued to build. We hadn't expected this from the weather forecast. Steve was towing his dinghy with his outboard on its stern. Since our incident in the Beaulieu River we hadn't experienced any problems towing. Generally we trailed a drogue behind the dinghy which gave it added stability, decreasing the likelihood of it's slewing from side to side or riding up our transom.

On a huge breaking wave Steve's dinghy surged up *Severance's* stern swim ladder and turned over.

"*Bagheera, Bagheera,*" Steve called urgently on the radio. "Will you stand by while I sort out my dinghy. It's flipped."

In these turbulent seas it took Steve and Mike considerable strength and balance to lean out over *Severance's* stern to try to turn the inflatable dinghy right side up. A couple of times we watched it almost go back, then flip upsidedown again.

"Oh no!" groaned the boys in unison, their eyes riveted.

Finally it was right side up and tied alongside. Next the outboard had to come off to be rinsed with fresh water. We watched anxiously as Steve tried to climb into the inflatable that was jerked abruptly on the towline and violently bumped into *Severance's* hull. One minute the dinghy was the same height as *Severance's* deck, and the next it was several feet below. Steve finally timed a jump, made contact, and crouched to the dinghy floor, clinging to the pontoons to stabilize his balance. Slowly he unfastened the Yamaha 8.8 horse power outboard and then, the most hazardous move yet, tried passing it up to Mike. Steve seemed to be standing in mid-air one minute and bent right over the next trying to stay level and close enough to *Severance's* deck, whilst clinging to the 30 kilogram engine. It was agony watching him go up and down and up and down but finally Mike strained over the side, grabbed the engine and quickly swung it inboard over *Severance's* lifelines.

There was an audible sigh of relief on *Bagheera*. But all was not done as the ring for the tow line had pulled out of the inflatable's bow and Steve had to jury rig a towing bridle.

Mike was quickly able to call us on the radio.

"*Bagheera,* can you see the red dinghy fuel tank in the water? We've lost it."

"We'll take a look, and see if we can retrieve it," was our immediate response.

We did get several brief glimpses of red as the can was tossed by the waves, and we started to head in its direction. As we approached we realized how precarious it would be for one of us to reach out with the boat hook and actually try to bring such a heavy item on board. Also we could not afford to go too close, for the steel tank could have done extensive damage if it had pounded into our fibreglass hull.

It was one of those difficult situations. We really wanted to help but the consequences could be far more severe and more expensive than a new tank. After a series of huge, breaking waves we decided to abandon

Sailing the European Atlantic Coast (off Cape St. Vincent)

the attempt. It was obviously the right decision but we did feel badly that a new inflatable fuel tank in Vigo was a horrendous $200, compared to the usual $40 in Canada.

It was to picturesque Bayona that Christopher Columbus returned in *The Pinta* after discovering the Americas in 1492. We pulled into the marina at the foot of the walls of an old, picturesque castle that had been tastefully turned into a luxury government-run parador, the Conde de Gondomar. The town is also charming with old, narrow streets and superb restaurants. We enjoyed some Spanish favourites: kidneys with sherry, squid stuffed with sausage meat, Spanish omelette with its potato filling and peppers fried in olive oil, although I nearly expired when I took a bite into the only spicy hot pepper of the dish. We all had a communal paella one night. The short-grained, golden saffron rice tasted crusty from the wood burning stove, and it was piled high with fish, shellfish, sausage, chicken and vegetables—a delectable combination of individual flavours.

Usually we would give the boys dinner on board, make sure Jamie was asleep, and leave Duncan and Colin reading with a 'lights out' time limit.

Our neighbours kept an eye on them and if there was a problem we were close by. This worked well until the boys found out that Caroline, from *Modus Vivendi*, was always going out with the adults. As a four year old, and an only child, Michel and Claudette were naturally used to taking her everywhere, and she did not have to get up for school in the morning. As a mother of three up early teaching school, I needed my time out! We compromised by taking the boys out on occasion for dinner but more often for lunch which was an incentive to finish school quickly and worked far better for Jamie than a late evening.

On the docks the boys learnt from the locals how to catch squid- it was a favourite past-time here—and the children would return, proudly showing off their catch, their faces as black as the dock from the squids' ink.

We all loved our time in Bayona, but temperatures were cooling. A fog descended just after I had done a massive load of laundry. It had been too thick for the sun to penetrate and the boat had been draped for a couple of days with clammy garments that clung like magnets whenever one ventured forward on deck.

"Lets get going," Andy urged us all. "I know I've got 'cape-itis', but I really do want to keep in the marvellous weather pattern we've been experiencing for so long. Autumn is here and we need to head south."

3. Portugal

Oporto, Nasare, Lisbon, Lagos, Vilamoura and the River Guadiana

We had to motor down most of the long sandy coast of Portugal as there was no wind and we frequently experienced fog. The flat calm conditions did however allow us to get some school completed while we were underway, for it was annoying for all of us that when we arrived in a new place and were dying to explore, school took up much of our time.

We were rather disappointed with northern Portugal for the towns were often scruffy and dirty, all the more noticeable when one has small children. Several sea walls had been recently built that weren't marked on our charts or mentioned in our cruising guides, and we had to time our landfalls so we still had good light on arrival. Although we enjoyed the sheltered harbours, so often sewage pipes flowed right into the best anchorages rather than a few hundred feet away in the free flowing current.

We moved on quickly to Leixoes where we found Americans Jay and Connie. They had commissioned their Nicholson 32, *Lively Lady*, in the marina in Lymington, at the same time as Andy. We compared notes about our trips down the coast and commiserated with them about their dinghy being stolen, although fortunately they had found a used one to buy.

Next day we took the tram to hilly Oporto where we toured the ornate stock exchange, the Palacio da Bolsa, tasted red and white Port wine in the caves and admired the traditional graceful sailing craft that transported the barrels downstream for shipping.

The sail, or rather motor, to Nasare was in particularly dense fog. We decided to keep offshore and then follow the 10 fathom (18 metre) contour line using our depth sounder which would bring us into the shore by the bay. *Modus Vivendi* followed in our wake. Meanwhile *Severance* chose to head into shore sooner, taking a more direct route. Suddenly they noticed the depth was rapidly shallowing on the sounder and eased back on their speed.

"*Bagheera*, this is *Severance*. Just to say we sighted land, but not until we were just about on the beach. The fog is unbelievably thick. We're now heading for the fishing port."

When Andy and I had visited Nasare on our honeymoon in 1973, they still pulled the brightly coloured, high bowed, Phoenician styled fishing boats up the beach with oxen. Now they have a big harbour with tractors for the smaller boats and docks for larger vessels. The docks were a pleasant surprise as the bay was an open rolly anchorage with the surge from the rollers crashing onshore, untenable for a safe dinghy landing.

The fishing industry here is extensive and many a fisherman was repairing his long lines along the beach. Beside, women in traditional long black dresses and head shawls were hanging the fish on racks to dry in the sun.

We came across a great character selling hot chestnuts and couldn't resist her lively gestures to come and buy. The aroma was wonderful and we peeled and munched them at once—quite delicious!

It was still attractive but the town had become touristy and we quickly moved to the back streets. Here we gazed into shops full of hanging bacalao (salted cod), the staple of the Portuguese diet and Andy suggested we purchase some so that he could create a favourite dish. One of Andy's father's pleasures in life was experimenting with different foods, particularly those of Spain and Portugal, and Andy had been captivated by his enthusiasm. He continues to love the exotic and extreme; for example if I have offal, the edible entrails of animals ('awful', the boys call it!) or tripe (the stomach of the cow) for dinner, Andy is ecstatic and quite happy to cook that night!

Most goods were still reasonably priced, especially food. We didn't even have to rationalize the price of eating out in Portugal; it really was as cheap as eating in and we took full advantage of the fact. One evening on our way back from a local's restaurant where they served steaming pots of caldeirada, the traditional fisherman's stew, Andy stopped dead in his tracks.

"Sshh, everyone, listen," he said quickly, "that's our outboard, I'm sure of it. Someone is using our dinghy."

As usual we had taken the dinghy to the beach side of the harbour to halve the walk into town. We rushed down the road and turning the bend, saw the dinghy was gone. It was heading to the far side of the harbour. We continued full tilt, picking our way through nets and building debris.

"Thank goodness it's rough today," panted Andy, "otherwise they might have headed out down the coast."

The dinghy had been zig-zagging around and when we reached the wharves it was close. We could hear children's voices above the whine of the outboard and suddenly they zoomed in front of us, just as the moon came from behind a cloud—it was three boys joy riding.

Andy called out. He and Mike rushed off after them again. Steve and I stayed put in case they came back. Almost instantly there was an eerie silence. We waited, expecting them to roar off again but the silence continued, not even a murmur of a kid's whisper.

"Don't you think we had better start looking." I said quietly to Steve at last.

We searched up and down the fishing boats, peering between and around them thoroughly. Our grey inflatable was not going to be easy to see, especially since the moon had disappeared again.

At last there was a shout from Andy.

"Liza. I've found it!"

What a relief. The children had gone alongside a large fishing boat but Andy had spotted the dinghy from the far side of the dock. It was untied but fortunately one of the boys had bothered to throw the painter onto the fishing boat and it had snagged between the nets.

We had been lucky, but it made us realize we should take some preventative measures. Andy fitted a wire line and padlock to the dinghy. Later he painted fluorescent stripes on our outboard, and identifying colours on our oars and transom. His theory was that a possible thief or joy rider would want a standard boat, one that couldn't be easily recognised, and would pass us by. Almost without exception, his theory worked.

Our neighbours on the dock were a delightful French couple. After a day ashore they called over,

"You must go to Batalha and Alcobaca. That's where we went today and they are both fascinating," they enthused. "They're monasteries and you can easily go by local bus."

It sounded appealing and we were ready for a trip inland. Many of our stops had been in tourist towns or ports and we felt we were missing some of the true flavour of the Portuguese way of life.

It was indeed a contrast to the coast as we travelled through the sweet smelling pine forests to visit the monastery of Batalha. King Joao I had made a vow to build the finest church in the land to honour the Virgin if she helped defeat the forces from Castile, and today it is still one of the most magnificent buildings in Portugal. It was started at the end of the fourteenth century and stands by itself in a huge courtyard, an impressive Gothic masterpiece of flamboyant towers, buttresses, arches, columns, and even decorative water fountains. The scene was complete as the monks filed out of the many tiered arched doorway in their long, white robes. The interior, however, was simple and elegant, with one magnificent vase of white lilies on the altar. The central nave whose height is thirty metres quite took one's breath away.

Alcobaca, situated on the Alcoa and Baca rivers is home to the grand Santa Maria Monastery that was built in the 12th century by King Afonso I to celebrate the defeat of the Moors. Majestic, despite its baroque facade, the interior was again awe-inspiring with its 100 metre long nave with chalk-white clustered columns like trees holding up the vaulted ceiling. The abbey was also vast and the boys were amused that the monks whilst roasting half a dozen oxen, could fish at the same time, since the stream ran right through the middle of the kitchen.

Another day trip took us close to Lisbon and some wind, at last, for a good sail. We planned to spend several days in the area as Andy had lived just outside Lisbon, at Monte Estoril, as a boy.

We anchored off Cascais. Andy remembered it as a small fishing village, now it has developed into a thriving tourist town. The boys were delighted to be taken to Daddy's favourite fishing rock, just missed by the new concrete sea wall.

The conditions looked perfect when we returned to the boat after an evening amble through the lively streets but the wind swung and increased during the night, producing an uncomfortable onshore swell.

We decided to leave early after a restless night's sleep, and Andy started to pull up the anchor. I motored up into wind and he pulled in the slack line by hand until it was vertical. Normally he would try pulling up the anchor and chain from the bottom too depending on the depth and therefore the weight. This time the anchor would not budge so he resorted to the manual anchor windlass which was efficient but slow, and still had no success. Andy signalled to me to motor backwards and forwards and around but the anchor was firmly lodged.

Michel from *Modus Vivendi* and Jay from *Lively Lady* came over in their dinghies to give a hand. As Andy and Michel were hanging over *Bagheera's* bow peering into the murky water, a huge breaking wave hit, lifting the bow way out of the water. Simultaneously there was a terrible grinding noise. To our horror, the anchor windlass had been ripped right out of the deck.

Not only was the damage infuriating but the anchor itself was still firmly stuck. Now the only way to get it free was for Andy to dive into the violent water and check it out. Climbing hand over hand down the rode, he found our hook caught under a huge ship's anchor chain, long since abandoned. It took several dives to dislodge it and Andy finally hauled himself up the swim ladder and back on board, thoroughly exhausted.

As we entered the Tagus River we passed the melon shaped domes and turrets of Torre de Belem, the beacon sailors have used for centuries when entering Lisbon. In white stone it looked a perfect miniature castle and brand new, but in fact dates back to the early 16th century. Beside it is the imposing 'Monument to the Discoveries'.

"But who are those people?" asked Colin, fascinated, for each face on the monument was a character with its own unique expression.

It was time for a quick history lesson for the boys and a refresher for us. It was from Lisbon that Henry the Navigator, King Joao II and King Manuel I sent ships into the uncharted Atlantic and down the coasts of Africa. Prince Henry's sailors, who set off from the Algarve, discovered Madeira and the Azores, and in 1487 Bartholomew Diaz unwittingly sailed round South Africa and discovered a new route to India. Later Vasco da Gama was sent to sail that same route and in 1498 reached Calcutta in India. These voyages were possible due to the skills of the Portuguese as navigators, and made Lisbon the richest capital in Europe.

We continued up river and two nautical miles past the bridge came to a guarded yacht harbour where we pulled in alongside the stone wall with several other boats. We were now in the Alfama, the old Moorish quarter of the city, a fascinating rabbit warren of narrow cobbled streets, winding passages, ramps and stairways. High overhead the laundry streamed in the breeze, strung across the alleyways between the wrought iron, geranium covered balconies. In places the eaves of the old dwellings that

Colin by Torre de Belem in Lisbon

were spared the earthquake of 1755 were almost touching. We could vividly imagine the scene painted by the poet Frederico de Brito in his lines, "Your house is so close to mine! In the starry night's bliss, to exchange a tender kiss, our lips easily meet, high across the narrow street." Our sense of direction was soon lost when we went exploring in this maze. Fortunately the city is set on a steep hill so we could always find our way back to the waterfront.

"How about going to a bullfight tonight," suggested Steve.

"Oh, can we come too?" called out Duncan and Colin enthusiastically.

"Thanks, but it's not for me," said Andy. "I can't bear to see or hear the poor bulls. But why don't the rest of you go and I will look after Jamie?"

Since the twelfth century the locals have revelled in the colourful, dramatic spectacle of the bullfight and in Spain the highly skilled matador still flirts with death with every swirl of his cape. In Portugal they do not kill the bull but it can be every bit as gory.

The boys were enthralled with the opening parade. The matadors entered the ring with a flourish, dazzling in their 18th century costumes and were followed by the cavaleiros on horseback. Next came the mocos de forcado, brilliant in their gold jackets, red sashes and olive-coloured trousers.

Then the fight began. The trumpets blared and the cavaleiro and bull thundered into the ring. The horseman and his steed raced towards the bull—swerving just in time to avoid a head-on collision—but passing close enough to thrust three or four darts into the bull's neck. As more and more blood oozed out, the bull became increasingly confused and infuriated, and the crowd roared wildly.

Colin clutched me tightly. We had both been watching in horror. By this time I was totally in agreement with Andy's sentiments.

Tension rose further when it was the turn of the tacklers, the forcados. "Eh, Touro! Eh touro!" their leader cried as eight advanced on foot to tackle the bull with nothing but their bare hands.

"No!" cried Colin, as the bull began to charge and we both hid our eyes.

It was all over. The bull had lost too much blood and he had no more strength left. It had been a memorable experience of local culture but one we would not be clamouring to repeat.

Another day we all rented a minibus and drove up to see Sintra, the high inland town used by royalty during the heat of the summer, and we were enthralled by its fairy tale castles, abundant waterfalls and lush forests. I had first visited Sintra with Andy in 1973 and it remains magical, almost unspoiled by time or invasions, whether the Roman or Moorish armies, the English or German romantics or, most daunting of all, the modern tourist.

We climbed to the top of the Moorish castle and the boys imagined they were defending the land. As we looked across to the imposing Castel da Pena on the top of one of the highest hills, Mike had an idea.

"Hey Duncan if you move over a bit your Mum could take a photo of you picking up a castle."

Duncan was thrilled when he got in position by the battlements and cupped his hand in line with the distant pointed turret of Pena Palace, silhouetted against the deep blue sky.

We were the first visitors of the day at the maritime museum, and to our surprise were waved in by the smiling attendant free of charge. Here the old maps and charts illustrated our history lesson and much more especially the intricate models, displays of old ships and royal barges.

It had been recommended that we visit the zoo. We were just discussing our distress at seeing the animals in such meagre, unhygienic cages when the boys rushed ahead to watch the gorillas being fed. Then one of the male gorillas looked up and suddenly went quite berserk. He grabbed and rattled the bars of the cage, rushed to the back and scrambled around briefly before bounding forward again. Crying out hysterically he hurled with all his might a handful of faeces straight at our friend Jay who had just caught the boys up. The gorilla continued in his fury, crying loudly, pulling the bars with great force, making no bones that he would try anything to get out. We all watched aghast.

Why had the gorilla's mood suddenly changed? The only reason we could think of was that he had reacted to Jay's outfit, as Jay was dressed like the great white hunter, in complete khaki safari attire, including the pith helmet. We felt sure that old memories of his capture had precipitated the gorilla's behaviour, which had apparently been unprecedented in the zoo.

It was not exactly the pleasant Sunday afternoon outing Jay had anticipated and we promptly climbed into a taxi, for a change of clothing was definitely the order of the day!

We had a final dinner with Michel and Claudette in a friendly restaurant in the old quarter, run by a charming father, son and guitar-playing girlfriend. Next morning we waved *Modus Vivendi* out of the harbour; they were off to Madeira and across the Atlantic. We were all sorry to see them go; the boys had enjoyed playing with Caroline, Duncan had been able to continue his French lessons with Claudette, and it had been great sailing in company and sharing new experiences together.

Having completed our chores, the most important being refitting the anchor windlass, and having satiated our cultural yens, it was time for us to leave, but not before visiting the wine store. Portuguese wine was cheap and very drinkable so Andy went to town. Eighty-three bottles later, averaging 80¢ a bottle, it was my turn to say,

"But where are you going to put it all?"

The evasiveness of his reply, "Never you mind, I've the perfect spot," sounded very familiar! He packed most of the bottles round the inflatable water tanks under our seats in the main cabin and for the next few weeks we always knew when we were running low on water by the clunking of glass.

We headed off to the beaches of Sesimbra leaving Steve and Andrea behind. The blades of their folding propeller had jammed on one side and they were waiting for a new one to arrive. We anchored off the fort and found the water so clear that Andy, Duncan and Mike decided to clean the bottom of the *Bagheera*. It needed it, we had lost almost a knot in speed. Meanwhile I cooked succulent swordfish steaks which we had just bought from the fishermen.

Next day after school the boys busily drew colourful turkeys to decorate the boat since it was Thanksgiving. Purchasing turkey and the ingredients for pumpkin pie was a challenge but we managed the turkey and an acceptable desert, almond tart.

In balmy conditions *Bagheera* rounded the 'corner' of Cape St.Vincent, the site of the famous 1797 sea battle where the British beat the mighty Spanish fleet. The boys discovered it was here that Nelson had first made a name for himself when, as a commodore, he had caused the surrender of two Spanish ships by turning his ship out of the battle line on his own initiative. They tried to imagine the scene from the pictures of the ships in our encyclopedia.

We would now be heading east rather than south as we sailed along the coast of the famous Algarve. The land here is very flat. The cliffs rise up out of the ocean impressively straight and high, with unusual shaped pillars and arched rock formations along the sandy shores. It was a great area in which to relax, the weather was hot, the beaches are accessible and the towns very clean. However tourism has become big business and the abundance of English voices was a little disconcerting.

Everyone particularly liked Lagos, an old town, which has been tastefully developed with an interesting museum with Roman and Phoenician artifacts from the area. Colin remembers it as the place he was given his first snorkelling gear, while Duncan got luminous yellow replacement flippers. The diving was almost tropical, but for Andy and Mike it was the beaches that won their vote. They loved the sight of the numerous bronzed topless girls and, usually unheard of, Andy actually suggested going to lie on the beach for the afternoon on more than one occasion!

We stayed a week at the marina at Vilamoura working on the boat, getting ahead in school, using the pool to further the children's swimming skills; and Mike gave Duncan some tennis lessons. The development was extensive with every sports facility imaginable and was rapidly expanding for the British package tourist. In its way it was attractive but to us very sterile. Mike spent his time here walking the docks and found a boat that would take him to the Caribbean. He was lucky as there were many people looking for an Atlantic passage and it was getting late for yachts to complete the passage and commission the boat in time for the Caribbean charter season. We waved our sad farewells—Mike had been with us for a long time—and set sail for Tavira.

Here Steve and Andrea came over to watch the eclipse of the moon. The boys were mesmerized and there was great demand for the binoculars. It made such an impression on Jamie that for weeks after whenever he saw the moon, whether day or night, he would call out "Look, the moon, the moon!" That night we had our first real raid by mosquitoes. As usual it was Andy and Duncan who were attacked viciously while the rest of the family remained almost unscathed. I made a note to buy repellent as soon as possible.

Our next trip took us back into Spain to the attractive border town of Ayamonte. Mediterranean in style, its whitewashed buildings are stacked up the hillside and palm trees grow along the front.

It was now the end of October and Hallowe'en. For days the boys had been getting us into the spirit. Duncan had decided to be a lizard, Colin wanted to be Shadow, the grey cat we had left behind in Vancouver, and Jamie was to be the good old standby, a rabbit, and decided to call himself Carrot. Andy even sacrificed an old and rather brittle chart for the ears. The boys spent most of the day on their costumes and making decorations. Bats, spiders and ghosts were produced in abundance from coloured paper, particularly by Colin, and we had to raid the school art supplies for the quantities of black and orange demanded. Soon creations adorned our main cabin to the boys satisfaction, dangling on thread from the deckhead and flapping eerily in the candlelight. A green, knobbly melon was purchased for a pumpkin and Andy helped the boys carve an acceptably gruesome face.

Some American friends dropped by in wild black wigs. Then we all went over to *Severance* for a 'trick or treat' treasure hunt and dinner. It was a different Hallowe'en to remember but the children had a wonderful time and the inevitable sugar 'high' the next morning.

The border between Spain and Portugal at this point is the River Guadiana, navigable for 25 nautical miles. Several people had told us it should not be missed so *Severance* and *Bagheera* we headed up river the next day. It was a magical trip. The river abounds with wild life, farm animals and varying vegetation. It seemed every moment there was something new to look at through the binoculars, from storks to vultures and from olive to pomegranate trees. Again it was interesting to leave the coast and go into the countryside, with all the small farmsteads and villages.

We anchored in the last navigable stretch of the river off the Spanish village of San Lucar, the two yachts creating perfect silhouettes in the totally still water. It was charming ashore, a white town with the whitewashed buildings gleaming in the sun. We patted friendly donkeys with bulging leather bags on their backs and watched the shepherds tending the sheep in the fields beyond, the muted bells gently clanging. We wandered to a deserted windmill and gazed up at a huge storks nest, three metres in diameter, which was perched on top. Andy found some over-ripe almonds and under-ripe olives, both as bitter as each other. Then Duncan found a perfect pomegranate, which hadn't been emptied by the birds. Not only was it delicious but it cleansed our palates again. We all fell in love with San Lucar, it was so serenely peaceful, and quite Andy's ideal lifestyle.

On the trip down river even more creatures were discovered and the children wrote a full page of what they had seen, under their chosen headings of four-legged mammals, arthropods, fish, birds and reptiles. We were impressed at their observations and memories.

We left for Cadiz at 4:00 AM. It was a cold, rough trip and we needed to get out sweaters and oilskins again. The sharp waves were hard work for the autopilot and for the first time it failed and went off course. The batteries were low because we hadn't realized how much power the autohelm had been using. We quickly started the main engine to recharge them.

I decided to take the helm anyway, enjoying the sensation of the boat as it surged along in the 25 knot breeze with the wind just forward of the beam. It is essential to have an autohelm when cruising as a couple and particularly when one has children on board. We couldn't have managed without it. There were times, however, particularly when the children were asleep and I could just be myself, I found it intensely exhilarating to be on the wheel, with a blustery wind on my face, long hair streaming behind, and my body moving effortlessly in complete harmony with the motion of the boat and the ocean.

On arrival at Cadiz we first went to the Puerto de Santa Maria as recommended in the guide, but found there was a terrible odour of sewage and a club fee of $20 a night. In town there was a welcoming yacht harbour. Their club had wonderful hot showers, particularly appreciated after the cold, wet trip.

It was raining hard the next day but a train ride to Jerez de la Frontera and a visit to the Sandeman sherry winery provided entertainment for all.

In contrast there was a warm perfect 12 knot breeze for our trips to Barbate and on to Gibraltar.

"What is Gibraltar like Daddy?" asked Duncan, awed by the huge rock that now soared up out of the ocean ahead.

"I have many marvellous memories of Gibraltar from my naval days but the last time I was here, Mummy and I had just sailed across the Atlantic together on the 72 foot Yacht *Eileen*, after we were married in the Caribbean in 1973. It's from Gibraltar that the British have controlled the entrance to the Mediterranean for nearly three hundred years. There's a lot to see, and great shopping for Christmas presents," he replied with a smile.

The
Mediterranean

4. Gibraltar and Spain

Granada, Alicante, The Balearic Islands and Wintering in Menorca

Gibraltar is the crossroads for boats entering and leaving the Mediterranean and an extended resting place for those deciding what to do next. There were two marinas jammed full of boats of every description and people were very welcoming.

As much as we had enjoyed the French, Portuguese and Spanish cuisines, good old English fish and chips and draft beer went down very well. I must say it was a relief being able to communicate in one's own language to get the chores completed: repairs to the boat, buying new clothing, stocking up on particular groceries, school supplies and new books. We were also able to buy charts and guide books secondhand. Andy returned one morning quite pleased with himself as he had bought 113 charts for $160, an incredible bargain as they were $15 apiece new. One can go through several small and large scale charts a day so it was a wonderful saving.

We were also able to glean several tips about Mediterranean cruising, although a comment from an old Caribbean acquaintance was typical.

"Don't count on good sailing, it's either a flat calm or blowing like stink with a rotten, sharp sea. But ashore it's marvellous."

Meanwhile school was going well with only the occasional expected moan and groan. I was pleased that Duncan had finished the Canadian northwest coast Indian programme ahead of time so we could study something a little more topical. I had also included several extra, fun activities—drama, calculators, problem solving and lots of physical education, as much to let off steam as for their skills.

The children had been good at coping with an erratic timetable that depended on our sailing schedule. Unfortunately, other than our foggy trips down the Portuguese coast, we had found it mostly wasn't possible to do anything underway—we either felt and looked green or gently nodded off over our texts—neither very conducive for producing successful assignments. The distractions on board, too, were endless. There were so many interesting things happening around us, people dropping by, or a weather forecast to listen to.

Andy was great at keeping Jamie occupied. Often they would go ashore to check out the fresh fare at the markets and their pre-lunch drink at a shoreside bar became quite a ritual.

As promised we went on an exploratory tour around the rock seeing the battlements, tunnels, guns and the outer cavern of the extensive limestone caves full of huge, long, dripping stalactites and bulbous stalagmites. Our driver was personable and a knowledgable guide but he particularly enjoyed taking us to see the apes which live on the steep slopes. They in turn greeted him like a long lost friend and were delighted to take his special goodies from the boys.

The flavour of the town had changed since our last visit as it was no longer a duty free port but it was still excellent for shopping. The boys loved wandering the streets looking at the toy shops and particularly at the electronic games. Finally Andy and I allocated an afternoon, left the boys with friends and set out for the usually dreaded task of Christmas shopping. Decisions seemed so easy, however, without the usual influence of peer pressure and television advertisements, so we had fun, completing our purchases in just a couple of hours.

It was hard to leave Gibraltar. The convenience of walking one's supermarket trolley down the dock, laundry facilities, a local pub, good company and friends for the children was enticing. However after a visit aboard the new British aircraft carrier, 'Ark Royal', interesting since Andy had spent many months aboard its predecessor whilst in the Royal Navy, we did finally bid our 'good-byes' on November 18th. Our departure was serenaded by a minute aerobatic helicopter which displayed its talents with loops and stall turns to the accompaniment of the childrens' excited waving.

It was then time for us to 'fly' up the Spanish Mediterranean Costas as we had a deadline in Menorca. Our daily routine was rising at 7:00 AM, starting school by 7:30 AM and being underway by 11:00 AM.

To Duncan's delight we had consistently good fishing, catching several meal-sized tuna which were quite mouth watering. One night, as we were eating another of Andy's delicious tuna creations, Duncan commented, "Did you know that not all fish are cold blooded, the tuna for instance?"

"But being cold blooded is one of the definitions of a fish," Andy replied.

Andy has always been very interested in fish, animal and plant life and always amazes friends with his general knowledge. This seemed a basic issue.

"But Daddy that's not what it says in YOUR book," replied Duncan defensively.

"Okay, you show me," Andy challenged.

Andy soon learnt not to contradict Duncan's specific knowledge so readily for on subsequent occasions Duncan would have the page number of his reference at his finger tips as well! It stimulated frequent research and a lively interchange of knowledge between the two of them.

This part of the Spanish Mediterranean coastline is dominated by high, arid hills and new tourist developments. We found the white arched concentrated developments attractive initially but they palled rather with their frequency and similarity, and were expensive.

Our first stop was La Duquesa, made memorable for the boys as they were allowed to stamp their own passports. We found without exception officials the world over love children. Even the immigration and customs personnel with the most formidable of reputations softened at the sight of a smiling wide-eyed Jamie whom Andy made a point of taking ashore with him.

The winds were light the next day and we motored to the fishing town of Fuengirola, enjoying a sunbathe. In contrast on the following day we had 30, gusting to 40 knots.

"Wow", Duncan exclaimed loudly, partly due to his surprise but also so he could be heard above the roar of the dancing, glistening wake. He had been sitting in the cockpit, clipped on at the stern, monitoring the speedo closely. "We've just gone over eleven knots. Now it's reading 11.4!"

That was indeed an amazing speed for our boat and especially exhilarating because the breeze was offshore and the seas still relatively flat. But the wind was also extremely cold and we became all the more aware of the snow on the mountains and that winter was approaching.

We reached our destination at 2:30 PM so decided to continue to a new marina further down the coast, described and illustrated in our Spanish cruising guide. It was supposed to have been completed the year before, but to our surprise the coast was bare so we continued on to Motril.

Steve and Andrea had been ahead of us with *Severance* for some days having had friends on board with flight deadlines to meet. As we approached Motril we called as usual at 6:00 PM, our radio rendezvous time, and were delighted to hear Andrea loud and clear. As Andy departed to clear customs his last words were "Now don't plan anything Liza, we have to move on tomorrow."

However aboard *Severance* were an American couple who convinced us we had to see the Alhambra in Granada.

It was a wonderful day. A taxi arrived to take us to the local bus station with seven passenger seats. It was too good to give up so we rode the one and a half hours to Granada in luxury. We drove up lush green valleys with the snow clad Sierra Nevada mountains beyond. After the plethora of new tourist developments it was again refreshing to go inland and enjoy the slower pace of life of the rural Spanish who frequently use donkeys for their transportation. Granada was cold and we thought of Vancouver as we stamped our feet in the frost.

The Alhambra dates back to the thirteenth century; although the hill was fortified in earlier times. It was the masterpiece of Mohammed ben Alhamar who made himself lord of Granada and transformed the barren wastes by piping water from the River Darro. There is water to be found everywhere, used to the maximum aesthetic advantage in the palace and gardens.

The site contains both the fortress, the Alcazaba, successor to the old Moorish castles, and the palace or old Royal House with its picturesque gardens. The palace is a fragile structure with many delicate arches and is covered with fantastic ornamentation in ceramic and stucco. It is only due to fortuitous circumstances that it has survived where others that were similar have long since become piles of rubble. The location overlooking the city and mountains is also magnificent and the boys were captivated by the cave dwellers who could be seen from the palace windows.

We spent most of the day at the Alhambra but later as we wandered down to the town to find our taxi, thoroughly enjoyed some other aspects of Granada. We admired the marquetry work, in ebony, brass, mother of pearl and various woods and watched the masters working at this famous local craft. Later we visited a pottery shop. The patterns were so attractive but alas, pottery is too impractical to have on board. It had been a fascinating day and, Andy admitted, well worth the delay.

From Motril we moved rapidly to Alicante with short overnight stops, although we did linger a couple of days in Mar Menor, an inland saltwater lake where the entrance bridge is opened at one's request. We explored the lake by dinghy, managing to avoid the many fishing nets but returned with somewhat disgruntled children. Although *Severance* and *Bagheera* had purchased identical dinghies and outboards, without doubt *Severance's* was much faster, and that would not do! Andy had his mechanical expertise tested that afternoon, carefully monitored by his two eldest sons, and they achieved some success in reducing the lack of speed.

Although close hauled (wind almost ahead), it was a pleasant sail into picturesque Alicante with its palm treed promenade and Ste Barbara castle high on the hill. The yacht club was hospitable and to our surprise we found there were six other Canadian boats along the sea wall. Several yachts were wintering here, five of us were from the west coast. Of course we all got together over the next few days and exchanged our plans and experiences—the delight of this lifestyle.

The Spensleys from Victoria became particular friends. The boys were thrilled to get together not only with other children but with ones who were also on the British Columbia Correspondence Education Programme and had lots to talk about—I would have loved to have listened in!

We all celebrated Andy's birthday together with a delicious five course meal of soup, salad, fish, meat and finished with three large, sweet tangerines each which had just come into season. The bill came to $4 a head including wine. The next day, after an energetic game of soccer on the beach, we went swimming—not bad for December 1st.

That night Colin pleaded, "Mummy, it's December now, can we please listen to Christmas carols before bed. Remember you said we could listen to one tape a day?"

The discussion had taken place several months previously. Christmas would obviously be different this year but the boys had been particularly concerned that in Spain they wouldn't hear any of the familiar carols. We were soon all boisterously singing away and for the next six years carols starting on December 1st was a ritual the boys never forgot.

After a good spending spree at the lively Alicante market, for wonderfully fresh fruit and vegetables, olives, chorizo, swordfish, octopus and meat—although we did pass by the half chickens with unlaid eggs inside—we proceeded to the Spanish Balearic Islands. Steve and Andrea stayed on the mainland as they planned to ski extensively.

We left at 5:30 AM for Ibiza from Moraira, just north of Alicante. The winds were light but it was a spectacular day and the island was breathtaking with its rocky hills standing out clearly against the deep blue, totally cloudless sky. We anchored stern-to the government dock late in the afternoon in peaceful Puerto de San Antonia. Then spent an interesting evening as 'voyeurs' observing the extraordinary mix of exotic people out serenading, arguing and flirting!

We decided to go north about Ibiza to get favourable winds but as we came round the coast so did the wind and annoyingly it remained on the nose, causing a swell and rolly night in Cala San Vincente.

Mallorca is another beautiful island and as we entered Palma harbour there seemed to be yachts everywhere. We decided to go to a new huge marina and gazed at the massive motor yachts as we wandered up the dock. It was back to tourists and the yacht charter world and large numbers of Brits in the pub. We stayed to explore the palace and cathedral in Palma, then on to a sleepy fishing village, Cala Ratjada. *Bagheera* arrived in Mahon (the home of mayonnaise) the capital of Menorca, on December 9th, two days ahead of schedule.

We came to love Menorca and stayed far longer than anticipated, not leaving until March 3rd. Nearly three months is an interesting period; you have time to be an extensive tourist, try many restaurants and almost become a local, form close friendships and even relax at times.

My sister arrived two days after us from England and we quickly moved ashore to her villa. The week flew by and in no time we were celebrating an early Christmas on the eve of their departure. The boat was hauled out of the water by crane for antifouling painting of the bottom—more than a little nerve racking—and soon it was Christmas itself. We were fortunate to have marvellous neighbours, the Rossers, and spent much of Christmas day with them. We left only to gorge on a five course traditional lunch at Scandal's which was thoroughly enjoyed by all, particularly Duncan who appeared to consume double helpings throughout. Andy and I dined that evening with the Rossers and staggered home after much port and Fundador (Spanish brandy), having spoofed most convincingly at 'Liars Dice' for several hours.

The Rossers became the best of friends to us and were most appreciated by all the family. The boys were thoroughly spoilt with cookies, ice cream and fun, and Andy and I were indulged with baths, washing machines, wine, good food and excellent company.

Menorca abounds with prehistoric remnants and we spent several days exploring these sights. Of particular interest were the T-shaped Taulas, constructed from two massive stones and about five metres high. Their purpose is debatable but they were probably either sacrificial tables or central support pillars of covered buildings. Around each monument is a horseshoe-shaped precinct constructed from large, vertically placed flat stones that abut perfectly. Taulas are apparently exclusive to Menorca. Also of interest are the Talayots, multi-purpose stone domed buildings used as dwelling places, defence towers, and as places of burial. We explored whole prehistoric villages, dating back some 4,000 years. It was fascinating following the development from life in caves to dwellings, well defined in the areas that were excavated. After the trip to Granada the boys were intrigued by the cave dwellers of the present and the comparison brought those of the past into clear focus.

We loved the green countryside and the twenty minute drive between Son Parc and Mahon always brought new discoveries. Early on the binoculars had been borrowed from the boat and they were always put to good use.

Duncan wrote in his diary, "We have seen lots of birds here— kites, plovers, robins, sparrows, vultures, eagles, hoopoes, blackcaps, sparrow hawks and falcons."

We returned to *Bagheera* in late January. After a few days Andy started renewing his muttering about electricity. He had looked at wind generators in England and again in Gibraltar but dismissed them as too expensive. As fate would have it a fellow yachtsman in Menorca had one for sale.

"There is just nowhere for it to go on my narrow stern," he said ruefully. "I didn't think of that when I purchased it, it seemed such a good idea. It's still new in its box."

After negotiating an agreeable price for all we became the proud owners of a British-made Rutland Windcharger.

The next two days were spent assembling the 'windmill'. Finally it was ready for testing but there was a flat calm. To see the water without a ripple near an island where it always blows was unbelievable so Andy's party piece that night was that he had the key to solving the Menorcan storms. The lull did not last long, however, and we were soon testing in a full gale.

The 'windmill' was a great success although not quite our image of 'yachty'. It produced power according to the wind strength, for example above 18 knots it gives four amps which ran the lights and helped with the 'fridge and autopilot. It became a great topic of conversation and even Malta radio called us to ask what the propeller was doing above deck!

We would thoroughly recommend a wind generator to anyone who plans long term cruising: it's efficient and satisfying to know one is tapping a source of free, natural energy. It is important, however, to consider the design. We mounted ours on a stainless steel post right in the stern at a height where the blades were above Andy's head if he was standing on the deck. Later we saw several boats with portable windmills that were generally rigged forward of the mast and quite low. When the blades are turning quickly they are not immediately visible and we have heard gruesome stories of people who had rushed forward to attend to dragging anchors, totally forgetting the generator was in place, with violent, gory consequences.

In early February my stepmother died and I returned to England. It was a sad but medically merciful death and I was pleased that I had been in frequent contact with her in the previous months. Maisie had come into our lives almost nine years previously and endeared herself to all the family. She and my father married when they were 72 and 78—an inspiration for us all! She was a remarkable woman who spoke seven languages and it was only at her death that I learnt that she held both the 'Member of the British Empire' and the 'African Star'.

Whilst I was in England it snowed hard, in fact the temperature did not rise above zero degree celsius during my stay. The boys were most jealous until three days later when it snowed in Menorca.

"It just shows you how the weather of the world is changing," an elderly woman in Cuidadella said to us. "Such a thing was unheard of in my youth."

Certainly the old, whitewashed Menorcan houses with their thick stone walls, slit windows and tiled floors seemed far more suited to keeping out the heat from the sun than giving comfort during the cold, windy, damp weather of the current winters.

I had returned to a most welcoming family and was immediately introduced to a newcomer at the sea wall. *Te Vega* was an American school yacht for learning disabled teenagers. There had already been much interaction between the two vessels, in fact we never seemed to see our boys. The yacht itself was a 130 foot schooner built some fifty years ago. Andy was most interested when she arrived as he had dived on her to help salvage efforts when she had sunk in Antigua, in the West Indies, in 1968. We thoroughly enjoyed the teachers, crew, students and Steve and Kim Wedlock who ran the ship and school respectively, and their two year old son, Ben. In fact the whole programme thoroughly challenged Andy's and my imaginations—was this a way to sail, we mused, where I could have a career and we could have our children on board? We had been two and a half months in Menorca and as much as we loved the island it was a large chunk of our intended cruising time, so we began monitoring the weather more closely. Menorca is in the stormy Gulf de Lyon weather pattern, unlike Majorca and Ibiza, whose climates are similar to mainland Spain and more moderate. Also our next trip, to Sardinia, involved passing through the confluence of several Mediterranean weather patterns and it is not to be fooled with so early in the year.

"It's far too soon to go sailing, especially to Sardinia. You're crazy!" were the words of yachtsmen and locals alike.

It seemed in immediate response to their words we were hit by a severe storm. Our barograph recorded it all, a sheet Duncan saved for his diary. It showed that on Tuesday at 1:00 AM the barometric pressure was 1018 and by Thursday at 3:00 AM it bottomed out at 977, a 41 millibar drop in barometric pressure in two days. During this time we had thunderstorms with heavy rain squalls and it became bitterly cold. Winds of 62 knots (115 KPH) were reported although fortunately we were protected in massive Mahon Harbour and winds only just reached gale force at the boat. Interestingly the water level in the harbour went up about half a metre due to low atmospheric pressure and of course it was in the middle of the night that our lines to the sea wall started creaking and straining, then screaming. In our bleary state it was hard to comprehend that the water had risen that far, for there is generally very little tidal movement at all in the Mediterranean.

All the yachts with us by the town steps were safe but the seas were much rougher round the corner at the exposed yacht club where boats broke loose whilst flooding made the streets impassable.

So we waited, completing more school, seeing friends and visiting our favourite waterfront tapa bars not infrequently. But after the weather had been stable for some days and *Te Vega* had completed a benign trip to Corsica we felt it was now time for us to consider heading out.

We were fortunate that the Port office generally issued a relatively up to date weather forecast but the fact it was rather generalized made a good excuse to visit the local bar at 9:30 PM (which was always entertaining as there was a brothel next door) for the TV forecast, in Spanish of course, but we did get the weather pictures. Also our dock neighbours, who were ham radio buffs, were generous in relaying weather information for the area from reports they were monitoring from various other

Prehistoric T-shaped Taula and Talayot in Menorca

countries. This cumbersome way of gaining knowledge regarding local weather predictions was certainly an argument for having a long range radio on board but it was not in our budget at this time.

Thinking of our imminent departure Andy decided to organize an advance party for me on this significant birthday—my 40th. It was a splendid evening starting with eighteen on board for Fundador brandy and champagne cocktails. Overcrowded you think? Well in typical party form the 'living room' was quite civilized with seating available but the 'kitchen', with its eight square feet of floor space, was packed like a can of sardines. As I horizontalized at 4:30 AM I thought what a great celebration it had been—I was not quite so happy when I awoke!

My actual birthday occurred whilst we were in Tunisia. It was also quite a memorable occasion but that will come later.

March 3rd, 1986 dawned bright and clear with good weather prospects brought to us by our dock neighbours in their various languages. It was time to bid our farewells.

In particular the boys would miss their dock friends Rebecca and Jan Kees and those who had been so kind to us: David and Marion Rosser at the villa in Son Parc, Anne and Clemente Oliver who had collected our mail and had frequently taken our children out and Dennis and Derika Courthope-Boas who had armed us with books and lent bikes and an Optimist dinghy to the boys for the duration of our stay.

It was a heart-rendering feeling as I looked up while taking in the fenders to see everyone on the dock waving. It had been a relaxing interlude in Menorca and so secure.

Again the nagging worry flashed through my mind, "Were we really doing the right thing leaving so early?"

5. Sardinia, Tunisia and Malta

Despite all the misgivings it was a very pleasant sail to Sardinia. It was the longest trip the boys had made other than crossing the Bay of Biscay when Mike had been on board to spell our watches. The winds were light when we left the huge Mahon harbour and initially we motorsailed, soon passing our German friends who had left earlier that morning on their yacht *Kismet*. Then gradually the wind filled in and we had a comfortable 10 knot breeze on the port quarter for the rest of the afternoon.

"Let's look for the green flash," suggested Andy as we were all relaxing in the cockpit watching the sunset after dinner.

"What's that? Does the sun go green?" asked Colin giggling.

"Well actually it can," replied Andy, much to the boys' surprise.

The green flash is a phenomenon which some people are apparently unable to see, so put it down to stimulated imaginations from sundowner concoctions. As the sun goes over the horizon, green is the last visible colour to be refracted. On a totally clear day with no haze, as the sun disappears the last flash of its light can appear momentarily a brilliant green. It is a rare event because often even on perfect evenings, cloud will form minutes before sunset obscuring the clarity that is needed.

Andy and I have seen green flashes in the Caribbean on several occasions, some with amazingly intense colour, but hadn't yet on this trip.

"You can only look at the sun just as it disappears," warned Andy, "otherwise it is too bright and bad for your eyes."

"Now you can watch—watch carefully—keep watching. NOW—THERE IT IS!" It was a weak green light, but definitely there.

"Wow!" declared Duncan. "That really did flash green."

Colin moaned, "Oh no, I missed it. Did it really happen?"

Colin was to experience many brilliant green flashes later in our travels, but he had learnt that the flash is so instant that a turn of the head or a blink of the eye at the crucial moment can mean that you have frustratingly missed it all.

As the sun departed so too did the wind and we again started up the engine. The night became an eerie pitch black and I was thankful when Andy came on watch at 10:00 PM as I had imagined all sorts of creaks, moans and ghostly ships during my three hours on deck. I had really looked forward to going below on the hour, to write our position, wind, speed, distance etc. in the logbook.

The night was cold and I had bundled up, feeling rather like a stuffed squid, but was comfortably warm. On one of my trips down the companionway my bulging jacket managed to flip off the auto helm control. Poor Andy woke abruptly as the forward cabin swirled round 360 degrees at high speed before I had realised, reacted and switched it on again. Not a commendable way to be woken up for one's watch it appeared judging from his reaction!

The next day passed quickly. Andy gave me the luxury of sleeping most of the morning undisturbed although I noticed he had commented in the log, "Jamie bumped his head. Colin and Duncan squabbling—just a normal day!"

He also had Duncan take watch for an hour and plot our position on the chart from a latitude/longitude fix produced by the SatNav. This electronic device receives messages at intervals from satellites that circle the earth. For an accurate fix information is needed from a satellite that has an angle of more than 10° and less than 70° above the horizon. How often these fixes occurred varied in different parts of the world but here in the busy Mediterranean there was at least one, if not several, during any hour of the day. It is a wonderful device and has the advantage over a sextant of great accuracy without the need for calculations and tables. It also operates regardless of weather conditions and visibility which so limit celestial navigation.

Duncan was stimulated with the activity and showed me his work proudly, when I finally got up from the forward berth having heard repeated requests for lunch.

"Land, I can see land," called out Colin excitedly, at sunset that evening.

It had been a much faster trip than we had anticipated. We didn't like going into unfamiliar harbours at night, particularly with the moon rising so late, but it seemed a long time to hang off at sea until light next morning. Besides, it was an open approach, so we decided to press on.

Friends in Menorca had recommended Sant'Antioco. We were disappointed to find that it was a commercial port rather than the small fishing village we prefer but the dockmen were very welcoming with their wonderful singsong "Buon giorno"—Italian words of greeting.

After clearing customs and completing school next morning, we could explore. We were thankful Jamie's stroller was still holding up, both to transport Jamie himself and to return with the groceries as it was quite a hike to go shopping. The town was small and clean and the main square busy with people brightly dressed and noisily passing the time of day. It was a new language for us again and we were all intrigued, listening and watching while the locals with wide friendly smiles uninhibitedly did the same to us!

"Guess what?" said Duncan, stopping to read a menu. "We can have spaghetti bolognaise, a real Italian spaghetti in Italy itself!"

"Oh yes, can we please?" was the inevitable chorus. "I wonder if it will be like yours Mummy?" Colin added.

It was already 1.00 PM, tummies were rumbling and this appeared a lively locals' restaurant. The price, however, was a real shock, for the meal was more expensive than the large three course lunch for ten we had enjoyed a few days before in Menorca, one of the most expensive places in Spain. Also the portions of both pasta and meat sauce were somewhat meagre, definitely not like mine they all decided.

As we returned to the boat the dockmen were busily loading salt. They called out a welcome and beckoned the boys over. They all had a fine time jumping in the large salt granules, and returned to the boat flushed and exhausted. It was to be the last physical exercise for a while as that evening the rain storms set in with little relief for days.

We made our way along the south coast of Sardinia taking short watches, trying to shelter from the blinding rain and cold wind under our small companionway dodger whilst still peering round to keep a constant search for traffic. Visibility was frequently down to a few metres.

The parent 'off duty' helped with the entertainment below. 'Upwards', a three dimensional scrabble type word game, was the favourite activity of the week with Duncan and Colin, while Duncan had become an avid bookworm, fast consuming our purchases from the bookstores in Gibraltar.

In the small fishing harbour of Teulada during a welcome lull we managed a refreshing walk amongst the brilliant wild flowers, then continued on to the capital, Cagliari. Founded by the Phoenicians from Tyre at the same time as Carthage, Cagliari was subject to many other conquerors from Barcelona, Pisa, Naples and Byzantium before finally being settled by the Romans in 238 BC. It abounds with Roman ruins, Spanish churches and medieval citadels and we were looking forward to a stimulating visit. We had also read of Cagliari's dramatic position between the sea and mountains in one of the most beautiful harbours in the Mediterranean, but alas we could see very little on our entry on April 8th as the squalls continued.

Maybe the rain had dampened our enthusiasm in more ways than one, maybe it was the high prices and Andy's inherent dislike of cities but we could not warm to this town. We found it dirty, buildings poorly maintained and the people impersonal and unfriendly towards the children. We were going to visit the museum next morning but decided instead to leave for Tunisia.

"Wow!" exclaimed Duncan as he came up on deck at 9:00 that evening for a final goodnight. "There are lights everywhere."

Seven ships were in sight. We were crossing the Mediterranean shipping lanes at right angles and I had been kept on my toes figuring out their relative positions. So far they had all been well clear, but if ships were coming worryingly close it was reassuring to know that I could always wake Andy for a second opinion regarding a course change. Also it was reassuring to have company when those huge towering hulls glided past at four times one's own speed, particularly on a black night.

We made our landfall at Bizerte in North Africa. The 70 square kilometre Lake of Bizerte created a natural harbour that had convinced the Phoenicians to build their Punic Port Hippo Diarrhytus at this site. In more recent times the port had been jealously held by the French and the Italians had feared it as 'a pistol levelled at the heart of Italy'. It was handed back to Tunisia in 1963.

The 123 nautical miles had taken hours due to the initial light winds. We tied up at the yacht club and were impressed. Everyone was so helpful and polite and the culture was obviously very different. Since the earliest times Tunisia has been a meeting place of middle eastern and Mediterranean peoples and subject to many European invasions— Phoenician, Roman, Vandal, Byzantine, Arab, Norman, Spanish, Turkish and finally French. Tunisian aborigines were the Berbers, a dark-haired, brown-skinned people about whom little is known. The result is a varied looking population.

The boys were first struck by the very different style of dress. The men frequently wore the long brown cloak, a burnous or a kashabia, a topcoat that was also woollen, hooded and frequently striped, while those in western attire topped their smart suits with a red fez hat. The women wore long lengths of white cloth draped around them called sifsaris, which held many surprises within their folds from babies to groceries to live chickens. They were used to coyly cover the face if confronted by cavalier men or pulled seductively tight to attract them!

We were now into the Arabic language with its fascinating script on street signs of which we had zero comprehension but fortunately most people could speak to us in French.

"Mummy, listen," whispered Colin urgently in the middle of school. "What's that weird sound?"

It was an unusual wailing noise which suddenly blared louder than life as the electronic amplifiers clicked in.

"That's the muezzin, like an minister, calling everyone to prayer." I replied. "Remember Tunisia is a Moslem country; I think this happens five times a day. Lets go on deck and see where it's coming from."

We easily identified the tall square minaret as the source. Coming below I closed the hatches as the sound was quite invasive for teaching school, to say the least.

As we explored ashore we made the mistake of asking our way once too often and were 'befriended'. Despite early efforts to get rid of our self appointed guide we began to find him very informative, and so gave in. He took us into the Casbah, the garrison area of the old city, via an intriguing vaulted passage built to hamper medieval invaders, then for a glimpse of the 17th century mosque of the Medina with its pretty tiled minaret before entering the Great Mosque. Fortunately we had read how to dress correctly, in long pants or skirt.

We found the mosques beautiful with their ornate work and well proportioned lines. Most of the minarets were square although some in Tunisia, apparently from a different sect, are octagonal. Our guide, ever full of stories in his broken English and French and with descriptive gesticulations told us that whatever the sect, they all feared the pagan evil eye; so the elderly woman burn incense and smash pots of gewgaws (trinkets) at births and circumcisions. He had some interesting gestures for the latter!

The winding lanes, white arched alleys, woman with black veils and shops with thousands of goods hung on display were fascinating. Colin was again in his element and hard to pry away. Then up to the Fort of Spain originally built by the Turks in 1573 and turned into an open air theatre in 1968.

Finally it was time to settle the fee our guide was obviously expecting and which we should have negotiated in the beginning but of course he hadn't been planned. We had a struggle on our hands and it was an expensive lesson learnt.

On the advice of our German friends aboard *Kismet* we moved on to the marina at Sidi Bou Saïd close to Tunis. The town itself is situated very high on the hill—or so it seemed when we hauled the family up the hundreds of steps—and is delightful. The white buildings are mostly low arabesque structures with arches and domes. They are highlighted by Mediterranean sky blue doors on which black shiny studs had been used to create the most intricate of patterns.

The day we arrived was March 11th, my birthday. Andy had planned a family dinner ashore and we found a good restaurant 'Le Pirat' which was fortunately close by, as there was another torrential downpour. We had a delightful meal with some eye-streaming spicy hors d'oeuvres and a bottle of excellent French champagne. But it was the bill that shocked us into how excellent; although the food was relatively reasonable, the total bill was vast—and we did not have that much money with us!

The moral of the story is to know your currency because what we had understood to cost 7.500 dinars, or $15, was in fact 75 dinars, $150. As Andy said at $50 for a bottle of champagne he would have been outraged but $150 was so ludicrous all we could do was laugh—hysterically!?

The management were not so happy as they didn't accept credit cards or travellers cheques. In fact it was our very helpful waiter who was in a total panic because the restaurant's policy required the waiter to collect, otherwise he paid. One and a half hours later, after we had explained that we were on a yacht in the marina and promised to pay as soon as the banks opened next morning, we were offered local liqueur on the house and spent an interesting evening at the bar with the locals.

Bright and early next morning Andy trudged up the hill, waited for the bank to open and presented his VISA card for a cash withdrawal. To his surprise he was greeted with "Visa, non." No problem thought Andy

A typical doorway in Sidi Bou Saïd

and presented his Mastercard but just as they were counting out the money some thirty minutes later (it always takes eternity for credit lines to be checked) they noticed the Mastercard had expired the day before!

Needless to say when Andy returned at 11:00 AM without cash, he was somewhat flustered. So then I set up the hill with my Eurocheques, special cheques with a personalized numbered card, that could be used as a standard cheque with an upper limit of $150.00. Instantly I had cash in my hand.

By the time I was back at 'Le Pirat' it was past noon and the waiter was obviously frantic, for as I arrived at the bottom of the driveway word was sent up to the restaurant and by the time I had reached the top, the sides were lined with staff cheering me on. I counted out the money to our now laughing, relaxed waiter, somewhat resenting, I have to admit, the appropriately sized huge tip I felt obliged to pay on top.

Incidentally I thoroughly recommend Eurocheques to anyone travelling in Europe, as they can be used in most shops as well as for cash in banks. In fact, we found they were accepted in most countries we visited around the world, although frequently only in banks, with the exception of North America.

We made some interesting trips from Sidi Bou Saïd by train, notably to The Bardo Museum in Tunis where they have the most intricate and largest collection of Roman mosaics, and to the old city of Carthage. Unfortunately the Romans razed most of the Carthaginian cities to the ground but a model of the old Punic Port was fascinating; it showed how the Carthaginians hid 220 warships out of sight from the sea. Who thought marinas were a modern idea?

Our next door neighbours on the dock were another friendly German couple who had just purchased a white budgerigar and an elaborate Tunisian bird cage. The children loved their bird and, I might add, their boat, as it had every gadget imaginable including an ice cream machine. They used the excuse of the boys to keep it in frequent use!

There was much pressure for us to get a budgie too and finally, to the childrens' surprise, Andy and I agreed. Andy thought it was a good compromise. The previous proposals had been a large terrapin or a piranha. I liked the beautiful, round, ornate wire cage, trimmed with olive wood that hung perfectly from the arched wood between the galley and main cabin. So we bargained for a cage in the Tunis souk and a yellow budgerigar named Sidi Bou became an additional family member. I have to admit that with his very endearing and tolerant personality and a little amendment to the cage to stop the spray of seeds in all directions, Sidi Bou became a delightful pet.

We could have spent months in Tunisia but now we had a deadline. Duncan had been invited to stay with his cousins in England to be shown some of the sights of London, and to spend a special time with Andy's family on the Isle of Wight. He was thrilled. To catch the English school holidays he had to leave in early April so we needed to be in Greece to take advantage of the favourable return fares.

We made a brief visit to the Italian island of Pantelleria, rather unattractive with black volcanic rock but the officials were welcoming. Jamie loved their dramatic uniforms, immediately going below for his pants with a red stripe too, much to their amusement. We stayed overnight then headed out early for Malta.

"Ssshh, sssHH—I'm sure they've just mentioned Pantelleria." said Andy later as he was listening to the news on the BBC World Service.

We were horrified to hear that Gadafi had ordered a rocket attack on the island just after we had left, one of the responses to the American assault on Libya. It was the first of several acts of violence that were too close for comfort. Overnight virtually all American ensigns disappeared from yachts in the Mediterranean and any Canadian ensign, however battered, was in great demand.

There was a crowd to greet us on the dock in Lazavetto Harbour, in Malta, even though it was only 8:00 AM; most were from yacht agents who after a lean winter pounced on a any new victim with gusto, but a couple were also ready to take our lines. They were waiting for friends who also owned a Beneteau 38s, but as soon as they heard our British accents they insisted we come back to their home convinced we must be dying for a bath. An hour later we were luxuriating. We found the city attractive with its buildings and garden walls constructed from limestone blocks with blending paintwork in varying shades of yellow to pink-beige.

Our new friends helped us rent a car inexpensively and we kept busy for two days touring the main island. The wild flowers were in dazzling bloom with golden daisies, yellow mustard, deep red clover and scarlet poppies. Typically Mediterranean, the island was rocky and the stones used for fences. In autumn the land would be brown but in spring the contrast between the brown stones and lush green undergrowth was stunning.

We saw the sights visiting the old capital, Medina, and the 'new' capital, Valletta. We wandered through the prehistoric megaliths similar to Stonehenge in England and visited a cave where elephants' and hippopotamus' fossilized bones were found dating back to the days when Malta formed part of a land bridge between Europe and Africa. Unfortunately it was too rough to visit the Blue Grotto but we did hang precariously over the cliff and caught a glimpse of some of the beautiful blue and green tones.

Andy also reminisced about his naval days so we drove past the now closed airbase, Halfar, and looked out to sea at the Islet of Filfla, his target for bomb practice. Walking down the old 'street of ill repute', now a tame, respectable family area was quite an anti-climax, shattering his vivid memories as a young midshipman!

At the quay there was another Canadian boat, *Blyss II*, a roomy catamaran with Anya and Ryan, children of Jamie's age, on board. One evening they were flipping through our photo album when Lydia exclaimed,

"Wait a minute, there are the Spensley's, where did you see them? We all came through the French canals together."

Such is the boating community.

In contrast to the usual daily charge for moorage Malta had a five week block charge, very favourable if one stays five weeks, somewhat expensive for us for one. Malta would have been another great place to spend the winter on the boat although cruising to other bays and islands is generally only allowed on a daysail basis.

Meanwhile school was progressing well although with Duncan's trip to England he was a little behind. However the children really had done some super assignments and become much more independent in their work habits. Duncan had mastered Italic writing and displayed a neat hand, far more legible than his parents! Colin was progressing well with his reading and Jamie knew all the right types of words, if not the logic.—"The time Mummy?: 10.17.2." In Menorca we were very fortunate in having a French-Swiss boat close by and we had exchanged children for French/English lessons for an hour a day. It was marvellous for me as Duncan could complete many of his set French Immersion exercises that I couldn't remotely understand. Also the kid language on the dock was French and it was great hearing him converse quite naturally. Certainly this trip demonstrated to the boys the advantages of having a second language.

Much of our time was spent discussing topical events—archaeological visits, nature, food etc., and I have to admit that sometimes these seemed much more relevant than the set programme. But they would be returning to the regular school system so we completed it all and like all school programmes some of it was a slog and some really quite fun. I have to admit, however, as mother/teacher I knew I would really appreciate our summer holidays!

We left Malta reluctantly after replenishing our supply of baked beans, Cadburys chocolate and other British favourites, for we had felt very at home here. Our Greek landfall was at Argostoli in the island of Cephalonia. It was a 140 nautical miles, twenty two hour passage with varied but passable weather until 25 nautical miles out, when the wind turned to a full gale on the nose. Why couldn't it have waited another four hours?!

6. Greece

Argostoli, The Gulf of Corinth, Delphi, The Corinth Canal, Athens, The Peloponneses, The Cyclades and Dodecanese Islands

Although we experienced several gales the temperature in Greece was perfect at this time of year. Even now at the beginning of April we frequently had 27 degrees celsius during the day but it was pleasantly cool at night.

We could have pulled in anywhere along the empty seawall in Argostoli, our Greek landfall, but barely had the lines been secured when Jamie called out excitedly,

"Look a bicycle shop, right here!"

Since borrowing his cousins' tricycles in England Jamie had been quite definite, he wanted his very own. He had managed to find so many bicycle shops in France, Spain and Portugal that even Andy was beginning to soften—but not quite enough to come to terms with having the deck of his sleek, pristine new yacht cluttered by such an un-nautical object which, he had rationalized, would be dirty, seldom used, and expensive, since soon it would be a rust bucket from the salty spray.

But now it was definitely advantage Jamie. Not only was it a bicycle shop but it had a large selection of cheap secondhand bicycles which, right on cue, were being brought out of the store for display on the pavement. They were right amidships, very few feet away, impossible to ignore. At that point Andy knew he had lost the battle and I must admit he gave in gracefully. Off they went hand in hand and for $5. Jamie

Jamie with new bicycle in Argostoli

became the immensely proud owner of a blue and white tricycle. He was in seventh heaven riding along the quayside. It was the perfect place except for the danger of going over the edge, not such a remote possibility we realised as by the afternoon he was uninhibitedly roaring up and down. We made sure he was firmly strapped in his lifejacket. With his constant big grin, his delight was infectious and he became quite an attraction with many a passerby stopping to watch and throw us a laughing comment.

At the end of the day he purposely came on board, laboriously opened up the lazarette locker, pushed it up further with his head, then with great difficulty hauled out the bucket. He clambered below to fill it, took out the washing-up liquid and cloth, and struggled back off the boat to give his new acquisition the most careful, loving, washing down. It was still just a bicycle sitting on the deck but a more immaculate one could not have been found.

We headed across the Gulf of Corinth to the town of Patras. Traditionally in Greece yachts go stern to the stone wall (known as Med-moor) after an anchor has been dropped from the bow to hold the boat in position. The manoeuvre is not difficult but needs practice. Andy let out the anchor whilst I took the helm, going slowly in reverse until I could throw the stern lines to the several people who were generally standing by. The boys held the fenders on either side which later into the season, when we had to push into the narrowest of gaps, was a very necessary and skilled job. Here one man on the dock was particularly helpful.

"I'm just on holiday visiting my family but now I live in Vancouver too," he told us, having noticed our port of registry on *Bagheera's* stern.

We soon learnt his restaurant was actually on our street just a few blocks away! I had to make some travel arrangements for Duncan and phone calls, all easily accomplished with Tom's help. I also found he was soon to return to Canada.

"How's your baggage?" I asked him "Any chance you could take some school papers back with you to post?" Sending the boys school work back to Victoria was an expensive business with the exercises and projects required but postage was free if mailed in Canada.

"No problem." was the unhesitating response.

It was great incentive to get paper 19 completed, only eleven more to go to the summer holidays!

In Menorca Andy had made a stern boarding plank by filling in a ladder with plywood. It stored perfectly across the transom by the stern lifelines and fitted into sockets in the stern when in use. This was the first time we had tried it out and it worked well although Jamie definitely needed some balancing practise. It became his new pre-school activity. Andy had also rigged wheels on the outboard end of the ladder so it didn't scrape on the dock with each wave, and had put lines up to the backstay so it could hang just above the dock when not being used. This, we hoped, would discourage the inevitable army of cockroaches who love not only to visit but become permanent distasteful guests with their unbelievably rapid rate of reproduction.

That evening the citizenry turned out for its evening stroll and our seawall was obviously a favourite part of the circuit. We had been a focus of interest all afternoon but it was when we were peacefully sipping a sundowner in the cockpit that the barrage of questions started. I soon retreated to prepare dinner whilst Andy politely battled on. The meal was ready.

"Why don't we eat below?" I suggested.

"Excellent idea."

Dinner was served, we were on our first mouthfuls.

"Excuse me, I want to ask some questions—I can see someone down there . . . I want to talk, come up."

We tried to ignore the continuous insistent calls but unfortunately a passer-by could peer right down into the boat.

Finally Andy stomped up the companionway bristling. The 'visitors' were soon gone and the companion-way hatch firmly closed but it then became stuffy below.

"Any idea where the wheel cover is stowed?"

"In the port lazarette, I believe." I replied.

"Good," said Andy "I will put it on right after dinner. That will give us some privacy at least".

Next day I took Duncan to Athens by bus to catch his flight to England. It was the first time he had flown alone and like all mothers I was having pangs of anxiety as he disappeared with the stewardess. I went to the line of 'phones and was just telling my sister in England that the flight was expected to leave on schedule when I was drowned out by a woman in the next booth.

She was screaming hysterically,

"Three people dead, blown out of the plane, THREE DEAD."

I tried to listen further and to my sister, couldn't make out either conversation, and finished the call. I walked away shaking. What on earth had the woman been talking about?

Back at the boat the BBC headlines boomed out—"Two bombs exploded in planes today. One was outside Tokyo the other near Athens. The bomb on the TWA flight into Athens caused the death of three people who were blown out of the aircraft . . . "

"Well that explains it." I'd already told Andy about the desperate phone call I'd overheard. "I hope Duncan didn't know about it, he would have been petrified." I continued.

I should have known better. When we phoned Duncan in England, he was 'full of beans'. "Guess what?" he enthused, "there was a huge hole in the plane parked beside us, right opposite my seat. It was really exciting!"

Navpaktos was serene with its minute medieval walled harbour, bordered by plane trees and guarded by an old Venetian castle glimpsed fleetingly through the wafting clouds.

To our surprise Tom was soon at the boat.

"I had no idea you were coming here," he said, "this is my home town, let me show you around."

Many people here had lived themselves or had relatives in Canada and we were treated royally with retsina wine—great after the first couple of wry sips—and marjoram lamb souvlakia straight from the charcoal grill. We were even given a large pork roast by the butcher. But it really made our stay to be taken by Tom to his family's villa which was so peacefully enclosed by olive and orange groves. Tom's mother could not have been kinder, insisting on loading us up with freshly picked oranges, lemons, lettuce and a jar of mouthwatering home-pickled olives.

We headed off to Trizonia Island and were charmed by the tiny hamlet with its lush green hills, wild flowers and the tinkling of goats' bells breaking the silence of dusk as we went ashore. The boys found a characterful 'talking' white duck and it was here that Andy and I were introduced to one of the delights of Greece; sitting in the square with an ouzo, overlooking the harbour and watching the world go by.

We soon learnt not to have ouzo on board, however, for this aniseed drink, as well as turning cloudy with water, turned our acrylic glasses opaque too. It made me wonder a little about our stomachs . . .!

We arrived in the small town of Galaxhidi early one afternoon and immediately headed into town to get some groceries. Whatever road we took we ran into a long funeral procession. The pall bearers were already staggering down the steep, rough road on our third encounter and we were just contemplating whether we could dash across ahead of them when one let out a cry, stumbled and fell heavily to his knees. We watched aghast as the coffin did a rapid cartwheel and the lid flew off. The body thumped to the ground and started rolling down the hill towards us gathering momentum by the second. We stood glued to the spot in horror. Then, just as we had come to our senses and were pulling the boys from its direct path, two of the bearers sprung into action. They tore down the hill, grasped the flaying legs and arms, unceremoniously dumped the body back in the coffin, shoved the lid back on and hoisted it back on their shoulders. Unbelievably they were all instantly back in stride, their previous composed, solemn expressions completely in place.

"Well," said Andy when we were out of earshot, "I imagined a lot of things happening on this trip but never thought I would need a contingency plan for being attacked by a corpse!"

The next morning we took the bus to Delphi. Our steep ride up an enormous valley, a solid olive grove, was an appropriate approach to this spectacular site amidst the sheer cliffs and rocky ravines of Mt. Parnassos. Delphi, the centre of the world of 'the ancients' derived its name from Apollo Delphinos, the God who was worshipped in the shape of a dolphin.

In April the hills were adorned with bright yellow mustard flowers which made the steep climb up through the old stone treasuries, temples and theatres all the more beautiful. It was relatively tourist free and I was delighted that for my photos we had the place to ourselves.

Unfortunately the museum was closed but we saw it eventually on our way back through Greece (when we definitely did not have the place to ourselves) and were impressed by the quality of the displays of vases, weapons, jewellery, statues, etc., all illustrating Greek art back to the 6th century, BC.

It was a sunny day for our passage through the Corinth Canal, and we videoed much of the spectacular 5 kilometre trip. The feeling of travelling a narrow 22 metre wide waterway with walls as high as 70 metres has to be experienced to be believed. It was an amazing feat of engineering for the times (1893), but we heard it had originally been started in AD 67 with Nero lifting the first clod of earth with a golden shovel.

At one point one passes under the road and railway bridge and in traditional style several people peered the hundreds of metres down at us, waving enthusiastically.

"Playmobil people!" Jamie shouted, after his favourite toy, so aptly expressing all our thoughts as we waved back to the tiny figures.

On our arrival at Zea Marina, Piraeus, we met an American family from Oregon on a Sweden 36 foot yacht, who not only had children similar in age to Colin and Jamie but who had discovered the local markets and sights. They toured us through the stalls heaped high with fresh meats, fruit and vegetables, and we gorged ourselves. The prices were reputedly the best in Greece, a country where we found most costs favourable. We were even persuaded to buy Jamie a 'plastic swimming pool', adding to the clutter on deck started by his treasured tricycle. Inconvenience aside these two items kept him entertained during school time in the months to come. His swimming pool also frequently became my washing tub and stomping the dirty clothing became one of his favourite activities—useful too.

We spent a day in Athens. It was strange to be in such a bustling city again; apparently half of the population of Greece lives in this area. We explored the Acropolis, with thousands of others, and enjoyed a display of Greek dancing, by peering down into one of the theatres.

"I wonder why there are so many Canadian flags around," said Duncan suddenly.

"How strange," replied Andy. "I know WE are visiting but . . .?!"

Later we met part of a group of several hundred Canadian travel agents. We were soon chatting about the latest news 'back home', and a couple of days later several came aboard at Aegina Island. Of course we sent many messages back to Vancouver, becoming more imaginative as the wine flowed.

The island of Hydra is famous for its natural harbour and stately 18th and 19th century stone houses. Also all the transportation is supposedly by donkey, although we did notice a building truck sneak in, and the boys were thrilled to tour the town on donkey-back.

As the harbour front was touristy we wandered up the narrow back lanes and steps on foot, stopping to admire the houses. Although seemingly random-built up the steep slopes, all had panoramic views and sunny terraces, already partially covered with bright green spring growth on the grape vines. But our visit was cut short as an on-shore breeze rapidly began to build. Some German charterers tied up alongside *Bagheera*, causing our anchor to drag, and our stern to grate on the rough seawall. We decided to leave this congested harbour and took three hours to cover 8 nautical miles, beating into a typical Mediterranean blow with short, sharp seas.

From Ermioni I took the Hydrofoil back to Athens to pick up Duncan. He had loved his trip to England seeing the sights and a show in London and had enjoyed taking a Springer spaniel for frequent seashore walks on the Isle of Wight. No excitements this flight except to spend the whole flight in the cockpit, being fascinated by the instruments and now not sure whether he wanted to be a vet or a pilot; maybe a flying vet will be the answer!

After two days in the attractive old harbour of Spetsai watching the local fishing boats, known a caiques, being built, we decided to leave to cruise the east coast of the Peloponnesus. Unfortunately it wasn't that easy. As we pulled up the anchor it became heavier and heavier and as it surfaced so did a veritable cats cradle of ancient, rusty chains, of varying shapes and sizes. But Jamie's new friends had been watching and soon their father was sculling over to help. He patiently untwisted the ancient pieces of metal, one by one letting them fall to the ocean bed, hopefully to be undisturbed for another one hundred years. Two hours later we were able to set off.

"Look, look!" cried Colin pointing to a dark object in the water ahead. He was on watch and we were just managing to sail in the light breeze. "I thought I saw it move."

It was a single turtle contentedly dozing on the surface. We gently picked it up in the fishing net and the boys were quite delighted as Andy held it, startled by its rude awakening but still quite docile. Duncan carefully put it back in the water and it scuttled out of sight. This kind of experience and Andy's knowledge and enthusiasm stimulated much spontaneous research in the various nature books on board. We were, however, disappointed to find the Mediterranean so dead from pollution. Fish were rare and tiny in the markets and diving unrewarding, serving more as practice for the Caribbean than immediate interest.

The cruising, in this southern part of the country, was definitely our favourite of all Greece. The villages were small and welcoming, the valleys fertile and well cultivated and behind the mountains soared steeply. Placa, the harbour for Leonidhion, for example was charming, with good beaches and wonderful freshwater streams. Kiparissia was a gem, another old village where all the women were busily whitewashing their homes for the summer, but as we had been warned a rolly overnight anchorage. At Ieraka we climbed through tall golden grass over Helen of Troy's ruined castle and paddled through limestone caves full of stalactites and stalagmites. That night it blew a full gale and Andy did frequent 'Jack-in-the-box' leaps through the forward hatch, to check our anchors, as the gusts blasted us. We found it typical in Greece, that although in a seemingly sheltered anchorage, the wind would funnel over and then accelerate down the mountains into the bay.

Our last stop on the Peloponnesus included a visit to the Gibraltar-like island of Monemvasia, connected to the mainland by a narrow causeway. We climbed up to the old walled town. Originally Byzantine, then Venetian, it was being rebuilt and we loved walking around the narrow stone lanes under the low arches. Later we had one of our best Greek meals of squid, feta cheese salad and retsina, but then had to run down the hill as the wind started howling yet again.

For the next two weeks we zigzagged through the Cyclades Islands. Although we enjoyed our visits, especially to the white choras, the old towns perched high up on the hills for defence, we found the islands very barren. All pretences of working the land had been abandoned in preference for the more lucrative tourist trade, but the old terracing stood out as a stark reminder of former days. During this time we often had strong, gusty winds from the north, frequently reaching a full gale. As we were mostly going across or down wind it meant good sailing but we felt sorry for many charterers who had deadlines in northerly Piraeus, right into wind.

As the wind filled in during the short hop between Serifos and Siros Andy dethrottled the engine and there was a resounding clunk which reverberated loudly below. I heard some revving and finally Andy croaked from the deck,

"Liza, I think the propeller has fallen off."

He was aghast, the Danish Gori folding propellers supposedly cannot come off after assembly and are very expensive. We sailed into Siros in a developing gale and managed to Med moor stern to the sea wall with Duncan and I taking a long stern line ashore in the dinghy.

Surprisingly we had a spare fixed propellor, as it's generally Sod's Law that you never need the spares you are actually carrying. When the seas had calmed down in the harbour, after blowing 50 knots for two days, when even the indefatigable ferries stopped running, Andy was ready to make the replacement. He gained quite an audience as he dove, using the inflatable dinghy pump tube as a snorkel extension, definitely not recommended, but the only way we could think of to get increased diving time. All went well except for a mild dose of carbon dioxide poisoning and moans about our future decreased sailing speed since a fixed pro-peller creates much more drag than a folding one.

During our wait in Seros we heard about the disaster at the Russian nuclear power plant, Chernobyl. One of the results of this calamity was that instantly all green vegetables had to be taken off the market, as it was felt that broad leaved vegetables in particular would be contaminated by the fallout which affected all of Greece. This meant the limited Greek cuisine was restricted further. We had been disappointed with Greek food since our arrival in Argostoli particularly because we had precon-ceived ideas. In Vancouver we live close to the Greek area and have introduced many to the delights of succulent roast lamb, fresh salads with chunks of moist feta cheese and spinach pie with wafer thin filo pastry. These were just a few examples of an extensive menu. In Greece we found the menus limited with the traditional fish now small and expen-sive, the meat often tough, the thin slices of feta cheese dry and salty. Now there could be no spinach pie. However some compensation was the flavours of the other fruit and vegetables which, although often knobbly and misshapen to the eye, were succulent and full of flavour to the taste.

When the wind had abated to a steady 20 knots we continued cruising, calling in at Delos, the capital and holy island of the 'ancients' for the Cyclades. Duncan and I went to see the site as he had missed Delphi and the Acropolis in Athens. Andy claimed to be 'ruined out' and much happier diving. We found some of the mosaics and the famous stone lions impressive although Duncan's strongest memory is of the enormous abundant lizards that delighted in performing gymnastics on our feet.

"Look Mummy! said Duncan, holding up an inquisitive, bright eyed baby.

"No, we don't need one as a pet!" I replied, forestalling the certain request.

"Pity," replied Duncan "Colin and Jamie would have loved him!"

It was a short hop to the popular Mikonos which, although touristy, was immaculately whitewashed and attractive with its contrasting trailing pink and purple bougainvillaea. We came across a noisy crowd of Australians, Canadians and British and a few hours later they all came on board *Bagheera*. Margaret, an Australian from Perth, stayed with us for a week and it was at her recommendation that we visited Amorgos, one of the islands in the Dodecanese chain.

We soon became friends with the local restaurateurs in the small village and Tony, also an avid fisherman, invited Andy, Duncan and Colin to go out with him to check the nets. Even Duncan managed to get up at 5:00 AM (he's our greatest slugabed, after his mother, of course) and they returned ecstatic. It was Tony's bumper catch of the season and he was soon blowing his Triton shell horn to announce the sale. Obviously we had been good luck, and we were all invited to lunch. After a vast meal we in turn invited the whole family on board for coffee and Fundador brandy. They were delighted, closed the restaurant for the first time ever during the season, they claimed, and arrived for the afternoon armed with a large box of Greek donuts. It was one of many relaxed, experiences with the local people during the early season.

We moved out of the Cyclades Islands to the Dodecanese. Simi, in some ways reminiscent of Hydra, had a wonderful natural harbour with attractive old houses in muted tones of rose, cream and blue stacked up the steep hillsides and was minimally developed for tourism. Tucked away in a back street we found a talented model boat builder. His models of old Greek trading vessels were minutely detailed works of art.

"Such a shame!" said Andy. "They are so magnificent, so precise, but we just couldn't stow one anywhere on board."

Unlike the wine, these would not fit in with the water tanks; alas, we would have needed a 100 footer to accommodate all the souvenirs we would have loved to purchase.

Two days later we entered Mandraki harbour, Rhodes, passing the bronze deer where reputedly one of the seven wonders of the world, the Colossus of Rhodes (the bronze statue of Helios, the Sun God) stood in ancient times. Ahead soared the old city walls, built by the Knights of

Rhodes, and to the east three windmills stood clearly against the deep blue sky. A picturesque setting and Rhodes hums; it's touristy but fun, and getting down to basics, it even has a laundromat.

We had American neighbours on our starboard side aboard 90 foot *Liberty*. Don and Grace had just completed a five year circumnavigation and hearing of their tales of the Pacific and Orient stimulated our imaginations. Optimistic estimations of bank balances were unfortunately too soon put in perspective when our mail arrived with current statements.

While Andy stayed on the boat to have the engine injectors serviced the children and I became tourists in Lindos, a medieval town with magnificent coastal views from the mini Acropolis within the well preserved castle walls. The boys loved the sandy beaches and the highlight of their day was to rent a dolphin paddle boat. Meanwhile I was entertained by the variety of sights on the beach; despite being only in a brief bikini, I felt conspicuously overdressed!

7. Turkey and Greece

Fethiye, Kas, Kekova Roads,
Marmaris, Bodrum, Istanbul,
Ephesus
Sporades and Ionian Islands

The wind on May 26th was a comfortable 10-15 knots and we had a relaxing sail to Fethiye, in Turkey, some 45 nautical miles to the east of Rhodes. It was a delightful landfall with the vegetation much greener than Greece and good marina facilities (even showers!) in one of the few organised yacht quays in Turkey.

On our first attempt to go stern-to, our anchor dragged in the muddy, weedy bottom. On our second effort Duncan, with his usual gusto, threw a stern line to a helper on the shore, but it snarled, falling in a tangled knot straight down into the water. Without it we drifted sideways into another yacht. Andy was not happy.

When the boat was secured Duncan, Colin and I went ashore with spare mooring lines to practice throwing. We coiled the lines, divided the coil in two, then threw, letting the rope in the first hand go slightly before the second.

"Remember to always coil ropes in a clockwise direction and to hold onto the end if it is not attached to a cleat," I told them. "Otherwise it can be very embarrassing!"

It became a game, especially when several other yachtsmen joined in, claiming they frequently had the same problem! It was another skill accomplished and successfully employed on many a future occasion, particularly when docking in strong cross winds.

The Moslem call to prayers was being chanted loudly from the minaret as we walked into a relatively new town, the old one having been flattened by an earthquake, in the 1950s. There were brightly coloured Turkish carpets everywhere, even over parked cars to keep them cool.

The market had a huge selection of fresh fruit and vegetables that were cheap and exceptionally flavourful. We soon learnt why Turkey is praised for the best cuisine in the eastern Mediterranean after some delicious mezes: snacks with yogurt, cucumber and garlic, stuffed vine leaves and white melted cheese in filo pastry. Then we were served a rich lamb stew. Even the boys had to refuse the sweet pastry soaked in honey that looked so good in the patisserie, but they loved its name "lady's navel"!

The heat was intense as we ambled slowly back to the boat, absorbing the different flavour of Turkey. Suddenly Colin called out,

"Look. A bear!" He was attached to his owner by a chain, and standing on his hind legs, performing. After watching and 'talking' to him at length, the children declared with relief that he seemed quite happy in his captivity.

Colin decided he would be my chaperon to a local hairdresser recommended by a fellow yachtsman.

"But it will be quite an experience," he'd told us.

We sat and waited while two men had their thick, shiny, wavy hair trimmed to perfection. After they were shaved the barber lit a bunsen burner and to our astonishment flicked it at the men's faces. Colin was mesmerized. Neither man flinched, it was obviously normal procedure. Was it to retard growth to their beards we wondered?

Finally the barber motioned to me to sit in the large leather chair and shyly showed me some pictures of glamorous western ladies' bouffant styles. They were hardly appropriate to our lifestyle! When I indicated that I just wanted an inch cut off all round, he seemed relieved and gingerly started cutting. Although he had welcomed me in enthusiastically it seemed he had little experience with long hair, but he worked with absolute precision and concentration. He would not take more than the equivalent of 80 cents.

Back at the boat the rest of the family were subjected to my hair cutting skills, which had improved along the way; although the boys were young enough to accept the result and Andy doesn't exactly have much of a thatch to attack.

We sailed south to the blue inland lagoon, Ölü Deniz and anchored at the entrance, because in the past yachts have caused pollution inside. Ashore we swam off the brilliant white sandy spit and Jamie for the first time mastered the skill of swimming horizontally. All the boys swam as babies with life jacket or waterwings. Duncan was an excellent swimmer and snorkeller at five. Colin was a little more cautious, but was now confident in most conditions. It was a relief to see Jamie becoming proficient in the water, and to enjoy his exhilaration. It was many months, however, before we felt comfortable with his swimming off the stern ladder without some kind of flotation device. I could never be confident in my ability to watch him in the water every moment.

We went on to Kas, past the now completely silted river and buried, ancient port of Patara, where Father Christmas, or Santa Claus, was reputedly born. Later we visited Demre to see the church dedicated to Saint Nicholas, apparently the patron saint of sailors, pawnbrokers, merchants, scholars, travellers and those who were wrongfully imprisoned! It appears that this Bishop of Myra, martyred in 655, was a very generous person and the locals claim he was the originator of the Christmas stocking tradition. The story tells how one day, wishing to remain anonymous, he dropped bags of gold down a chimney for dowries—and it so happened that the daughters of the house were drying their stockings in front of the fire and of course the gold neatly fell into them!

The Kas and Kekova Roads area was our favourite part of Turkey, its scenery wild and primeval, with rugged mountains split by ravines. Lying at the foot of arid slopes the whitewashed Kas was an exotic oasis, the bougainvillaea a dense mass of pink and purple, the deep blue convolvulus bells trailing the terraces and the gold and red lilies a spectacular contrast of hue. We stayed several days, really enjoying the Turkish lifestyle.

The people are helpful, hard working and very friendly. The town is kept immaculate, with garbage bins emptied several times a day. We ate out often, frequently ordering the cooked hot and cold salads, inexpensive and quite delicious. Many that are made from aubergine, or eggplant, a vegetable we seldom use at home.

The children couldn't believe their luck when they found ice creams were only 5¢ each. How could one refuse—especially as the purchase included a 'show' as the brightly attired vendors flicked with a flourish scoops of mouth watering flavours into the cone.

During school Andy and Jamie became regular customers at the local grocery stores. 'Ka and Karry' got most of their business. One day, to his embarrassment, Andy found he didn't have enough money.

"No problem," they insisted. "Take your food and pay at your convenience!" Generosity indeed, especially to a 'here today and gone tomorrow' yachtsman.

On the dock beside us, with their car and caravan, were a retired Australian couple. They had just spent several months touring the eastern block countries. We really admired them. Their long-legged dangling furry monkey puppet was a great hit with the boys and when they brought it out on the wharf the usually solemn local children gathered around in delight. It broke the ice and soon the boys were learning the locals' fishing techniques and their new young friends were shyly, but inquisitively, coming on board.

Many of the Turks spoke English. We asked if they had learnt any other languages, the Germans seeming to be the most common visitors. Usually the response was "No, just English, everyone speaks English."

The world over we found this to be true, which was useful, but we had hoped to become versed in other languages as well. Often we didn't get past the basic hello, goodbye, and thank you. At first this bothered us but with so many languages and dialects we found it became too confusing to learn much more.

Ten minutes from town was a deserted Hellenistic theatre. It was serenely peaceful, especially after the bustling Greek sites. We climbed up the stone seats to the top and it was easy to imagine the enjoyment of 'the Ancients' in this idyllic setting overlooking the wide deep blue bay with its many inlets and islands. In the distant haze floated the Greek island of Kastellórizon. While we were in Kas many of the Turks mentioned with bitterness the islands which lie close to Turkish shores, that now belong to Greece. These used to be owned by Turkey and were, they felt, geographically far more logically Turkish.

We made our customary trip inland, catching a mini bus to Gombe, up 1,500 metres in the cool mountains. A local lady eased in beside me dressed in the typical gathered, baggy, floral pants, full blouse and head scarf knotted to look like a hat. She finally managed to wriggle her huge basket onto her lap. It was laden with produce, topped with large sprigs of wild rosemary. Its pungent bouquet wafted through the bus, mingling with fragrance from the oranges which she had peeled for the boys.

We walked for miles, counted rainbow trout in a hatchery and were invited to join the villagers for tea. Lunch was a delicious lamb kebab and cooked salad in the town square. As we cooled down with the light pilsner

Turkish Efes beer we watched the husbands leading laden donkeys; the subservient wives trailed behind, bowed down with the leftovers.

"Quite their rightful place!" Andy declared.

"Dream on!"

The breeze was behind us, as we travelled east, the strong Meltemi wind blowing up, as was common, around lunchtime. We anchored in crystal turquoise water in the miniature cove of Tersane on Kekova Adasi. It remains a favourite with its tiny sandy beach and ruined stone church, a haunting memory to Christianity in this Moslem country.

"Mummy, there's a fisherman here. Let's buy some fish for a barbecue ashore," Duncan called down the main hatch as I was finishing up school with Colin.

We hadn't had any success fishing ourselves and decided on a fat grouper from the friendly fisherman and his wife. Andy and the boys built a barbecue using some large white boulders from the many ruins. As I loaded the food into the dinghy Duncan hailed,

"Can you bring our shoes, please? It's slippery on the rocks."

"Okay, anything else?" I replied.

"Yes, garlic and salt," called Andy. They are two essentials in his diet.

Opening up the cockpit locker for the shoes I was confronted by unabashed, cheeky, beady eyes. I admit I dropped the lid with a scream! I had only had a momentary glance but it had to be a rat. Not only are rats not my favourite creatures but we had heard horrendous stories of their going on board yachts and making life unlivable. They are impossible to catch, as they can disappear to the most inaccessible corners of the bilge. I rushed below, grabbed a handy tennis racket, then rapidly shut the hatches. Feeling prepared, I gingerly opened the lid again.

There he was, as audacious as ever. A quick scoop and bat and he was overboard. I felt a little guilty as he hit the water until he nonchalantly swam for shore!

Andy twitched all night, leaping out of the forward hatch a couple of times, convinced he heard scratching along the fibreglass deck, but seeing nothing. However the next morning tell-tale droppings and large holes in our new plastic mosquito netting were proof enough. Later we were told that the rats on this island had learnt to tightrope walk along the stern lines boats tied to the shore. Large funnels fed through the mooring lines, with the wide opening facing the shore, presented satisfactory obstacles to these unwelcome visitors.

We spent many days in this peaceful area climbing the Genoese Medieval castle above Kale Köy with Jamie often on our backs, and examining the massive stone Sarcophagi, old Lycian burial tombs with peaked Gothic looking lids. Many were still erect on their pedestals after four thousand years and interspersed with old gnarled olive trees, ancient themselves. Looking down from the miniature theatre within the castellated ramparts, we could see the sunken parts of the old city, rendered thus by one of the earthquakes which are so frequent in this area.

It was time to head west, then north, as we had friends joining us in Marmaris on June 19th and we wanted to spend time in Fethiye Bay on the way. During the trip, to his delight, Duncan caught five tuna and easily sold four to other yachtsmen. We managed to rescue one for ourselves!

He returned elated, displaying his new wealth.

"Everyone thought they were very cheap," he said. "But I got the price of your hair cut Mummy for each one!"

"Terrific, but remember to spend it in the next couple of weeks before we leave Turkey," I replied.

We had found as we moved quickly from one country to the next that the children were often left with pocket money they could no longer use. In Menorca we decided it would be best if I acted as banker. I kept a record of their pocket money in my diary in Canadian dollars. When they wished to make a purchase I would give them money in the right currency and deduct from their running total. They saved far more than they ever had at home.

Fethiye Bay is another relaxing area in which to cruise. Colin had finished his school year and to celebrate we went to lunch on Tersane Adasi amongst the Byzantine ruins. The restaurant was at the waters edge, a few tables with crooked posts supporting an awning, on an island sparsely covered with olive trees and the occasional palm. Goats wandered everywhere and a large tortoise immediately attracted the boys' attention.

Our waiter served us on the double, literally jogging back and forth to the kitchen in one of the ruins. We wondered how he had the energy in the intense heat, particularly as it was during Ramadan. Ninety-nine percent of Turks are Muslims and Ramadan is the required month of fasting between sunrise and sunset. The waiter told us that Islam was a gentle, understanding religion in Turkey and God understood that he had to eat and drink during Ramadan to perform this job to support his family. He did, of course, remember to pray five times a day—usually. Muslims must not eat pork or drink wine, although, he told us with a grin, Mohammed said nothing about raki or beer! Raki, the national drink

Andy

Liza

ACTIVITIES ON BOARD

Duncan and Jamie. Lego and this Spanish Tente were some of the many toys and games frequently played

Colin sorting shells in Fiji. Collecting gems, fossils and foreign coins was also popular

Jamie giving a news broadcast. The BC correspondence school programme included many innovative activities

Duncan's farewell party in the Basin, Australia. Jumping from the spinnaker pole, climbing the mast and swinging in the bosun's chair were favourite activities when at anchor

PORTUGAL

Batalha Monastery

The fishing harbour at Nasare

Hanging fish to dry on the beach in Nasare

TUNISIA

Our budgie, Sidi Bou

Tunisian olive wood bird cage

Buying the cage in the Souk in Tunis

GREECE

The Corinth Canal with Lyn (Andy's sister) on board

Simi

Delphi

TURKEY

Sarcophagi (tombs) at Kale Köy

Going up the Caunos River past Lycian tombs

Ruined Christian church in Tersane, Kekova Adasi

BAGHEERA'S INTERIOR

Forward cabin

Aft port cabin

Main cabin

Galley

Navigation area by chart table

after tea, is a clear, aniseed flavoured spirit similar to Greek Ouzo and French Anis.

A trip ashore in Göçek coincided with the President's visit and the military was out in force to control the crowds. Turkey has a large army, particularly to guard her many borders. Although all was orderly, the soldiers frequently swung their guns up and down towards the crowds. Many of the soldiers were just in their teens, and after a couple of them had pointed their loaded guns right at us for several moments, presumably to impress the obvious foreigners, I grabbed Andy.

"Let's get out of here, this is scary."

"I agree, we can forget shopping for today," he replied.

We were thankful to be able to take off in the dinghy. What a contrast to go to the peaceful miniature cove of Ruin Bay. The boys became proficient at taking other boats' stern lines ashore, tying them to the dense pine that covered the slopes right to the water's edge. They enjoyed meeting the new boaters and going aboard their yachts. In particular we became friends with some New Zealanders and South Africans. Again dreams of exploring far distant horizons haunted our thoughts.

For Duncan's tenth birthday we chartered a local boat to explore the Dalyan River, having been advised we would get lost if we took our inflatable dinghy. The boys sat right up on the bow and loved weaving through tall reeds up to the ancient city of Caunos with its theatre, which surely had inspired the design of our stadiums at home.

We saw hawks, herons, kingfishers and sandpipers and an abundance of large terrapins. At Iztuzu, by the river mouth, the loggerhead turtles stop to lay their eggs. This is one of the few places left in the Mediterranean with the right conditions—fine loose sand, south facing and an absence of noise and bright lights. Sadly it was being threatened by the building of a resort.

Up river there were Lycian tombs at every turn. These memorials are designed like temples, carved out of the vertical rock cliff faces and one can actually climb inside. Built about the second millennium BC they are a lasting reminder of this ancient civilization while other more recent structures have perished in the earthquakes.

In 1798 Nelson's fleet put into Marmaris for repairs and relaxation from the hectic business of pursuing Napoleon around the Mediterranean. It is nowadays a fleet of charter vessels that fills the quay to capacity with travellers who enjoy the facilities of a booming tourist town.

As we were about to drop anchor, to back into the only small gap left along the wharf, a German 50 foot boat laden with guests charged up to us.

"Get out of my way," roared the skipper. "That is my reserved place." But the locals called from the shore,

"No, no. You *Bagheera* come in."

"Let's go for it," said Andy.

The locals laughed as they took our lines. Competition for the tourist trade was hot; this was a small victory over the large foreigner. There was no such thing as booking your spot!

Along the waterfront were wall-to-wall restaurants displaying attractive but sparse arrays of very expensive fish. Even the locals were admitting that the Mediterranean was virtually fished out, and it was a dilemma; seafood was the traditional Mediterranean fare. Our 'Local' was run by a vibrant character and although we were eating aboard he insisted we should stop by later for a raki.

We were glad his sales pitch had been persuasive. At the next door table there was a noisy celebration—twenty men and one woman—with a band consisting of an extra long 'clarinet', an eleven stringed 'lute' and a versatile small drum set. They were playing infectious lively Eastern music and at midnight we felt we had to get Duncan out of his bunk to enjoy the party.

Somehow someone learnt it was his birthday. Suddenly exotic candle and fruit creations arrived for him and before long he was invited to dance with the Turkish men. I must say he rose to the occasion amazingly well and was soon stomping around in unison with his hands above his head.

The next day some people from Istanbul came to the boat with a huge birthday cake, anxious to know if Duncan's name was spelt correctly. What trouble they had taken. All was correct and they were most interested to come on board, amazed how much room there was below. At dinner that night, in the same restaurant, the band came especially to play 'Happy Birthday'.

"How can it sound so normal?" whispered Duncan.

We were also surprised, it didn't seem possible that the previous night's eastern wails had come from the same instruments.

Everyone was clapping enthusiastically and as the guest of honour they gestured to Duncan to dance. Characteristically someone at the next table immediately jumped up to join him.

"Fun," said Duncan as he whirled past our table, grinning from all the attention, "but can I do something a little more normal next year?!"

Marmaris is a shoppers' paradise and it was hard to keep away from the stores with soft leather clothing, hand painted brightly coloured ceramics, copper pots and pans, ornate Ottoman jewellery, fascinating Meerschaum (the white soapy stone that is carved into mythical shapes for pipe bowls) and hundreds of Turkish carpets and flat woven kilims.

Looking at carpets and kilims was a ritual that could easily be an all day affair. Outside displays usually carried inferior stock but once inside, seated with tea offered, an honour you should not refuse, then the most wonderful creations would appear, even though we made it quite clear none would fit on the boat! I particularly loved the dense silk carpets, but alas they were far beyond our means. Still it was wonderful to be able to examine these works of art.

Our English friends from Lymington, Simon and Jenny Collyer, arrived as scheduled and we headed west. We lunched in the almost landlocked natural harbour of Serçe and were offered dinner by the local restaurateur.

"What's on the menu?" inquired Andy.

"Goat," replied the restaurateur pointing to the goat that was running around in front of us. We declined!

The village of Bozburun is the Turkish sponge fishing centre, maybe because of this area's stark, hard-baked land. The sponge boats leave from May to September to cruise the coast and divers go down over 60 metres. The boys were happy to find a couple of small brown sponges on the surface and brought them aboard to dry. After a couple of hours in the sun the stench was terrible!

Along the new wharf were local 'gulet' boats in every stage of construction: some just ribbed, others being planked and some almost finished with decks being laid. With the original design adapted to have a wider beam and stern they were in great demand for tourist boats as they are very roomy, usually having four to five comfortable guest cabins and a huge afterdeck, with large dining table. We saw these boats everywhere. Made from pine, with bowsprit and wooden masts, with their white hulls and brightwork gleaming, we thought them very attractive. The rigs were short and many had only excuses for sails, but they mostly motored, generally in the mornings before the Meltemi winds had filled in. Charter boats were busy and prices amazingly low. For example, one German told us that, including the return fare from

Germany, a two week charter with good food, trips and drinks was costing him about $1,000. It seemed great value for an excellent holiday, especially if you could get your own group of eight or ten together.

We visited various bays on our way to Bodrum, particularly enjoying Keçu Bükü. The boys spent hours playing on the long sandbar before we walked to the village. The smiling local children frequently gave us posies of flowers as we wandered up the road and we chose vegetables that were still in the ground.

That night we celebrated the end of Duncan's school year. It was June 22, not bad, a week earlier than the regular schools back in BC!

An old amphitheatre providing a picturesque anchorage by the isolated city of Knidos. It had been abandoned in the Middle Ages. Ashore we examined some excavations and Andy was fascinated by the water pipes.

"Every bit as efficient as today's plumbing," he declared.

The harbour in Bodrum was shadowed by the giant Castle of St. Peter, whose huge medieval silhouette dominates the town. Over the water we could hear the bustle of activity ashore.

Within the castle walls a Yuruk nomadic herder was dressed in colourful traditional costume with an equally bright kilim on his camel. The Oceanographic and Archaeological museum inside the castle had fascinating displays from ancient wrecks.

"If only we could find a sunken ship too," Duncan yearned.

The market was vibrantly alive with its farmers and tinkers, their woven baskets bulging with goods. Fruit and vegetables of every variety were piled precariously high, vegetables often meticulously bundled, leaving no doubt why Turkey is called the market-garden of Europe. There were village cheeses, succulent green and black olives, mounds of dried fruit and nuts, overwhelming aromas from herbs and spices, gleaming pots and pans, and brightly coloured cloths and carpets, with the live chickens, ducks, and sheep and cattle all contributing to the noise and activity. We wanted to buy it all but we had decided to leave the boat in the marina and go away for three days.

Immediately on arrival in Bodrum we had set to work to arrange a quick trip to Istanbul. We managed to organise the bus and hotel but it was fortunate that the arrangements were spontaneous. The prospect of travelling on two 15 hour bus trips in 60 hours would have been too daunting if dwelt upon. We left at 8:00 PM, had four 15 minute stops to grab prepared food (it took the first stop to figure it out!) and slept well in between. At 9:00 the next morning we had our first glimpse of that famous fantasyland skyline, with its architectural heritage of Byzantium and the Ottoman Empire, and towering pencil slim minarets.

We had two days and we 'did the town'—visiting the busy covered bazaar and crossing the Bosporus from Europe to Asia by old fashioned ferry. We studied the outstanding jewels in the Topkapi Palace, including the emerald dagger, toured the Harem, visited the Blue Mosque, Ayasofya, Dolmabahce Palace and the Hippodrome. This whirlwind tour culminated with our friends buying a Turkish carpet. The visit had quite lived up to our expectations, although Andy definitely lacked enthusiasm when we suggested we try to find the belly dancers who whirled tassels from each breast in opposite directions—one of his favourite reminiscences of when he had visited Istanbul as a midshipman.

Alas our dashing around was too much for Jamie's stroller and while making a quick exit from the bazaar, of course with a bevy of vendors at our rear, it dramatically collapsed—a heap of metal, screws and salty cloth. It had done sterling service during the last year, being dragged over the roughest terrain with many an overload of groceries, and it would be sorely missed.

"But never mind there are three strong boys to do the carrying now," Andy remarked. The three boys gave him the predictable response!

The bus trip back was completed in record time. 'Might is right' was the attitude of our cavalier driver as he swung out round the frequent blind corners at top speed. He had insisted we tourists should have the front seats. I clung to the rail with clenched knuckles constantly white!

There was a note from Steve and Andrea Bayly on our return. We had last seen them in Spain before they went skiing and it took the evening to catch up on all the news. They had experienced far poorer weather than we, and had been held up by squalls and rain storms as they crossed the Med.

Another Canadian, Richard Naylor, dropped by the next morning,

"It's my birthday. How about joining a group of us for a barbecue tonight?"

Andy had sold Richard his boat *Happiness* about seven years before, in Vancouver. What a surprise it had been to see him on the dock in Gibraltar, waiting to take our lines. We all headed off to a nearby bay, sang songs by firelight, and battled at water fights although the Bagheera's lost abysmally as they ran out of outboard fuel.

Next morning we arrived for Joan Newman's breakfast party dressed in tiaras and bow ties. Joan, a great Australian lady, provided just the excuse we needed to carry on cruising far beyond our two year plan.

"You just have to be in Australia in early 1988," she told us, "so you can join in with the Tall Ships' events commemorating Australia's Bicentennial."

"But would we be eligible?" I asked.

"Absolutely. I've been on several of the committees," she informed us, "and will have you sent an invitation. It's going to be enormous fun and incidentally one of the perks for participants is an unrestricted one year working visa."

It was the quickest mail we ever received and after reading all the glossy invitations, from the Prime Minister, Bob Hawke, and the Premiers of the participating States, and considering all the welcoming events planned, we were very tempted. But we were back to the problem of cruising the Pacific with the huge distances between the groups of islands. Although the boys had been terrific on the boat, never complaining they were bored and seldom sea sick, the two-day crossing of the Bay of Biscay was still their longest passage. We decided that before replying we should see how they fared on the Atlantic crossing which, with an approximate distance of 3000 nautical miles, would take two and a half to three weeks.

As Steve and Andrea on *Severance* departed south, *Bagheera* hurried north, overnighting at the marina in Kuadasi to see the famous Ephesus (Efes). A personable, informative guide took us through the site, one of the best preserved of ancient Roman cities, although originally founded by the Greeks in the eleventh century BC. It provided a great insight into a very different way of life.

As we walked down marble streets avoiding the ruts made by chariots, we learnt about the rich merchants' buildings; the boys tried out the ancients' toilets for size; we all peered down into the theatre with seats for 25,000 and had our imaginations stimulated by the passage between the Colsus library and the brothel. Then off to visit the site and ruins of another of the Seven Wonders of the World, the Temple of Artemis.

Our guests Simon and Jenny left that night. It was on my night watch as *Bagheera* deadheaded north the thought struck me.

"Oh, no!" I exclaimed.

"What's the matter?" Andy called up the companion way.

"We didn't have a Turkish bath!"

"Yet another reason to go back."

Turkey remains one of our favourite countries for cruising: great people, delicious food and the best prices in the Mediterranean.

Two days later in Greek Khios Andy's sister and cousin arrived for

The Celsus library at Ephesus

two and a half weeks. We headed west visiting some small communities before arriving at the popular Northern Sporades. These islands are quite developed, but enjoyable, and the compact group with good harbours and beaches makes an ideal area for family cruising.

Alas my memories are few as I became really ill with the 'flu and was unable to throw off the infection in the heat. The boat was continuously over 32 degrees celsius and I found it thoroughly debilitating. This was one of only a handful of occasions that I was ill during the six years. In fact, we were all very healthy throughout. In contrast, since returning to heating and air conditioning systems, and the constant circulation of viruses, we seem to catch every 'bug' going around.

Health was a major issue which we had addressed before we left Vancouver. Several medical sailing friends had helped compile a medical 'chest', that filled several plastic containers. We were able to cope with all the regular cuts and bruises, ears, nose, throat and common digestive malaises, and had cartons of specialized salves, solutions, pills, bandages and 'equipment'.

On Jamie's last visit to the orthopaedic surgeon in Vancouver, an old friend who had felt Jamie should have Dennis Brown boots and splints before we left as he 'intoed', I was presented with a final stuffed brown bag.

"Thought these might come in useful."

I opened it up. On top was a long, thin plastic tube.

"Oh, that's in case Andy gets caught in the middle of the ocean with a prostate problem," he replied in a matter of fact voice.

It was one of my moments of panic. What was I letting myself in for? Could I really cope with something so extreme? But I reassured myself. In reality we were going to civilized countries, with good medical facilities and where we would always be able to find someone to translate to the physician.

When I couldn't shake off the 'flu I finally went to a very helpful Greek doctor who prescribed more antibiotics and suggested I eat ice cream, as I couldn't get anything else down. It seemed to work and of course Andy was never without company to the ice cream stands! The doctor was fascinated when he came down to see 'Bagheera' at the end of his clinic. He had charged only a minimal fee.

At this time an incident occurred that shocked us all. An Australian nurse was found to have codeine tablets in her handbag when she was leaving Greece, and was arrested and imprisoned as she had no doctor's prescription with her. We were stunned as codeine is sold over the counter in several countries, and particularly concerned as we had many drugs on board, including morphine. In future we always made sure to keep prescriptions attached or to have labels that distinctly documented the countries of origin with a pharmacist's notation and date.

We rushed through the Northern Sporodes: Skantzoura, Alonissos, Skopelos, Skiathos. My main memories are of flowers and lines of octopus hanging out to dry. We had caught many octopus throughout the Mediterranean and Duncan had become our expert pounder. One hundred throws on a rock and they were tenderized to perfection. After a quick visit to Piraeus we travelled back through the Bay of Corinth, again a pleasant place, but where the local people were quite jaded compared to the spring, and already longing for the tourist season to be ended.

In Patras Frank joined us and Lyn and Audrey departed. Frank was the brother of Mark who had joined us from England to France. We made our way up to the Ionian Islands, also a favourite charter area, although showing signs of complacency with ready-made customers. We did find some deserted spots around Meganisis, however, and Duncan was delighted to find blackberry brambles up the River Achebos, the longest river in Greece.

"Let's pick lots," he encouraged us enthusiastically, "and then we can make a blackberry and apple crumble, just like the ones in Desolation Sound at home."

It was an industrious afternoon picking fruit, then crumbling the flour, butter and sugar. The crumble filled the roasting pan, serving for dessert that night and for many a school snack to come.

Sandy beaches are not plentiful in the Mediterranean so we made a point of visiting Anti Paxos, arriving early to pearl white sands and a brilliant turquoise sea. Not for long. By midday it was a seething mass of tourists. Andy was all set to leave and Frank started to pull up the anchor.

Suddenly he stopped and a "Wow" of wonder rather audibly escaped his lips. Dozens of bikini-clad girls were pouring onto the deck of the charter boat which had just anchored beside us. In any other circumstances it would have been far too close for comfort but this time Andy decided that it was just fine for the next couple of hours, definitely worth a delay!

Homer had praised Corfu as a lush paradise which cast a spell over its visitors and we also found the island delightfully green and full of old world charm. As we ordered a beer by the park some cricketers arrived. It quite brought back Andy's youth in England and took us right into Gerald Durrell's world. Close by was a large supermarket and I stocked up well, not sure what I would find on the shelves in Communist Yugoslavia.

As we set off north at 6:00 AM it was hard to believe that our Greek travels were over. In all we had spent two and a half months on the mainland and in the islands, and really enjoyed the cruising, especially in the Peloponnesus, and particularly in the cooler pre-season. Prices were reasonable and moorage charges minimal. Although there was a limited menu for eating out, shops were well stocked, and Greek yogurt (10% fat) with pine honey is unbelievably melt-in-your-mouth.

There is nothing quite like a Greek village where you come stern-to, wander to the nearest taverna, down a beer or ouzo, and watch the world go by.

8. Yugoslavia

Bar, Kotor, Dubrovnik, The Islands, Sibenik, and the Krka Falls

As a rule the Meltemi dies at night but of course it didn't on July 29th and *Bagheera* crashed through short, sharp waves close-hauled up to Yugoslavia. Heading north, we tacked back and forth across the Adriatic Sea, coming quite close to Italy on the west side and making sure we kept outside the twelve mile mined zone off the Albanian coast on the east.

It was one of 'those' trips. My 'ear patch' for seasickness fell off. The children felt ill, and to crown it all the 'hat' was pounded off the diesel furnace outlet and sooty water came teeming down into the main cabin; all over the cushions, books, my bedding and me. It even got inside the picture matting, just to show you that it's not all gin and tonics on the afterdeck. The Copelands at this point were not all sweetness and light. Fortunately all bad trips come to an end and we made our landfall at Bar.

This was our first visit to a European Communist country and we wondered what facilities we would find ashore. Bar is a new town, rebuilt after an earthquake in 1973, and has modern shops, a department store and a supermarket. The racks were almost empty in the department store, whether in hardware or clothing, and designs old fashioned, but we were pleasantly surprised by the well stocked supermarket shelves—until Duncan quickly pointed out the extent of duplication.

"Mummy, the whole of these two aisles is filled with apricot jam!"

It was the same throughout Yugoslavia. Food was available but limited, and buying food was a chore. To purchase bread one had generally to line up at the meat and cheese counter where everything is sliced SLOWLY, and a line-up for a Yugoslavian is purely a challenge to queue barge. Not being able to speak the language was a definite disadvantage and I felt far too inhibited to elbow the tiny old ladies out of line, although they had just done it to me! The markets were colourful but the produce less flavourful and more expensive than in Greece and Turkey. Juices were thick and fruity, and the local inexpensive wines could be excellent, but the crude glass bottles weighed 'a ton' to carry back to the boat. They also shattered easily as I found to my embarrassment when the handle of my supermarket basket broke and the contents and splinters of glass from four bottles devastated the entire shop.

When stowing our purchases Duncan noticed that cans and packages had contents and instructions in four languages. It was a graphic introduction to the diversity of cultures in the country. It soon became evident that although we had thought of Yugoslavia as one country, Yugoslavians did not.

As one man put it, "We've had a few conflicts in our time, and what can you expect in a country that has two alphabets, three religions, four main languages, five principal nationalities, six republics and a border with seven countries!"

It was time to read our cruising guide and reference books again to get the background of this unbelievable mix.

When the Slav tribes entered the Balkans during the Dark Ages they came in waves under different leaders. They were at once subject to diverse influences as they settled across the dividing line of Eastern and Western Roman Empires, Byzantium and Rome. A particularly bitter division was the dispute between the Roman and Orthodox churches. The Croats and Slovenes chose Roman Catholicism, whilst the Serbs, Macedonians and Montenegrins adopted the Orthodox creed from Byzantium. After the Ottoman conquest in the 15th century, the Bosnians in large numbers became Moslems. Then for centuries the country was torn by conflicts between East and West, split between the Ottoman Turkish Empire and the Hapsburgs of Europe, with the Venetians also putting in their spoke down the coast. Topography was also a factor, with isolating mountain ranges to the north and south, and the Dinaric chain running parallel to the coast.

Although by the nineteenth century the various strands of the Slavic kingdoms were beginning to interweave, it wasn't until the end of the

First World War, on Dec 1, 1918, that Yugoslavia officially became a single country—the Kingdom of Serbs, Croats and Slovenes. The name Yugoslavia, meaning Land of the South Slavs, was first coined in 1929. However, the country came into existence with a monarch and under western supervision, and faced as many problems as it solved. Yugoslavia became a federation of different republics, after being devastated in World War II. The success of building a socialist state and achieving a semblance of balance between nationalities was largely due to the personal authority and charisma of the wartime partisan leader, Tito.

Thus the country of Yugoslavia ended up with two alphabets, the Roman and Cyrillic, after the split of the Roman Empire. The Roman or Latin is used in the northern and western Catholic areas and the Cyrillic in the southern and eastern Orthodox regions. The third religion, Islam, came with the Turks. The four principal languages are Slovene, Serb, Croat and Macedonian, although Croat and Serb are very similar. The five main nationalities are the Slovenes, Croats, Serbs, Macedonians and Montenegrins, with sizable groups of Albanians, Hungarians and Romanians, and form a population of over 20 million. The seven national frontiers are with Italy, Austria, Hungary, Rumania, Bulgaria, Greece, and Albania.

True to its reputation, the Dalmatian coastline is utterly spectacular with its gaunt white limestone mountains dropping sheer to the sea. The scattered islands seemed tossed along the coast, and many are adorned with fairy tale castles and churches. It was delightfully green and fertile after the eastern Mediterranean, well cultivated too, and the villages of 14th century stone buildings were charming and refreshing after the rubble of the 'Ancients'.

As we cruised up the majestic fiords to Kotor, Andy informed us he had chosen the perfect anchorage for the night—a remote uninhabited island, according to the chart.

The deep, dark water was glassy calm and the boys and I relaxed with cushions on the foredeck. Suddenly Colin jumped up.

"Look at the island. Aren't those roofs?"

Looking through the binoculars there were definitely many roofs with huts to go with them. Far from being our deserted island this was a bustling 'Club Med'! With over 80% of visitors heading straight to the coast we found new tourist developments springing up everywhere.

We had been expecting Kotor to be a beautiful old town, but instead only a few of the old buildings were completely intact and there was a lot of rubble. Our guide book was printed in 1977 and in 1979 Kotor had suffered a devastating earthquake. Restoration was much in evidence, and one of the first buildings to be completed was the Maritime Museum in a refurbished 17th century mansion. The boys loved the display of ornate weapons and model ships, and we were amazed that the Seaman's Guild of Kotor, one of the oldest in Europe, has records going back to 809 AD.

Behind Kotor soars Mt. Lovcen. It seemed impossible that a road could be built, let alone a bus scale the heady slopes, but we had been told a trip to Cetinje on this route was a must. It was a slow crawl along cobbled roads, our bus snaking its way up through dozens of hairpin bends, often achieving only a few feet a turn. Then there was the frequent hair-raising backing down to allow overtaking, to avoid rockfalls and a wrecked car that hung precariously over the edge. But shattered nerves aside the panoramic view of the gulf that opened up in postcard clarity was breathtaking. At a height of 1,000 metres we entered the Lovcen pass and suddenly were in the limestone 'karst' and the totally contrasting lunar landscape of crags and boulders, that is found throughout the country.

"It's just like a sieve," a local explained. "All the rain and melting snow just disappears through the limestone and all we get is this thin patchy vegetation. And our rivers just disappear down holes and flow for miles underground."

On our way out of the Bay of Kotor we stopped at Perast, a model town of Venetian Gothic homes. For half a millennium Perast was the muscle of the Adriatic maritime strength and it is famous for its sea captains. Offshore lie two picturesque islands, one a Benedictine Abbey, formerly a fort, which commanded the passage up to Kotor in Nelson's day, the other, originally a reef, was built up in the 17th century by sinking pirate ships filled with stones.

We motored north to Dubrovnik in stiflingly hot, humid weather and decided to keep up the big awning generally only used at anchor. As it covered the cockpit and cabin, almost to the mast, it kept the interior much cooler but we couldn't use the mainsail, as the awing goes over the boom. We promised ourselves more interior fans. The small German Hella ones are excellent, being both quiet and durable, and by the end of our trip we had eight on board. The children love the cool and comfort they give and turn them on automatically. (So much so that last winter in Vancouver Jamie was cocooned in two duvets in our berth, in very chilly conditions, but the two fans were still blasting down on high speed!)

The city walls of Dubrovnik, made from the local limestone in the

14th century, are massive and look unbelievably brand-new. Strategically located in the Adriatic, this city has always tried to keep in favour with the dominant power—whether Venice, Hungary or Turkey—and Denham notes in his cruising guide that six centuries ago Dubrovnik adopted a number of humanitarian reforms far in advance of other western nations. There were old people's homes, laws abolishing slavery and torture, public assistance for those in need, a public health service, town planning and a number of schools. It is tragic that after centuries of negotiation to keep the town neutral the recent cultural conflicts have brought devastation.

Gruz harbour is noisy but conveniently next to the market and (what bliss) an air-conditioned supermarket! It was a quick bus ride to the immaculate old medieval town, its strict geometric plan softened by the Renaissance lines, sculptured dome or tower and faded pastel patchwork of roofs.

Some of our most pleasant memories of Dubrovnik are from our stay at the Dubrovnik Marina, a few kilometres out of town up the Dubrovacka Inlet. The setting was classic, opposite a monastery and by the old Palace of Sorkocevic, now a luxury hotel and garden restaurant.

We tried the restaurant that night. At the next table were Ricardo, an Italian, and Clare, his wife, an attractive English model. They had sailed down the coast from Italy and finding we had sons of similar age we all planned to stay an extra day. Our boys hadn't been with children who spoke English for a while and changing our plans to accommodate other children was always our practice.

During the meal we marvelled at the wonderful harmonizing singing, at which the Yugoslavian men excel. Often a group would wander into a restaurant and sing for a beer. The clarity and volume were always perfect, never overwhelming when close-by but always reaching the farthest of tables. On this occasion they were accompanied by small five string guitars.

The next day the children had a great time with their new friends, fishing and roaring up the river in our inflatable dinghy. Duncan also went swimming in the icy river water; his new skill at free diving was going to be tested. As I had stepped ashore I heard a plop in the water, and peering down I caught an instant flash of my watch before it sank into the gloom. We checked the depth sounder, over 9 metres. Duncan was sure he could get it and on his second dive, with just mask, snorkel and flippers, he came up triumphant.

While the children filled up on spaghetti, Andy and I went out to dinner with Ricardo and Clare, and acquired two valuable pieces of information. First we were introduced to rock borers, 'ductori'. Rather like mussels but with oval brown shells, these mollusks are dug out of rocks and are over 30 years old. They are considered a delicacy and are quite tasty.

The second tip proved invaluable.

"I know this is hard to believe," Clare told us laughing, "but we've found that the best way of judging restaurants in Yugoslavia is by looking at the waitresses' shoes!"

They had noticed that the government run restaurant employees all wore high ankle boots with cut out toes and heels. With no incentive most of these restaurants have indifferent service and food, whilst most privately run restaurants are excellent. So from then on shoes were perused before menus and with good results.

We were interested that, although a Communist country, private enterprise was allowed if there were less than five employees. Many of the restaurateurs had been overseas for several years, to learn the trade and build up some capital. They loved to chat into the night and were generally lively, personable characters with an objective outlook about their country.

They told us that Yugoslavia has its own brand of Communism, which they prefer to call Socialism. The key is workers' self-management. Instead of State ownership most enterprises and services were owned and managed by the people who worked for them. In return for their labour workers get not only wages, but the right to participate in decisions affecting every level of the organization of the enterprise.

This came about after World War II. By the end of the war Yugoslavia had lost 10% of her population with 1,700,000 dead. Nearly a million homes had been destroyed and 3.5 million people were without roofs over their heads. Two thirds of the hospitals had been totally razed, two fifths of the industrial installations were in ruins and thousands of miles of railway lines, roads and bridges had been bombed out of existence.

Fortunately Yugoslavia is rich in raw materials such as coal, iron ore, crude petroleum and chemicals as well as having large fertile plains and river valleys. Agriculture is highly developed, and 85% is in private hands although land ownership is limited to 10 hectares (25 acres). With Tito's guidance in this socialist philosophy the change in economic development after the War was dramatic. Yugoslavia was not subservient to Russia and while the Soviet Union was the country's most important single customer, the EEC was the biggest economic trading group and there was also substantial trade with the United States.

Unfortunately the system that put the country back on its feet could not stand the test of time. The economically limiting size of the farms, the negative aspects of inefficiency and duplication in the self-management system and a slowing world economy were having a profound impact on the country, causing spiralling inflation and the shortage of supplies we had experienced. For the locals there were subsidies for such basics as bread and dairy products. Boards with two price systems, for locals and tourists, were usually displayed.

We headed north, with more northerly winds, but they were light. We had been looking forward to cruising the Dalmatian Islands which radiate out like fingers from the coast and anchored at Polace on Mljet island, next to a fourth century Roman palace.

It was a two kilometre walk to the beautiful cool, clear seawater lakes in the Mljet National Park with butterflies continuously dancing in our path.

"Look, a mongoose," whispered Colin.

It was right ahead. Later we saw many more, and the boys were delighted, although mongooses, being originally imported to reduce the snake population, have now become pests.

Back at the anchorage one could hardly hear oneself over the cicadas. Their great hum came in waves, with magnificent crescendos and diminuendos.

Hvar is supposedly blessed with more sunshine than any other city in the Adriatic, an average of seven hours 365 days of the year, according to the brochures. The advertising had been successful; it was seething with tourists. However, from the water the old city of Hvar was enchanting; its stone walls contoured around the bay, guarded by a fortress towering high above the red roofs, with a backcloth of green hills exuding pungent aromas of rosemary. Ashore I had my longest wait for bread, one and a half hours!

The harbour was a beehive of tourist ferries and yachts, the turbulence abruptly tossing us around. We spent the night by the green Pakleni Otoci Islands, by-passing the popular ACY (Adriatic Club Yuvoslavia) marina at Palmezana for the anchorage on the south side at Vino-gradisce.

There were lovely country walks which provided great exercise and stimulated more local research. We saw sharp-snouted lizards with their blue undersides and cheeky attitude, and Dahl's whip snakes, slender reptiles easily identified by the dark spots on the side of the neck. The most common of the often dense butterflies were the cleopatra and the southern white admiral. In the ocean a profusion of marine worms wafted their fans from their long calcareous tubes several inches high, and slimy sea slugs (that Jamie loved to pick up) were everywhere, browsing away on algae.

We left early for Ravni Zakan, planning to get a few miles under our belt while the boys slept, but soon were surrounded by dolphins, and the boys wouldn't have forgiven us if we hadn't wakened them. At their most playful at dawn, the many dolphins leapt and dove around and under the boat for twenty minutes, an exhilarating sight to start the day.

In stark contrast to the green rocky southern islands the Kornati chain are conical, brown and bare.

"Just like a lunar landscape," Duncan commented aptly.

Ravni Zakan was fascinating for a night, but eerie, and we were pleased to be back to the green landscape of the mainland at Sibenik. Having entered the channel, typically guarded by an impressive stone fort, we explored the ancient centre that clung to the side of the hill, a steep warren of alleys, steps and arches.

In Corfu some Yugoslavians had suggested an anchorage at the end of the lake; blissfully we had it to ourselves. The boys bathed in the river, fished and picked more blackberries. I organised and cleaned the boat from top to toe for our next guests, sorted the school books for the following year and hung such quantities of laundry on deck, that the boat sailed around at anchor. Meanwhile Andy completed some maintenance and repairs on the boat. Despite the image of an idyllically relaxing lifestyle the chores still accumulate with the same monotonous regularity, and most are done slowly and inconveniently by hand!

In Skradin we were made very welcome at the Adriatic Cruising Club marina. Here we were joined by Paddy, Chris, Scot and Nicola Thompson, old English friends. It was a picturesque setting at which to arrive and our trip up the green valley and vineyards to the Krka water falls the next day was exhilarating for all. The water plunges in a series of cascades over 50 metres and from the lower pool one can swim behind the teeming falls themselves, although several very deep breaths are necessary. Although I found it quite nerve-racking the children couldn't have enough. It cemented a great friendship and they had a active ten days, swimming, fishing, playing games or 'zotting' off in the dinghy to explore new sites for forts or camps ashore.

"Can we rig the spinnaker pole?" was a frequent request.

Colin and Andy with one of the many turtles found sleeping on the surface in the Mediterranean

Spinnaker pole jumping had become a favourite activity with children and adults alike, a great way to cool off in the debilitating 32 degrees celsius. We rig the spinnaker pole horizontally from the mast, attach a line with a loop to the outer end and swing out over the water from the bow descending to the cool depths with a jump, dive or belly flop.

There were some memorable visits ashore, sampling local wine at the small island town of Primošten—absolutely lethal—and wandering the peaceful old stone island town of Trogir before the tourists came out in force. Its elegant palaces belied its long list of invaders that included the Romans, Venetians, French, Austrians, Italians, and Germans not to mention endemic malaria, pirates, Saracens and the constant menace of the Turks. Vrboska, on the island of Hvar, was a sleepy little village, sprawling along the side of one of the island's deep bays and Korcula a mix of buildings from different eras piled together. This time we stopped at Pomina on Mljet island, finding an uncrowded anchorage and a much shorter walk to the lakes. *Bagheera* had strong head winds on the final sail to Dubrovnik, because yes, as soon as we reached Skradin, the winds turned southerly. So much for the great spinnaker runs we were going to have with the extra hands on board!

The Thompson's visit had been stimulating for us all and a successful experiment with nine compatibly on board. We sailed round to Gruz to spend our final dinars and found that Canadians Bernice Betts and Jim Lozej on *O'Desiderata*, a Beneteau 375 like *Severance*, had just arrived. It was great timing; we were able to give them our cruising guides, in particular the new Yugoslavian National Guide to the Adriatic, a publication that is well illustrated, translated into English and a bargain as it includes all the necessary small and large scale charts. They, in turn, suggested a stop at Taormina in Sicily. We rapidly caught up on Vancouver news, and were pleased to learn that our paths should cross again soon in the Canaries.

9. Italy, Spain and Morocco

Sicily, Straits of Messina, Lipari and Volcano
Menorca, Ibiza, Ceuta
Tétouan

We deadheaded south, motor sailing into the light wind. With a brief stop to refuel at Crotone on the Italian mainland, we arrived at the port of Naxos, in Sicily, three days later. Exhausted after many early mornings and late nights during the Thompsons' visit, the boys slept a good deal of the time.

It was stifling in the harbour so the boys and I took to the rather stony beach. It was divided off for individual hotels, seething with puce coloured tourists and we could barely walk along the water's edge. Tiny ice cream cones cost $1.40 each. This was reality with a vengeance.

Back at the boat Andy was working in the cockpit, so the children climbed below through the forward hatch onto the berth. Inevitably the bedding was covered in sand which is why we generally discourage using the hatch as a door! It was the beginning of a comedy of errors. It was only when we climbed into bed that I felt the abrasive feeling that I knew from experience was going to irritate all night and never go away by itself. So I gathered up the sheet and shook it vigorously over the side. 'Plop', went my glasses, which I normally never take to our berth as I only need them for distance, down into the oily depths. No problem, I delved to the bottom of a locker and hauled out my spare pair. These promptly fell off the table. Just a mere 30 centimetre drop and only onto a wooden floor but they cracked. This was getting serious, so Duncan and Andy went diving the next morning. They surfaced in despair.

"There is so much garbage on the bottom, and the water is so murky we'll never be able to find them. Also I really don't think we should go on diving, it's just too dirty," said Andy.

My last resort was wearing contact lenses, if I was going to see anything of Taormina. Before starting our trip I had worn contacts for over ten years incident free, except for the odd hunt around the bathroom. Since boarding *Bagheera* in England my eyes had smarted and streamed. I consulted an ophthalmologist who suggested it might be a chemical reaction to something on board. But where would I start looking with all the paints, varnishes and glues in such a confined space? I was also interested that our friends on *Lively Lady* were having similar symptoms and we had wondered if our eyes were reacting to the howling, salt-laden winds. I had finally stopped wearing contacts altogether and had resorted to prescription tinted glasses.

Whilst we were visiting Taormina I had no tears from wearing the lenses but within five minutes of returning to the boat my eyes were streaming. I visited the head frequently for eyedrops and cold compresses. By now my eyes were on fire.

Realization suddenly dawned.

"Andy," I called. "The chemical that's affecting my eyes has to be in the head." We looked at the shampoos, the sun and hand creams, the detergents and through the medical chest.

"I know what it is," said Andy at last. "I bet it's that air freshener you put in the head in Lymington." It had been bought our first day on board!

He was right. It had only taken us a year and a half to analyze. I had more tinted, prescription glasses made for spares, and actually continued wearing glasses most of the time, finding them far more practical than contacts. Being quick to put on they were far easier for three hour watches and they protected against dust and sun; even with contacts I'd still had to wear dark glasses. Also taking contacts in and out with a heavy sea running wasn't great for the stomach, and I didn't have to worry about solutions and infection. (Although now, with extended wear and disposable contacts, I might think otherwise.)

We took the bus up the steep road to Tormina. Ornately Italian, with wrought iron railings, arches, columns and elaborate doorways and windows, the old town, although touristy, was very attractive. We gave the Greek ruins a miss; even I was becoming 'ruined out'. Instead we admired the many churches and multi-coloured mansions, then relaxed in a cool cafe and indulged in thirst quenching drinks of fresh lemon and crushed ice. We were entertained by flamboyant Italians and tourists' comments as they wandered by, flashing their cameras. One of the most magnificent sights was Mount Etna, soaring in the distance with a hint of snow on its peak. Although seeming serene against the deep blue sky, Etna has erupted eight times in the last three decades. "Sometimes at night", a sparkly-eyed old lady told the children, "it shoots flames to the sky". It was the perfect backcloth for this rather theatrical town.

Mid-afternoon we set sail for Reggio on the Italian west coast. For half an hour we pounded through sharp waves with the 25 knot wind on the nose. It wasn't fun at all, so we turned around and flew back downwind to the harbour. Ironically this wind would have been perfect two days earlier on our way south.

Setting sail next morning we experienced a flat calm and arrived at the small marina at Reggio at 1:00 PM. That afternoon we completed our first day of the new session of school. I had been summoning energy for days, now well aware of the commitment needed for the next ten months, but the boys were full of enthusiasm.

Early the next day Duncan and I headed into town to shop. Our dock neighbours told us the supermarket was good. It was refreshing to find prices clearly marked and some 'specials' besides. But we waited fifty minutes in the bank to change Eurocheques and the taxi fare was $15 for a five minute ride. As I was arguing with the driver Andy returned, enraged that he had been overcharged for fuel. A yachtsman and marina attendant sorted out the taxi driver but we left with poor impressions about the treatment of visitors.

To the northeast of Sicily lie the volcanic Aeolian Islands and we headed to Lipari, the largest of the group. It was a serenely calm day so we motored through the Straits of Messina.

Andy looked at length through the binoculars.

"There's an extraordinary vessel ahead," he commented finally. "I just can't make it out."

"Look at the bowsprit," cried Duncan a few minutes later. "It's huge and there's a man right on the end."

"And look at the top of the mast. There are lots of men up there," called Colin.

In Lipari we found out it was a swordfish fishing boat. The bowsprit appeared well over 50 feet long, and when fully extended was longer than the boat itself. The man on the end manned a harpoon. He responded to shouts from above. With their increased elevation, the men in their 'nest'

Sword-fishing boat in the Straits of Messina

at the top of the mast had a greater range of vision so could see the huge fish as they basked on the surface. The helmsman was also at the top of the mast for quick response. We watched him turning the boat as they sighted their quarry, with the man on the end of the bowsprit flying through the air at unbelievable speed.

At this time the world's yachting media was focused on the latest technical go-fast antics in America's Cup design.

"What a great spoof a photo of one of these vessels and an article about a new America's Cup boat could be," said Andy. "We could call it *Good Godmother*, a high-tech yacht put together by a Sicilian syndicate!"

"Back to school," decreed the schoolmarm. The distraction, as always, had been fascinating (and educational!), but it was time to get back on task if we were going to complete the school programme.

Our neighbours in Lipari had just spent three weeks sailing east across the Med. The wind had been behind them all the way; some people have all the luck.

The island was dramatic with the red lava rock and 16th century castle and 17th century cathedral standing on the plateau above. They were some of a varied collection of ruins.

The boys insisted we climb the volcano on the island of Vulcano, which rose out of the sea in 183 BC. It was a steep climb and a hot day, but the children were full of energy. As we neared the summit sulphur steam from the rock fissures abruptly hissed at us. We had to be careful not to touch the yellow stained vents with a steadying hand, as the steam was burning hot.

All went well until the path narrowed to a one person track, with a long drop of loose scree beneath. As I peered down the steep slope I was having my doubts about three year old Jamie; we could no longer even hold his hand when the path came to an end and the vertical climb began. At this point we decided Jamie and I should opt out. Andy, Duncan and Colin continued, climbing the large rocks, and soon disappeared.

"It was fantastic, Mummy," Duncan called down half an hour later. "We went right into the crater. It was really steaming."

"And we did need the wet facecloths," Colin added. "We would have suffocated if we hadn't had them."

"Yes, the sulphur fumes were terrible," Andy agreed, "but what an amazing sight, and we learnt that the name volcano actually comes from here."

Later we bathed in a sulphur pool close to the boat and covered ourselves with mud. It dried pasty white and was reputedly good for the complexion.

"Oh Mummy," said Jamie looking worried. "You look just like a ghost!"

Our jacuzzi was a natural one; the hot air bubbling up through the warm ocean. As promised our skin did feel wonderfully smooth. Wonderful, that is, until my husband commented,

"You know it's only because our pores are full of mud!"

Eating out for a full meal was expensive so we bought some irresistible rich cakes and savoured 50¢ mouthfuls. We left in the early evening hoping to glimpse the volcano of Stromboli perform. We had been told the view from the sea was truly awe-inspiring with the stream of incandescent lava flowing down the flank of the mountain into the sea. But alas, there were no ribbons of fire that night as we headed for the island of Ustica. After refuelling the winds were light but picked up along the south coast of Sardinia.

"Maybe we can risk not going into Cagliari for more fuel," said Andy.

"It would save a lot of time and we should make Menorca in time for the Mahon fiesta."

Andy calculated we required at least six hours of a brisk sailing breeze to supplement our fuel. It shouldn't be a problem we rationalized. Sods Law again, for as soon as we had cleared the Sardinian coast the breeze deserted us and there wasn't a breath for two days!

Mid-passage we met a Spanish yacht in a similar predicament, only they were short of oil. We gave them oil and they promised to tow us when we ran out of fuel. To our surprise we didn't need their help. By cruising at 1500 revs (giving about 4½ knots) we almost doubled our cruising range compared to our normal 6½ knots at 2,200 revs. It was an interesting exercise, with frequent looks of disbelief at the fuel gauge, and we easily arrived in time for the traditional Mahon Nuestra Senora de Gracia fiesta.

This celebration dates back to the 13th century, when Alfonso III of Aragon conquered Menorca and drove out the Arabs. He was helped by the ancient Order of San Juan who initiated the celebrations that apparently have changed little over the centuries. At 5:00 PM the handsomely dressed 'knights' rode through the town on their sleek dark Menorcan horses with colourfully braided manes and tails. True to form the spectators rushed out making the horses rear, their thick black manes streaming and the riders having to use every skill to manage their steeds through the dense crowds in the narrow streets.

Other aspects of the fiesta were not quite so traditional but fun for the boys. They enjoyed bashing each other in bumper cars, devouring huge candy flosses, watching the dazzling firework display, while the highlight was a visiting circus.

Coming back to Menorca was like returning home. We were welcomed everywhere by old friends and local tapa bars and Anne and Clemente Oliver gave a wonderful party with all the trimmings for Colin's eighth birthday. He was thrilled that Steve and Andrea on *Severance* and other Canadian friends, Peter, Lydia, Anya and Ryan, on *Blyss II*, (seen in Malta), could also share it with him. His presents included more characters for Playmobil, a well used toy on board, and drawing and colouring sets. In our recent longer passages Colin had been spending hours at the main cabin table designing, drawing, colouring and building more creations out of paper. Always small, very detailed and usually involving animals and birds, they gave him great enjoyment and satisfaction. We were fascinated and delighted, and frequently found an excuse to go below, to watch the progress.

Over a week later we dragged ourselves away from Mahon, leaving at 6:00 AM to sail around to the Calas Covas, a series of fiord like inlets, flanked by well-wooded cliffs and full of caves. Once inhabited by prehistoric troglodytes, the caves are still popular as dwelling places today, especially during the summer months. As we sat at anchor eating breakfast in the cockpit we watched the community gradually come to life.

After brief stops in Puerto Colom, Mallorca, at Ile Esplanada for a romp on the long sandy beach, and in Ibiza for a shop and water (a mistake, as it turned out to be brackish), we left for Ceuta, a Spanish owned town opposite Gibraltar on the North African coast. It was a superb sail with easterly winds, interestingly always stronger at night, and we arrived on September 22nd. En route we had heavy shipping traffic, saw some pilot whales, many dolphins and caught a 14 lb tuna. When we were pulling into Ceuta Colin commented,

"But we can't be here already. I thought it was going to be a long trip!"

It was hard to believe we had been out for two nights, except for the busy watches. At 22.00 on the first evening I wrote in the log 'Five ships converging—help! Duncan has come to keep me company.'

We had been told of the cheap wine and liquor in Ceuta. Remembering the frequent sundowner parties but high prices in the Caribbean we wanted to stock to capacity. With staggeringly low prices such as $2.00 for a 40 oz bottle of gin and $2.50 for a 40 oz bottle of Fundador brandy it was hard to restrain ourselves, but we did have to keep some room for food!

We had promised the boys a brief visit to Morocco, and took the bus to the border, some 10 minutes away. Here a charming taxi driver persuaded us to visit Tétouan 40 kilometres inland. It was a pleasant trip through sand dunes and eucalyptus, and we stopped at the roadside for the boys to have their first ride on a camel.

Touring the town we noticed that the minarets were short and square, whereas in Tunisia they were tall and square and in Turkey they were round. I was fascinated too by the variety of women's attire, from western style to hooded long robes with mouth scarf, and another rather flamboyant rig with red striped long skirt and large bell-shaped straw hat.

Inevitably we ended up in the bazaar. Having rather regretted not buying a Turkish carpet we were interested in the choice here and over many mint teas found a silk carpet visually and economically much to our liking. We were surprised that in Morocco silk is cheaper than wool, and although there are fewer threads per square inch than the Turkish, the pile is longer and more luxuriant. The boys were delighted.

On our return, while approaching the border, I took a photo of Andy and the boys beside a local who was wearing a huge straw hat piled high with buns. A typical touristy memento, I thought, until whistles sounded and a uniformed official aggressively insisted I give up my camera. Apparently the area was restricted, no cameras were allowed. The long and the short of the next hour was being hauled in front of the hierarchy of security officials and finally taken to the internal police, as I really didn't want my film destroyed. They flatly refused to call any Canadian or British authorities and as time went on I must say it did cross my mind that I would give up the film rather than end up in a Moroccan gaol. Finally, at the end of a monotonous tirade of, "Give us your camera," we unexpectedly heard the word "Go". We MOVED.

Later we were asked why we hadn't offered an incentive to speed up the process, but as we only had 80 pesetas on us, just enough for the busfare back to the boat, it wasn't a realistic option! We also have strong feelings about bribing and didn't succumb to it in all of our world travels, although on occasion Andy's patience was more than pushed to the limit.

The boys were excited about returning to Gibraltar. As we motored over from Ceuta we were welcomed by as many dolphins as we'd ever seen. They seemed also in a particularly happy mood, diving around the boat for an hour, many in pairs leaping the bow wave. It was as though they and the recently sighted gannets, lesser blackback gulls and stormy petrels were welcoming us to the Atlantic beyond, for we were now at the end of our Mediterranean travels. In the last eleven months we had realised all our expectations and more in ancient culture and magnificent cuisine. As hoped, the cruising had been perfect for the children with the short trips, and they had thrived in the varied adventures ashore. Now our thoughts were on planning the big trip west; heading out into the Atlantic to Madeira and the Canary Islands, then the three thousand nautical mile journey across to Barbados in the Caribbean.

The Atlantic

Jamie on the Atlantic crossing

10. Gibraltar, Madeira and the Canary Islands

Porto Santo, Funchal, Rudder Damage
Lanzarote, Fuerteventura and Las Palmas, Gran Canaria

The docks were humming when we pulled into Gibraltar. Everyone was in a frenzy of preparations. With our captain keen to start our long list of chores, we immediately joined the fray.

Within a week we found crew for the Atlantic crossing, hauled the boat, painted the bottom and our three water line stripes, fitted a new folding propeller, installed a new refrigeration unit under warranty, sold all our Mediterranean charts and bought secondhand Atlantic and Caribbean ones, had the life raft tested, sails repaired, and instruments checked. Andy fibre-glassed in a horizontal bulkhead under our mattress to increase strength at the water line forward should we run into a solid object; a semi submerged container or oil drum is a constant concern. He put carpeting (poor man's baggywrinkle), on the spreaders and shrouds to prevent chafe on the mainsail when running downwind, extra chafe patches on the sail itself, and plastic tubing and toggles on the genoa bowline knots to stop wear, particularly when it was poled out.

I queued endlessly at the washing machines conveniently located on the dock, and finally managed to launder and bleach every washable item on board down to the last pillow. For the most part I had handwashed for the last eight months.

"And don't forget Pooh Bear," Jamie admonished me. "He hasn't had a wash since we were last in Gibraltar and he needs one!"

Having been lovingly dragged around nine European countries, he did indeed.

In the main cabin, surrounded by chaos, the boys tried to complete school. One morning after yet another interruption Duncan complained,

"It's impossible to get any work done here and anyway none of the other kids are doing school."

"I agree, its really frustrating," I replied, "but how are we going to get this term finished? The other options are school at sea or we could skip a Christmas holiday in the Caribbean."

"No way!" they chorused. These were my sentiments exactly.

For the next few days, while Andy had the main cabin apart for the various projects, the local cafe became our schoolhouse. With few other customers during the morning hours both Duncan and Colin completed their assignments in record time, working at separate tables and motivated by praise and free drinks from the manager!

I always find it ironic, and frustrating, that when we are docked and would like the boat presentable for people who are constantly coming by, it is generally in bedlam. At sea of course it is always immaculate as everything has to be stowed for the motion. When Andy went to England for a week to see his mother, who was now over 80, the boat returned to its normal state—until I started buying stores.

One of the major worries of the Atlantic crossing for many was the provisions required. There were endless conversations revolved around special boat menus, and the quantities required. A 40 footer like ourselves could easily take three weeks to complete the Atlantic voyage from the Canaries to Barbados. If there was some disaster, such as a broken mast, it could take much longer. I always have provisions for at least an extra month, with emergency supplies in special containers and in the liferaft, for considerably longer.

Having cooked on charter boats in the Caribbean for several years, when I usually had to shop in advance for at least a week's supply of gourmet meals, and also having provisioned for an Atlantic crossing some years previously, I wasn't as concerned as some. Nevertheless the size of the task was onerous. I decided to write out a list of menus mainly because I wanted our new crew, who were responsible for half the food preparation, to do the same. We had been pleased to find Jacques and Jacquie, and also to learn that Jacques was a highly qualified French chef, as we always like to eat well.

I had barely completed my list, of specific meals and quantities demanded, when Andrea from *Severance* came by. She took one glance at it.

"Can I borrow this Liza, I'll just photocopy it, and then return it."

The list did the round of the docks and I didn't see it for days. More to the point was Jacques' list. Every lunch and dinner included another mouth-watering fish creation.

"But Jacques, what if we don't catch any fish?" I queried.

"Pas de problem! Zee ocean is full of zee fish."

"But what if we don't manage to catch them?"

"It is a problem," he replied thoughtfully, shaking his head. "I will think again."

We found it was easy to tire of fish, even Andy the fish enthusiast. As we couldn't freeze the left-over fish, rather than throw it back in the water, which seemed a crime, we would eat fish for every meal, including pickling and drying some. After two or three days of this regime no-one wanted to catch another fish for a week.

With our regular butane/propane stove with oven I never required special 'boat' recipes such as pressure cooker bread or pulse stew. However without a freezer we did have to adapt to using canned and dried goods. A varied supply of British canned chicken, beef and lamb stews, salmon, crabmeat, tuna and vegetables, and dried mince meat, soy, cheese, peas and beans etc. were available at Lipton's supermarket at the end of the dock. These were enhanced by Spanish goods: octopus, squid, ratatouille, olives, pimientos . . .

Friday, October 3 dawned bright and sunny. It was to be a long day. At 8:00 AM I was already shopping in the Spanish La Linea market, then a friend drove me to the hypermarket 'Continenti'. It was hard to believe my eight trollies of goods would fit into her mini, besides her own shop, and that we would make it back over the border with no customs charge—but we did. Then off to two local supermarkets.

"Mummy, do you really have more buggies for us to wheel down the dock?" Duncan asked incredulously. "Where will it all go?"

"Oh, I'm sure it will fit," I replied optimistically, although I was beginning to wonder myself.

"Is it okay if we go up to the sports club with Lance and Miles?" asked Colin.

Their new friends' parents had discovered a club close-by that had good facilities and was free of charge. It also had abundant hot showers.

"Of course. What about Jamie? Where is he anyway?"

Jamie had become very independent in the last few days, making many friends on the dock and catching up on a deprivation in his lifestyle—TV time!

"I'm here" said Jamie peering down the companionway. "What a mess, Mummy. I hope you're going to clear it up soon!"

I had to laugh, he had one on me this time.

"I've been invited to Blyss for supper, with Anya and Ryan. Is that okay?"

"Wonderful." I breathed a sigh of relief, I did not want to think of dinner.

"How about we have fish and chips?" Duncan continued knowing his timing was right.

"Great idea, but get some for Jacques and Jacquie too."

It became the rule. We always eat out the evening of a provisioning session. It is the only way to keep one's sanity.

Jacques, Jacquie and I worked diligently into the night: labelling, listing and stowing. Duncan helped by writing the contents of the cans in permanent marker. Although we do not have a bilge area in which to stow goods, it is a good policy in case labels get wet and come off, an undesirable true pot luck would be the inevitable consequence otherwise.

Finally, by midnight, Jacques and Jacquie had their canned and dried goods stowed in a locker behind the main cabin cushions, with the remainder forward under our berth.

I still had a lot to do, but I am a night owl and with the boys asleep I had total peace and quiet. This is my productive time of day; quite the opposite to Andy who likes to rise and work with the sun. Sometimes we almost cross paths in the small hours!

The remainder of the food was categorized in three cardboard boxes, carefully checked for cockroaches before being brought on board. They fitted along the outside of the aft port double berth. We had asked for the mattresses for this bed to be divided lengthwise down the middle with this in mind. The inner half of the bed was still wide enough for the boys to sleep on and we had a leecloth that kept the boxes in place. I could also fit in all the bulky items such as cereals, paper towel, sugar including the 'strong' bread flour (40 kilos), which was liberally sprinkled with bay leaves to keep away the weevils.

By 3:00 am every item had disappeared. I felt very virtuous, but not always sure what might come out with the socks!

The chores continued, but interspersed were some delightful times. Having RNSA (Royal Naval Sailing Association) prominently on our stern we were invited to the local chapter's cocktail party. This led to several other parties, some of the few occasions when the dresses, suits and jackets we squashed into our lockers, came into their own. I even used an iron, on my neighbour's boat, on occasion.

We had five west coast Canadian boats on the dock and our 'private' VHF radio station hummed. The boys made many friends, frequently watched videos and enjoyed looking in the toy and electronic games shops. Visiting the famous apes also kept them out of mischief. We all visited the local sports club most evenings. Duncan took pleasure in beating his mother at badminton but had some expertise to gain in squash. Jamie made the most of the last of his tricycle to visit his friends, as Andy felt we didn't have room to carry it across the Atlantic.

There was also a Royal Naval Air Show, and as the marina is next to the runway, we could watch the practice sessions. In fact, we found the practices almost more interesting than the show itself.

"You must come up on deck," Andy called down frequently during the morning.

He became quite nostalgic when the 'Red Arrows' aerobatic team soared over in perfect formation, and some 'oldies' arrived that he had previously flown. It was the Harriers, however, that were the most impressive, demonstrating their vertical takeoff and stationary hovering abilities, completing their performance with an elegant bow. The show ended with the parachutists. Jumping at 4,000 metres they all landed within a 15 metre span, having created intricate red and white smoke designs during their descent.

Our English friends managed to procure tickets for us to hear the Bugles, Bagpipes and Band of the Royal Irish Rangers perform in St. Michael's cave. It was a vibrant, varied programme from military to folk music, from classical to Irish dancing. The effects of using the perfect acoustics of this large cave, full of illuminated stalactites and stalagmites, were breathtaking. None of us, as the children were there too, will ever forget the glorious sound of the full band playing 'The Chariots of Fire.'

Finally we were ready to leave—or, as the expression goes, as ready as we would ever be.

On October 19th Sven Rasmussen arrived from Vancouver to join us for our first leg to Madeira and the Canaries. We held a final party, the food courtesy of our French chef, and bade our farewells to many new friends.

On our last morning 'disaster' struck.

"Mummy, Daddy," called Colin frantically, "Sidi Bou has flown away."

With our lives so hectic we had forgotten to trim our budgie's wings, to inhibit his upwards flight. So long as Sidi could only fly level or downwards he would stay in the cabin. As usual as soon as he was up Colin had taken him out of his cage for a walk-about. Instead it was a fly-about and our pet was now perched, chirping cheekily, on the boom of our absent neighbour's boat.

The boys rushed on deck calling him by name but to no avail. Andy unfastened the cage and slowly climbed over the lifelines and along the deck towards him. Within inches of success Sidi soared into the air then landed on the boom of the next boat—and so he progressed, with Andy in hot pursuit, down the next five yachts. The boys were in despair.

"We'll never catch him, and it's all my fault." wailed Colin. "And now he's going to go in the water."

Sidi did have a dilemma because there was no next door boat to fly to. Whether he actually worked this out, or whether he was just plain exhausted we will never know, but at this point he graciously condescended to hop into the cage. What a relief! I was already envisioning the upset and trauma, to say nothing of the delay to find a substitute.

We left Gibraltar on an ideal wind, a 15-20 knot easterly, and it was a perfect trip 600 nautical miles out into the Atlantic. As usual we kept three hour watches. With Sven on board we always had the luxury of six consecutive hours between watches for sleep. With Duncan and Colin in charge of one hour watches in the afternoon, sometimes there were eight blissful hours to relax after our hectic time in Gibraltar.

Our landfall was Porto Santo, a small semi-arid island 20 nautical miles to the north east of Madeira.

"Just look at that beach," called out Duncan "it goes on for ever."

The 11 kilometres of sugary sands were one of the reasons we stopped here. After a three day trip the boys needed a good run. We had a long hike along the bay and finally exhausted them, and more so ourselves, with a game of soccer. It was a wonderful full nights sleep and we woke at 9:00 AM to find Duncan had cooked us all French toast.

This island was the first on which the discoverers of Madeira, Joao Goncalves Zarco and Tristao Vaz Teixiera, landed in 1418. These captains took refuge here when they were blown off course in a storm. They named the island 'Holy Port' to express gratitude for their survival. The island's main claim to fame is the rough stone two story building where Christopher Columbus is said to have lived shortly after his marriage to the daughter of one of Prince Henry's navigators. It is situated in the island's capital, Vila Baleira, a small cluster of red-roofed white houses, with church and shops around the pebbled square. I went into the butcher shop and chose some pork. I was touched that the butcher carefully cut off the choice cuts for us. The price was reasonable and the meat melted in your mouth.

On our way to the big island of Madeira we saw a yacht dead astern, so weren't surprised to hear them call us on the radio. We were surprised, however, to hear that they were unable to see us on their radar screen. They were only about four miles away and with our Firdell Blipper mounted on the mast we should have shown a strong image.

"I can't believe it," said Andy to Sven and myself. "The Firdell has a stack of reflective surfaces and European tests showed it to be the most effective radar reflector on the market."

We had the reflector attached about 11 metres above deck on the forward side of the mast. What was wrong? As this yacht was dead astern when they called all we could think was that the mast created a blind spot. This theory was confirmed when we talked to the owners later. As soon they were no longer right behind we showed as a strong blip on the screen. To overcome the problem we hung a simple aluminum double reflective surface reflector from the backstay. It always surprised us that many cruisers neglected this most important piece of safety equipment. After this lesson we decided that on future boats we would have twin reflectors on the mast to eliminate the blind spot.

When we arrived at the marina in Funchal, the capital of the big island of Madeira, it was overflowing; full of boats who like ourselves soon were to set off on an Atlantic crossing. We elected to anchor outside. Our choices were a clean but rolly anchorage or moor with a stern line ashore to the seawall in relative shelter. We opted to stay outside, but this turned out to be a catastrophe twice over.

We were overwhelmed by this beautiful island with its soaring jagged mountains, lush vegetation, agricultural terracing climbing up the slopes, and tropical and temperate flora. Portuguese in nationality, Madeira was recognized as a gem when it was discovered in the fifteenth century.

Funchal is an attractive city with beautiful old architecture and lavish use of Portuguese tiles and stone patterned pavements. There is an excellent fruit, vegetable, meat, fish and flower market, and eating out is inexpensive. Typical fare is Espada, the long eel-like black fish with sharp teeth which, we were told, are hauled from great depths of over 925 metres. They are good eating and most distinctive with their long tails dangling from trestle tables in the market.

Hallowe'en in Madeira with Steve, Jacquie, Andrea and Sven

We explored with Steve and Andrea Bayly from *Severance*, and looked at the famous Madeira lace and embroidery (exquisite in detail and price), tasted the local wine (too sweet for me), bought the rich Madeira cakes (great as they last for a year) and rode the wicker sleighs down the steep cobblestones (I was petrified). We celebrated Hallowe'en and also toured the island by bus, enjoying the spectacular scenery bathed in different hues of green.

It was idyllic until after dinner one night. Sven went up on deck to smoke his pipe but returned rapidly,

"It's disgusting," he exclaimed "there's oil everywhere."

An oil slick covered the water, smearing everything black in seconds. Not only was it hard work to remove the next morning but it played havoc with our newly painted waterline and boot top stripes.

Our second misfortune was worse. During our trip around the island, *Bagheera* ended up on the rocks. Evidently a Swedish yacht had come in and dropped his anchor, apparently intending to anchor stern-to the seawall also. On finding there wasn't room to squeeze in, he decided to lift his hook again and leave. Unfortunately his anchor had tangled with ours, which had been firmly embedded for a week. When our anchor came up too, the other boat blithely discarded it. On the next squall *Bagheera* hurtled into the rocks astern.

Neighbouring yachtsmen met us as we returned in our dinghy.

"The boat is okay," they said, "but we wanted to tell you what happened before you saw the three anchors out and panicked."

They had seen *Bagheera* drag and had acted rapidly, calling on the radio for help, then rushing over to our boat. But the anchor would not grab as they hauled in the rode. *Bagheera* drifted backwards, pounding several times on the large boulders of the sea wall before it was towed off by another yachtsmen who had rushed over in response to the radio call.

Ironically our engine key was in place and they could have motored out of trouble. I mention this not as criticism, our fellow sailors did a sterling job for us, but in case anyone is faced with a similar situation.

There was a hole right through the hull just above the waterline on the starboard side. The next morning Andy dove to assess damage to the hull underwater.

"The rest of the hull and keel are almost unscathed but the rudder is shattered. About a third has disappeared and above that the fibreglass has split away from the stainless steel," he reported several dives later. "We'll have to haul out."

He went ashore to make inquiries and came back an hour later looking despondent.

"There are no hauling out facilities for yachts and the shipyard is booked up with fishing boats until after Christmas. There is nothing else to do but to go along the wall in the marina and make the repairs ourselves, with the boat in the water."

We went into the inner harbour, and after organising ten boats to move out, moored against the wall where there was a stairway to the water's edge. An hour later, with several lines around the rudder whose ends were held by willing helpers at our winches, we were ready to lower the rudder carefully. The depth was about 6 metres. Everyone held on tightly, we lowered it about a metre and finally the stock was free from the lower bearing.

"I don't believe it," Andy laughed from the water, "the rudder is floating."

Although extremely heavy to carry on land, what was left of the interior foam was surprisingly buoyant. Andy worked non-stop for four days: cutting, filling, taping, fibreglassing and sanding ... and fibreglassing and sanding ... But the true comraderie of yachtsmen came to the fore with many stopping to help with the unpleasant job of working with fibreglass. Others came by with tools and materials. Invaluable was a gift of two-part polyurethane foam, that had been a stumbling block as it was unavailable locally. It was needed to fill the rudder when the new fibreglass shells were formed.

A large crowd gathered to watch the refitting of the rudder which was indistinguishable from the original. This time we had a problem getting the rudder to sink, particularly with its extra buoyancy. It finally took the weight of a 8 kilo Danforth anchor and 1.5 metres of 8 millimetre chain to get the stock vertical and reinstalled.

We all agreed, however, that if this had to happen, Madeira was quite the best place to be, in fact the longer we stayed the less we wanted to leave.

One of the joys was the climate, sunny and pleasantly warm during the day but cool in the evening. This has encouraged a winter tourist trade, particularly for the energetic, as Madeira offers wonderful walks beside the levadas, the irrigation ditches which cover the island.

"We've just heard there's a spectacular levada walk from Curral das Freiras. Why don't we do it before leaving?" suggested Steve one night at dinner.

It was Number 2 in the tour book, and rated difficult.

We consulted our friends.

"It's fine," they assured us, "the boys will love it."

We took Duncan and Colin and went up by bus high in the mountains. Built inside the crater of an extinct volcano the nuns had escaped to this village from the pirates in days of old. The air was bracing as we started our descent, finding the levada easily from the instructions, with a path beside. Soon we could walk only on the levada retaining wall, about 25 centimetres wide. On our left was the levada, about 45 centimetres wide and fast running, with an occasional cliff behind, good for hand support. But on the right there was frequently a sheer 300 metre drop into the valley.

To say that my heart was in my mouth for the safety of the children was an understatement, thank goodness we had left Jamie behind. Occasionally there was an outcrop where we could pause, breathe freely and admire the steep green valley with a brilliant rainbow adding to its splendour, then on again in trepidation.

In places the wall was covered in green slime and as I saw Colin skid I couldn't help calling out,

"Colin, be careful and go slowly."

"It's all right, I'm fine." He called back predictably.

He had on plastic water shoes with no grip. I promised myself that I would buy him new running shoes the next day, even though they tend to rot on boats in the tropics.

Finally we made it to the banana belt and the path widened to a lane that brought us to the residential area of attractive houses and colourful gardens. In all it was about a 15 kilometre walk.

"How was it?" we were greeted with on returning to the boat.

"Great!" the boys replied.

I was still shaking.

At the beginning of November Chuck and Gail Croft arrived on their beautiful 73 foot Deerfoot, *Interlude*. Chuck was a rival from our racing days in Vancouver. We caught up on local news and enjoyed a tour of their palatial, magnificently equipped yacht. Two days before leaving Sidi Bou, our budgie, went walkabout again. We had put his cage up on deck and with all the people crossing our boat, with ten rafted outside, he had received plenty of attention, but the hook on his door had come undone.

The boys were distraught. They spent hours going from boat to boat saying mournfully,

"Have you seen our yellow budgerigar? He's flown away." To no avail. They even took off in the dinghy to boats anchored off, a remote possibility but all had to be checked out.

The next day a man came by to tell the boys that there was a bird just like Sidi Bou in the bird cage in the local park. Andy and boys rushed off and there he was, or so we like to think, chirping away happily, a mate at his side. On the way back Andy took the boys into a pet store and they returned with 'Malmsey Bou', named after the sweet Madeiran wine. Although Colin commented wistfully,

"I wish we still had Sidi Bou. I wonder if Malmsey will sit on my shoulder for school work and nibble Daddy's ear?"

We left Madeira sadly despite our misfortunes there. Although not a great cruising area it is one of the most beautiful islands in the world and remains a favourite. Charter flights from England are cheap and if any of you do visit you may find our *Bagheera* panther logo still painted, with many other yachts' displays, on the seawall.

The Canary Islands that we saw were a stark contrast. Bare in the extreme with curious striations in many of the rocks in golds, pinks and yellows. Our first stop was Gracioso Island and then we went on to Arrecife in Lanzarote. We anchored off the town, convenient and more picturesque than the commercial harbour but depths were unpredictable, holding was poor and we had a problem with the fixed moorings that were on a short rode.

Here we saw our Menorcan friends Anne and Clemente who were opening a new holiday accommodation office as Lanzarote, with its sandy beaches, was booming. We toured the island by car. The children swayed on camels on the lunar like slopes of Timanfaya and we explored some of the intricate lava caves, which stretched over 4 kilometres to the sea. The rock formations were fascinating but spookie, especially when all the lights went out!

We moored at Castillio, in Fuerteventura, a new German development on a pretty sandy bay. It is an alarming entrance with reefs on either side, but the attractive, small marina even had a travel lift, for up to about a 40 footer, in case anyone comes this way who needs to haul out. Here we met up with Vancouver *O'Desiderata* again. We last saw them in Dubrovnik, Yugoslavia.

Also on the dock was British '*Adhara*' with John the bagpipe player. We went over and congratulated him on the harmony of his latest wails.

"Well if you think it sounds good here," he said with a grin "you should hear me in the washroom!"

So we all trooped into the white tiled men's washroom, John making sure no-one was going to be caught unawares! The resonance was quite deafening. The next time we heard John play we were in the Caribbean, and his bagpipes had gone out of tune—the tropical humidity or was it the rum?!

We arrived in Las Palmas, in Gran Canaria island, a week before the start of the Atlantic Race for Cruisers, as the rules stipulated. The harbour was packed but we were able to raft up with our group of west coast Canadians. Lydia, from Blyss, was helping out in the race office. Mid-afternoon she rushed back to the boats.

"Heh guys, there's a fashion show tonight. Its supposed to be a crazy evening, we'll help you dress!" she announced.

The Canadian men turned themselves out 'beautifully'. Some strategic balloons added the finishing touch as they minced across the stage. Needless to say they stole the show, although the fashionable girls who turned up were rather less impressed!

11. The Atlantic Race for Cruisers

Las Palmas to Barbados

The Atlantic Race for Cruisers (ARC) was the first ever rally for cruising boats to cross the Atlantic to the West Indies. It was organised by Jimmy and Gwenda Cornell "to provide a fun race, to add zest to the long passage and increase safety and confidence." It was appealing to many, a high percentage of whom were crossing the Atlantic by boat for the first time.

As one lady expressed it,

"I was terrified of being all alone with my husband and child in the huge Atlantic Ocean, but with all these participants I feel we will be part of a big family out there, and we can just call on the radio if we have any problems."

Within two months of the announcement the original estimate of 60 to 80 entries was exceeded and at the final count 209 crossed the starting line, representing 24 nations. The boys were pleased that 22 boats had children on board, several being their ages. The youngest was a New Zealander, born in Las Palmas only two months before.

The final week was a blur of boat preparations, shopping, school, parties and specially organised events.

Before Jacquie moved on board I broached the subject of seasickness. Jacques and Jacquie had travelled down from Gibraltar on *Severance*. Jacquie had suffered so severely from sickness that Steve and Andrea questioned the wisdom of her crossing the Atlantic at all, convinced she would be incapacitated and a liability. Being a connoisseur of sea sickness myself (what fame to make a claim to!) I ran through the standard precautions. Had she abstained from alcohol and not eaten rich foods the night before a trip, (I knew Andrea's rich spaghetti bolognaise was a favourite), and not cooked or eaten bacon or drunk coffee the morning of the passage? In particular had she taken medication at least the specified time in advance?

She failed on almost every count! Knowing we had a base to work from gave me some hope, along with Jacquie's very positive attitude and determination to make the crossing.

"I have to admit," I said to Andy later. "I think she is just a 'regular case' and she will probably be fine if I give her an ear patch and she eases her way into eating with crackers and bland foods. I think we should risk taking her, after all people were very good about taking me!"

Andy did a final check of the rig and boat equipment. To his horror, when he moved the liferaft a 'clang-clang' sounded.

"Liza," he called urgently. "Listen to this." He moved the life raft again and once more the 'clapper' sounded.

"I don't believe it," he continued. " That's the warning signal that there is no CO_2 in the bottle. That means our life raft won't automatically inflate."

Andy had bought a new carbon dioxide bottle in England leaving it empty, as required, for the flight. The person servicing life rafts in Gibraltar had assured us he had remembered to have the bottle filled. We were aghast. This unforgivable error could have had tragic consequences. Andy quickly removed the canister and had it filled in town.

The boys finally finished Paper 10, the term's work was over conveniently before the organised day of water sports. The dinghy race was a highlight. Duncan and Colin joined their new friends and along with the rest of the participants were copiously floured and showered from the shore. All, that is, except one girl who determinedly rowed from start to finish around the water fight that ensued and was an easy victor, much to Duncan's disgust!

Meanwhile I replenished the stores. Despite rumours of indifferent shopping in Las Palmas there were two good supermarkets. They were used extensively judging by the constant parade of delivery trucks down the quayside. As the week progressed the pace heightened and with it many crew's level of anxiety, reduced only by yet another visit to the shops. It wasn't surprising that many people who had expected to lose weight during the 'gruesome' crossing complained of waistbands being rather tight when donned again in Barbados!

"Don't forget lots of 'Long Life' milk," Colin called out as Andrea and I left to face the supermarkets ourselves. "Please don't get any of that powdered stuff again, its horrible!"

I was pleased that 'Long Life' milk was available and inexpensive. We had used the heat preserved long life milk since the sixties in the Caribbean. Then it had tasted half way between fresh milk and evaporated milk. It has improved over the years and is now almost indistinguishable from fresh milk, and comes in various grades from homogenised to skim. It is acceptable in tea or coffee, and when chilled, excellent for drinking or in cereal. It is a luxury we treat ourselves to, as none of the family can stomach the powdered variety.

Also available in litre cartons was Spanish wine, which became known as 'Chateau Cardboard'. The red, white and rose were all palatable, especially since they were under 60¢ a litre. The cases of wine and milk filled the last available corners of the aft head.

Two days before leaving Jacques, Jacquie helped me in the market. We spent over $100 on fresh fruit, vegetables and meat. There was a good choice and produce was in its natural state, straight from the fields. This is just what we wanted, although cleaned supermarket vegetables look pristine and inviting, they generally don't last long. These potatoes were covered in earth, carrots not machine washed, lettuces crisp and green vegetables fresh and dry. Apples were unbruised, bananas underripe, oranges and grapefruit sweet but firm. We were also able to buy fresh eggs, that had not been refrigerated. This is important for longevity, and with a thin smear of vaseline to seal the shell eggs will last for weeks.

Our bags were full and baskets piled high. Fresh produce is often the greatest challenge when stowing on a crowded boat because to last well it must be exposed to circulating air. After a thorough sun drying, the uncrushables such as cabbage, squash etc., went in bins in the cockpit locker. A sack of potatoes went in one lazarette locker in the stern and a sack of onions was squeezed into the other. The lockers were opened daily for an airing and produce checked. Any soft or bad fruit and vegetables are removed as they quickly contaminate the rest. Jacquie carefully wrapped the apples in paper towel to prevent bruising and they fitted snugly along the shelf in the main cabin. One large basket of fruit had to live on our cabin floor, the other went under the table.

Our last day we rented a car. The children loved Palmitos Park with its exotic cacti and colourful parrots. The bird show was most entertaining and the unlikely skit of a parrot windsurfing, wandering up the beach to recline in a deck chair, donning dark glasses and reading the newspaper, had the entire audience in fits.

Meanwhile various discussions/arguments could be heard on the dock concerning the race. Although a relaxed rally in concept (the name was changed from race to rally in subsequent years) even some who had appeared die-hard cruisers were taking it very seriously; shipping in racing crews, off-loading heavy cruising gear and announcing that mothers and children should fly instead. Intricate ratings were eventually issued on the final evening but as measurements had been supplied by the owners and instructions were to estimate any unknowns, there were many discrepancies. *Severance*, for example, found she had to give two days to a similar Beneteau 375, but Steve was told it was too late for any adjustment. Also the basis of the rating scale was kept a close secret, although it appeared that displacement, sail area and waterline length had not been taken into account. These are all critical in a downwind race. There were several protests before the start and even at the finish many yachtsmen were extremely annoyed that in the final analysis motoring was not penalized. Those who had motored on the first night and through one particular day of calm had a huge advantage. But it was hard for spirits to remain dampened, we were after all on the eve of the big crossing.

As we returned to our vessels Colin called out,

"Look at all the boats with their flags."

The forest of masts, with signal flags flying in the brisk wind, was silhouetted against the glow of the dying sunset. It was a magnificent sight.

By 11:00 the next morning most masts had gone from the harbour, they were heading out to the starting line. The start was scheduled for noon but where was the committee boat? Finally a Spanish minesweeper came charging out of the harbour at full pelt, firing the starting gun whilst still on the move and far from the official line. Amazingly, despite boats charging in from all directions, there were no serious collisions, particularly as the organizers had decided that yachts should only observe the 'international rules for the prevention of collision at sea', and not the IYRU racing rules.

Gradually the chaos sorted itself out and the fleet divided, some going north-about whilst others decided that going south round the island would give them the edge. Spirits were high aboard *Bagheera* as we surged along at 8 knots under spinnaker, going north about Gran Canaria with all the Canadians except *Severance*.

The wind had dropped by late afternoon and we drifted through the night. It allowed us time to settle into the routine. With Jacques and Jacquie as our crew we each could each have a relaxing system of three days of a three hours on/six hours off watches with the fourth day on cooking and clean-up. This also gave a theoretical full nights sleep every fourth night, although as neither of the extra crew were too experienced it didn't always work out that way. By dawn the next morning there wasn't a yacht in sight. So much for having to dodge yachts all the way across the Atlantic that we'd talked about. But yachts were very much in evidence on the radio later that morning particularly as it was Andy's birthday. He got his quota of tuneful and tuneless 'Happy Birthdays' and witty and 'roasting' rhymes, then it was time to break open the champagne.

"C'est magnifique," said Jacquie holding up her glass "I did not dream it could be like this."

Jacquie had put on an ear patch the night before our departure and was feeling great. She could hardly believe it, and that evening happily tucked into the birthday dinner of rabbit and cheesecake.

"There's another celebration too, you know," reminded Duncan.

At 12:54 PM he had written in the log '*Bagheera* has done 10,000 miles'.

"How much is that in kilometres?" asked Colin. "It always sounds so much better."

"About 18,000," said Andy.

"Wow!"

Mid morning on our third day we saw another yacht on the southern horizon. Like ourselves they were flying their spinnaker, and after watching for a while we realised we were converging and on a collision course. The British *Oyster Lady* was on starboard tack (wind blowing on the starboard (right) side of the boat, sails to port). We were on port tack, so they had the right of way.

"I don't believe it," laughed Andy. "The only boat we've seen for days and we're going to have to alter course for them!"

"Hey *Bagheera*," their crew called out as we converged, "look this way for a photo."

"Great, we'll do the same for you," we called back.

"See you in Barbados," called Colin as we rapidly pulled apart.

With the exception of two faint spinnakers on the horizon and two ships, we didn't see another boat until the finishing line exactly two weeks later.

For the next few days we dipped south, heading approximately 20 degrees north and 30 degrees east, theoretically to find the steady trades, then to use a great circle route. These winds provide the best sailing of all, and once found generally give a fast Atlantic crossing.

Initially the winds were up and down, but everyday seemed to get a little warmer. On the fifth day Jacquie commented in the log 'Enfin le climat tropical. Beau soleil et mer superbe.' Next day Andy wrote 'Trade wind clouds at last'.

We had crossed the Tropic of Cancer two days before. King Neptune, our worthy captain, had adorned a silver crown and had given the children and Jacques an initiation, using copious quantities of shaving cream.

Our seventh day was the most memorable of the voyage. At 7:00 AM we caught a mahi mahi. It wasn't our first fish of the trip, we had enjoyed tuna and bonito, but this was our largest at about 25 pounds and a challenge to pull in on 10 pound test fishing line. Andy had decided not to use heavier line as big fish would be too difficult to get aboard with our reverse transom. The theory sounded good but in practise we lost many fishes and lures. This fish gave use a real battle.

"Turn on the engine Liza," Andy gasped at one point. "There is too much load. The line is going to break. Go in reverse."

I laughed. Andy is generally a very competitive racer. Although with our laden vessel we were hardly in racing trim going in reverse was not what I had expected to hear!

But his attention was on the immediate battle at hand and like all battles the more one fights the more one is determined to win. Andy seemed to play the line for hours, winding in then letting it go free whilst our monster fish took a run, then winding it in again slowly. After an hour in reverse it was victory at last, a magnificent iridescent blue and gold mahi mahi (otherwise called dorado or dolphin fish).

A technique we'd learned in Las Palmas greatly helped get our prize on board. Pouring a little gin, or any other alcohol, down the gullet and on the gills of the fish works like a dream, the fish instantly go limp. Some fight once more but after another anointing and it is game over. Not only does it give a quick painless death but there is no need to bash the poor fish over the head with a winch handle, (which I could never stand to look at or listen to, let alone do), and no splatters of blood. With warm blooded tuna that bleed profusely that is a major bonus. As we used our gin from Ceuta it was hardly a financial burden, although we used so little it was always worth the price.

Since midnight the wind had gone flat, except for a half an hour when it blew at 20 knots under a black cloud. Ancient mariners were driven crazy by the cracking flap, flap of the sails. Eight hours was enough for us, we started motoring at 9:00 AM. As we talked to boats within a 30 nautical mile range on the VHR radio we found everyone around us was motoring, and had been since the early hours.

One of the positive aspects of a flat calm is discovering sea life that is normally invisible. As we were admiring the sparkling transparent sails of the Portuguese men-o'-war jelly fish Duncan suddenly called out,

"Whales. Look, lots of whales."

There were two groups of sperm whales, about fifteen in all. We slowly headed towards them, finally shutting off the engine and drifting to within metres. They seemed unconcerned, especially the young. We watched from the bow, totally in awe as they glided slowly through the water around us, occasionally blowing through their spouts, their dark streamlined bodies glistening in the sun. The males were large, maybe 15 metres in length. They allowed us seven privileged minutes, then lazily ambled away and dove to the depths. We waited until the last one had gone, not wanting to miss a second of this magnificent visit with nature.

It seemed a crime to turn on the engine and break the trance but we had to find some wind. We were still suffering from the doldrums of the Horse Latitudes, so called after the 16th century Spanish conquerors. It was in these latitudes that they lay becalmed, watching their drinking water run low and finally in desperation heaving their dying horses overboard, a last resort to save water for their dying men.

Our problem wasn't with water, we had used little from our tanks and had extra jerry cans on deck, it was with the wine. As Jacquie went below for a snooze she realised her baggage on the cabin floor was awash, in red wine. I went into the aft head to investigate. What a calamity, the cases of long life milk had been too heavy for the cartons of wine. The aroma was overwhelming as I mopped up the excess, it was a good test that I had got my sea legs back again. Fortunately only a few cartons had burst, the rest were just bruised. I put them aside for immediate use, as the one glass a day we allowed ourselves as a sundowner.

It became hotter and hotter and finally Duncan asked if we could go for a swim. We had told the boys that we had swum mid-ocean on our first Atlantic crossing and it had made a lasting impression. This did seem the perfect time.

"Why don't you go in with the boys first Liza. I'll stay at the helm and keep watch," suggested Andy.

We threw a polypropylene line behind the boat, as it floats it made a good grab line.

Then everyone tumbled over the side.

"C'est merveilleux!" cried Jacques coming up gasping.

It was wonderfully refreshing, the boys couldn't get enough but splashing can attract sharks so the swim had to be a short one.

Later Colin was studying our fixes (plotted positions) on the chart.

"Do you realize," he told us, his voice full of wonder, "the chart shows we had 2,700 fathoms (5,000 metres) of ocean under us when we swam." How insignificant were our 10 metre dives beneath the surface.

Duncan had also been busy, reading up about sperm whales.

"Good thing we didn't try to harpoon them," he commented.

"My book says when they are attacked they can be very dangerous, that when harpoons were thrown by hand from small boats often the men were tossed into the sea as the boats were upset by the whale's tail thrashing. And Moby Dick was a sperm whale and he bit off a man's leg!"

"I'm glad you're telling us this after our swim!" I replied.

Mid-afternoon we felt a whisper of a breeze, ripples appeared on the water, the mainsail started to fill, we unfurled the genoa and stopped the engine. By sundown we had 15 knots from the north, soon to clock to the north-east.

"Cheers! Welcome to the trades, and a downwind sleigh ride to Barbados," said Andy. Holding up his glass of wine he continued, "And here's to 'Chateau Cardboard pressé'!"

A sleigh ride it was, with the winds constantly over 15 knots, frequently 25 and gusting up to 40. The seas became huge, welling up behind us, a massive wall of water, but our buoyant stern soared up over them all. We never suffered a wet dousing let alone being 'pooped'—the feared filling of the cockpit, and sometimes even the main cabin, by a breaking wave from behind. Our speed was phenomenal. For days on end we never dropped below 7 knots giving several 180 nautical mile days, even though the genoa was frequently furled.

We sailed mostly 'wing-on-wing', the genoa poled out one side and the mainsail on the other. The boat was remarkably stable with Otto van Helm doing a fine steering job in the confused seas and we experienced only once the frightening downwind 'deathroll' with boom and spinnaker pole alternately dragging in the water. We had been caught by a squall and overwhelmed, with our spinnaker still flying.

Our dead downwind course was tricky for our inexperienced crew, especially when the line squalls came through and we felt steering by hand more prudent. Hand steering in these conditions required considerable skill, especially when the waves came at us from three directions and it was fate as to how the bow of the boat would come down off a peak. If the boat rounded to windward the sails would flap. This is generally not a problem unless the boom touches the water, but the other way can allow the wind to get behind the mainsail and cause a gybe, when the boom slams over to the other side of the boat, a killer if your head is in the way and a great strain on the rig.

On the thirteenth day our boomvang broke as we broached into wind and the clew of the mainsail, at the end of the boom, tore out. It was blowing hard, 25 knots gusting 35. We had to go into wind to bind the sail and tie in a permanent flattening reef, which also had the advantage of making the boom about a foot higher at the outer end.

I stood at the wheel needing 2500 revs on the engine to hold the boat into wind. Andy pulled in the main and struggled with the flogging sail. Beyond him the waves, that had been huge walls behind us, were now mountains crashing down on us from ahead. That five minutes went by very slowly and left a lasting impression. I would never want to go around the world east about into wind. Just the thought of it makes me shake and feel ill!

Besides the permanent flattening reef we had also rigged separate light preventer lines and fittings on the boom, rather than adapting the robust boomvang. Thus if the boom dragged in the water, or we gybed inadvertently, the preventer would break rather than the boom itself. Several sad looking pieces of boom arrived in Barbados aboard other yachts, including the one from *Severance*.

We had been anxious about the boys enjoying the trip, even with the enticing idea of visiting Australia which was now firmly embedded in our minds. We need not have been concerned. They loved the exhilaration of the big seas and sensation of speed, and had no problem with the motion. Even when us adults had to take care to hang on as we manoeuvred around the cockpit, Jamie walked around without a care in the world.

Duncan and Colin became bookworms. I had bought a new book a day for Duncan in Gibraltar, but Colin also 'took off' reading for pleasure too. Instead of the adventure stories that had been Duncan's early favourites Colin plunged into fantasy starting with T.S.Lewis's 'The Lion the Witch and the Wardrobe'. Both boys also spent much time with me up in the forward cabin learning new knots for macrame and sewing colourful cross-stitch animals. They were able to give several creations for Christmas presents and drew cards to go with them. Jamie listened to his tapes and spent hours playing with his Fabuland Lego, when possible in the kitchen sink. I spent hours reading to him, whether on the deck or in the forward cabin, and if Andy or I were having an afternoon snooze he could usually be persuaded to join us for a nap too with the constant soporific motion of the boat.

We caught more fish, Duncan often being in charge, and frequently had flying fish for breakfast. We spent hours watching the ever increasing numbers of birds: petrels, tropicbirds, frigate birds and boobies, who would visit for a while, hovering, soaring and plunging for a morsel. The white-tailed tropic birds were the noisiest with their harsh, shrill 'kak-kak-kak'.

One afternoon Duncan was on watch when he called below urgently.

"Daddy, come up quickly, we've caught a bird on our lure."

Andy took one glance and started the engine.

"We'll have to go in reverse or we'll drown it," he explained.

Slowly he pulled in the line then let it free to give slack. Again and again he tried, finally to our relief it was unhooked and flew off.

"I do hope he'll be okay," sighed Colin. Everyone had rushed up on deck at Duncan's call.

"Why do you think he did that?", said Duncan.

"I wonder if he thought the lure was a fish?" said Andy.

It seemed the only explanation, so when birds were around we watched the stern and made a point of calling out, trying to frighten them away if they started diving by the lures.

The boys liked to help make the bread. With the excellent 'strong' bread flour from Gibraltar and instant yeast it couldn't have been easier. We put all the ingredients together, gave them a quick knead, left the dough a maximum of an hour to rise in the 24-27 degrees celsius temperatures and it took forty minutes to cook. No yeast pre-mixing, no double risings and it was quite delicious. The only problem was it never seemed to last too long . . .

Christmas was frequently mentioned. We were getting in the spirit, like it or not, because December 1st had passed and Christmas music bellowed from our cockpit speakers everyday.

"Will we be able to get a Christmas tree do you think?" asked Duncan concerned.

"I'm sure we can find a substitute anyway." A comment I was to regret. It took us two days in Barbados to find a tree to Duncan's satisfaction.

"But what about our messages to Santa?" asked Colin. "We have no chimney to send them up." This had been a family tradition at home.

Ever resourceful, Andy said quickly, "Well why don't you send them by sea? Santa will understand."

Work started immediately. Egg cartoons were suggested for the ships. Mother dutifully emptied out the eggs, it was omelettes for dinner that night! They were designed and painted, masts fashioned and sails cut from coloured paper. Finally lists were neatly scribed.

As we admired the finished products Andy and I squinted at the sails to read the crucial details, although we had completed our main Christmas shopping in Gibraltar. Then the boys dropped their vessels over the stern. Miraculously they all landed right way up and were dramatically swept away on the crest of a wave.

Jamie's most frequent words for the next few days were,

"Do you think Santa found them? I hope they didn't sink!"

Although we saw few yachts or ships we never felt alone as we could talk to several boats at any time on the VHF radio.

In particular *Severance* and *Mover* were almost always in range and we shared our positions and daily excitements.

We delighted in *Mover's* first catches—two large mahi mahi in one day. Duncan couldn't believe it had only taken them five minutes to wind in a 1.2 metre fish with their 200 pound test line on a winch. Three days later we helped them out with some recipe suggestions when their enthusiasm for fish was definitely waning. We also shared concerns. *Severance's* autohelm, for example, was only working intermittently and that meant heavy work for the crew in the fierce seas.

Everyday at 12:30 PM GMT we turned on our short wave radio and monitored the race 'Rawhide' Ham net, run by Peter on *Blyss*. This gave us a wider perspective of the positions of race participants and an updated weather forecast. It was through this medium that we heard of the arrival of the first yacht, a 54 foot trimaran, '*Running Cloud*'. At our current speed we estimated we were only three days behind.

Expecting to see a convergence of yachts as we neared Barbados we began to realize that we knew most of the boats ahead. Andy flippantly commented that we may be in the first twenty and we were, in fact, twentieth boat when we arrived during the afternoon of December 16th—our only claim to fame being that we were the first boat in with children aboard.

Our only 'real' race was at the finishing line with a 33 footer who had come north about Barbados. They had taken a rhumb line course from the Canaries, rather than the more popular southerly route that we had taken, and it had definitely paid. The rhumb line course saved about 400 nautical miles on our logged 2,700 nautical miles, however they took the risk of getting stuck in the doldrums.

The welcome in Barbados was overwhelming, to all yachts at whatever hour they arrived, with rum punches and a bottle of Mount Gay rum for top-ups, fresh bread, water and mail. I really cannot praise the Bajans more for their organizations and kindness, and for keeping up the enthusiastic welcome to the last.

We read our mail avidly but we had one important letter to send ourselves. The children had more than passed the test for long ocean trips. I felt that now 've were 'out' it was easy to stay out cruising, the arduousness of packing up the house still clear in my mind. I could easily continue teaching the children and time had passed so quickly none of us were ready to end the trip. We wrote to Australia and confirmed we would be happy to accept their gracious invitations to take part, as Canadians, in the Tall Ships events during January 1988, which were part of their Bicentennial celebrations.

It was Jamie's classic comment that won the day. After all the preparations and conversations the crossing of the Atlantic had naturally made a deep impression. Two days after we had arrived he came to me looking serious,

"But Mummy, when are we going to do the Atlantic ?!".

For him it had been a wonderful time with unlimited attention.

Jacques and Jacquie packed up to leave, Jacquie throwing away at least half of her possessions which poor *Bagheera* had lugged all the way across, as they were too heavy for her to carry! Andy departed to immigration to sign them off the boat. As they had arrived in Barbados on our vessel we were responsible for them having a means of leaving the island. We were well aware of the rules and had checked that they had money for airfares. As they were French this could be to the closest territory of France, the Caribbean island of Martinique. However, although Jacquie had lived most of her life in France she was not officially French we found out, she was Belgian, and the authorities wanted her to produce a ticket back to Europe. She didn't have enough money to pay for one.

It was a tense afternoon until they found a yacht that was sailing up to Martinique. The owner was willing to sign them on. We had been lucky; we should have been more diligent. To have been safe we should have held the money for the flights, and have been sure of nationalities. Several owners have come to grief because they were inhibited about asking for the cash or travellers cheques in advance, feeling it implied mistrust. One skipper in Barbados had paid his crew and they had moved ashore. The wages were far more than air tickets but they drank them away. The boat owner was still responsible for their flights home.

We completed a rapid clean-up, boat re-organization, massive laundry on the dock, consumed many rum punches, and on December 21st our Vancouver friends, Jane, David, Jason and Emma Heukelom arrived. They looked luminously white that evening but rapidly toned in. Then it was December 23rd and Jamie's fourth birthday. He celebrated it with several 'boat kids' on the beach.

On Christmas Eve Jane and I decided to join some friends for midnight mass. As we were negotiating Goergetown's swinging area of disrepute we were accosted by the police. It didn't help that we'd been soaked by rollers whilst coming ashore by dinghy in Carlisle Bay, and that I'd been given the wrong name of the church!

"You won't find church services here," we were told bluntly. "You should move on quickly and hold onto your bags tightly."

We followed their directions to the nearest church, fortunately the one we wanted.

The service was entertaining with the colourful population wandering in, out and around at will. Jane and I sang Christmas carols volubly, although after two hours were still feeling soggy and getting a little hoarse. With no end in sight we decided to take our cue from some locals and followed them out. Safely back on board we pulled on our Santa hats to fill the stockings.

Christmas morning with the five children on board came around all too quickly.

As they delved into their stockings and ripped open their presents Duncan said with a grin,

"What do you think Jamie? Do you think Santa found our boats and messages?"

"Oh yes he did," replied Jamie happily.

The day passed quickly with 'funnelator' water fights, many rum punches and finally Christmas dinner on the beach.

By now we had been ten days in Barbados and were anxious to show our guests some of the 'crème de la crème' of Caribbean cruising, the Grenadines. We left Barbados on the afternoon of December 26th thus missing the prize-giving on January 1st. Although our friends were there to represent us our participation plaque and prize were forfeited, particularly disappointing for the children when they heard it was a 'ghetto blaster'. But for the most part the ideal of the race had been accomplished. Over 200 vessels had crossed the Atlantic successfully and a special comraderie had been achieved. As we cruised up the islands we were to have many a good evening with a number of our newly made friends.

The Caribbean and the Galapagos Islands

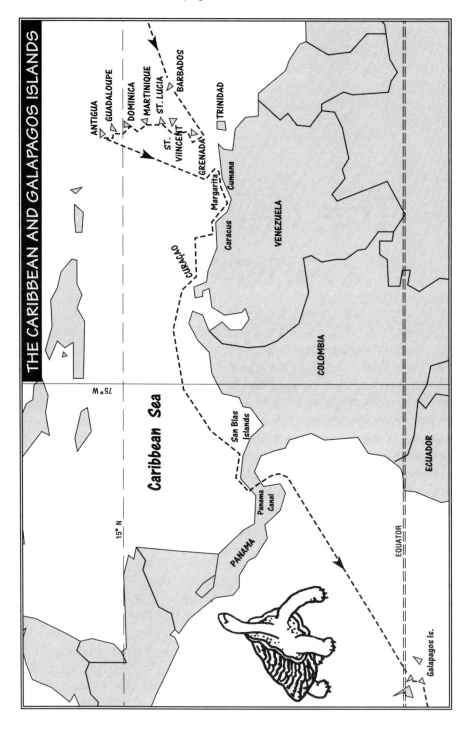

THE CARIBBEAN AND GALAPAGOS ISLANDS

ANTIGUA
GUADALOUPE
DOMINICA
MARTINIQUE
ST. LUCIA
BARBADOS
ST.
VIINCENT
GRENADA
TRINIDAD
Margarita
Cumana
Caracus
VENEZUELA
CURAÇAO
COLOMBIA
75° W
Caribbean Sea
San Blas
Islands
15° N
Panama
Canal
PANAMA
EQUATOR
ECUADOR
Galapagos Is.

12. The Windwards and Leewards

Grenada, the Grenadines, St.Vincent, St.Lucia, Martinique, Dominica, Guadeloupe and Antigua

The Lesser Antilles are a chain of islands nearly 600 miles long that curve from Puerto Rico to Venezuela and divide the Caribbean Sea from the Atlantic Ocean. The Windwards, Grenada to Martinique, and the Leewards, Dominica to Anguilla, form the southern part of the chain. This area is a second home for us, after our chartering days in the West Indies in the early 1970s. We think it includes some of the best cruising in the world.

The islands are close yet are varied in topography and personality. The winds are on the beam (easterly with a touch of north or south) providing exhilarating, but comfortable, sailing in the usual 10-25 knot trades.

It was an overnight trip to Grenada. The moon was high and the sky dense with stars, a perfect introduction to a tropical passage for David and Jane. At 7:00 AM the 600 metre high mountains were beginning to emerge from the haze. A lush, colourful island with its native people full of laughter, Grenada has always been one of our favourites.

Jamie and Emma woke early and came up on deck.

"What's that smell?" said Jamie "It's like banana bread," he continued with a hopeful smile.

"Sorry, no such luck!" I replied. "The smell is from the island and you're right it is the same spices that we put in banana bread like cinnamon, nutmeg, cloves and allspice. That's why Grenada is called 'The Spice Island'."

We made our landfall and cleared customs at L'Anse Aux Epines (Prickly Bay) on the south coast, visiting the Calabash Hotel for a traditional banana daiquiri. Flowers trailed down from the ceiling and tiny hummingbirds gathered nectar from bright pink hibiscus.

Dave was at the helm when we arrived at the capital, St.Georges.

"What an entry!" he exclaimed. We had been motoring between two hills; suddenly the harbour had burst into view. The Carenage is a volcanic crater, a dramatic setting reminiscent of the Greek Hydra with the town stacked up the steep hill. We shopped in supermarkets that were well stocked for the charter business, then went over to Grenada Yacht Services in the south lagoon.

It was discouraging to see that the marina which used to harbour the elite of the Grenadines' large charter yachts had fallen into disrepair, begging development. Hiking up the hill behind we were deafened by the sound of the tree frogs.

"How big are they?" asked Jane. "They are so loud."

"Tiny," said Andy laughing. "Look." The green frog was all of two centimetres long.

Our West Indian meal at 'Mama's' started with callaloo soup, the spinach-like leaf of the dasheen, and continued to an array of spicy meat and fish dishes, including such local delicacies as barracuda and opossum. It was a delicious spread and we were graced by the presence of Mama herself, larger than life in pink satin splendour.

The Grenadines stretch some 70 kilometres, lying between Grenada and St. Vincent. Unlike their neighbours they are relatively low, so generate little rain. Instead of the lush green vegetation of the high islands they have a cactus scrub; but the short sails between islands, the superb diving and sandy beaches more than make up for the arid interior.

We left early for Carriacou, and had a good trip on a passage that can be to windward and uncomfortable, especially off north Grenada, at 'Kick-em-Jenny'.

"Why is it so rough here?" enquired Dave.

"Turbulence and even riptides can occur at the north and south ends of the islands due to the effects of wind and tide," Andy explained. "Both are generally strongest down here at the southerly end of the chain, and there is often an uncomfortable chop between the islands on the flood when the current is setting east against the wind and continuous equatorial flow."

"How strong can the equatorial flow get?"

"Generally not much more than a knot here, but it is stronger off the South American coast. A lot of people don't know about it. I remember one yacht that sank off here in the seventies. The skipper had estimated his position but he was found 40 nautical miles to the west. He was really lucky. He was on a sunfish sailing dinghy that was also just about to sink."

Several native children hailed us as we arrived in Tyrell Bay. Some were swimming, others rowing in dinghies.

"Well, who shall we pick?" asked Andy.

It is always wise to select one local lad to secure the safety of your vessel and dinghy, and collect supplies.

"I think the boy who swam out the farthest," said Duncan.

"But how is he going to get to and fro?" replied Andy.

"Why don't we employ two", suggested Jane, "the one who swam out the farthest and the first one who arrived by dinghy."

It was settled and the pair couldn't have had wider smiles or be more willing. They rowed off with the garbage and as requested came back with a bag of the small, flat, but tasty mangrove oysters.

"Do you think we might get a visit from Super Skyscraper and the Hot Boys?" we asked.

On our last visit Super Skyscraper, who was all of 1.5 metres tall, had given a lively performance to the thirty people who climbed aboard our boat.

"He got his own bar now," was the reply "but he gone off the island presently."

That evening we commiserated with Jamie Dobbs, an old English friend of Andy's who we had last seen in Guernsey in the Channel Islands, about the challenges of chartering.

"It's a disaster," he groaned about the charterers. " 'He' wants strong Columbian coffee, cigars and champagne and 'she' is a vegetarian, but we received no forewarning of these preferences from the agent. As you know there's hardly any shopping until St.Vincent and they don't want to go back to Grenada."

It brought back many memories of the 'joys' of the charter business. It was not a lifestyle for me, the sentiment held by many of the women, but Andy, like most men, loved it. He had often hankered to be back, forgetting the problems of maintaining the boats, the eighteen hour days, the constant gourmet meals to be served and the agony over the lack of charters in a poor season.

"You are so lucky to be able to do your own thing on your own boat."

"Don't I know it," replied Andy "To be sailing in the Caribbean and not have to work is my idea of heaven. We're so looking forward to showing the islands to the boys and taking them diving."

It was the first time I glimpsed the difficulties Andy would have in readjusting to the 'real' world on our return to Vancouver.

Petit St. Vincent, known as PSV, is an island hotel famous for its 'jump-ups' and a perfect spot to celebrate New Year's Eve. The island is to the north-east of Carriacou but first we had to go up to Union Island, to the north-west, to clear into St. Vincent waters.

As we wove our way through the yachts at anchor I automatically looked for the famous charter boats of old: "*Ticonderoga, Lord Jim, Fandango, Panda, Blue Leopard, Eileen* . . . The 65 foot converted 12 metre racing yacht, *Flica II*, which we had run, was often one of the smallest.

"It's unbelievable," I said to Andy. "All these boats are about the same size as *Bagheera*. The largest must be only 50 feet. How things have changed."

"It's mostly because of the bare-boats, I suppose." Andy replied, wheeling round again trying to find a spot to anchor.

In recent years we had chartered bare-boats ourselves. It was much cheaper, and more fun, than taking a large crewed yacht, although not the same pampered holiday. But it was a shock to see the bare-boats take over Petit St. Vincent, the oldies always looked so grand here.

The traditionally sleepy bar and restaurant was humming with guests, access now made easy by the new airport on Union. But the island with sandy beaches and scattered unobtrusive guest cottages was as attractive as ever.

The steel band also performed as loudly and vibrantly as in our memories and we 'jumped-up', dancing the night away—including forty minutes of Auld Lang Syne. It was a family band with the men, women and children all playing with gusto. Gradually the young nodded on their drums as the hours crept by.

On our last serving of banana daiquiris Andy held up his glass. "Here's to 1987. David, Jane, welcome to the wonderful West Indies."

We had hoped to have a lobster barbecue for our guests so when the fishermen came by next morning with lobsters for sale we bought their entire catch—five lobsters for a total cost of $5. The boys collected wood and coconut husks, and built the fire for a barbecue on the beach. Lobster with garlic butter sauce was a sumptuous dinner for the first of the year, but we made a mental note to start earlier next time, as all nine of us

Steve Bayly from *Severance* in the Tobago Cays

ended up huddled around one small flashlight trying to dissect our food from the sand. We were still adjusting to tropical time with darkness by 6:30 pm.

We went to all our favourite islands and back again: diving for and barbecuing more lobster at the Tobago Cays, where the emerald and sapphire hues of the sparkling sea are almost unnaturally brilliant, and indulging in rum punches in the rustic elegance of the Cotton House in Mustique, by the old bougainvillaea covered sugar mill.

Off its northern shore lies *The Antilles* a ship which had been the pride of the French Merchant Marine. It was wrecked by a captain flying high on his maiden voyage and its back was broken on the reef. Now it is gradually disappearing but when I first saw the wreck in 1971 it was still smoking, but that hadn't deterred the lads I was with trying to get aboard. The disaster happened during afternoon tea and a favourite memento became one of the teapots that were still to be found on the afterdeck.

We particularly enjoyed Salt Whistle Bay, a beautiful powdery white sand cove. The resort is set back, well hidden by the palms and flowering shrubs along the shore. Here the locals taught the children to make palm frond hats and birds.

The west side of Mayreau was always good for diving and the boys found their first queen conchs here. They were thrilled by the size of these shells and the shiny pink mouths. They collected several and, after I had managed to remove the bodies before they became rank, had fun selling them boat to boat to many ARC friends.

Admiralty Bay in Bequia was full of yachts and thriving with Rastafarians selling their wares, but it still retained its sleepy atmosphere. We were pleased to find the model boat builders still creating beautiful products. Many years ago they had built us a replica of *Flica*.

Another visit to Bequia had coincided with the catching of a whale. From 5 miles out we had smelt the pungent blubber being boiled. We were staggered that the humpback whale had been caught by a hand harpoon when we saw the huge carcass on the beach with its mammoth mouth. Instead of teeth these whales have a row of long horny plates, called the baleen or whalebone, that hang down from the roof of the mouth on each side of the huge tongue and act as giant sieves.

Duncan was fascinated by the 'Whaleboner', where the bar is made from a jawbone and the stools from vertebrae.

"Guess what?" he announced later. "The old whalers found the baleen whales easier to catch than those with teeth like the sperm whale and the killer whale as they swam much slower, also people wanted to buy the baleen plates. That's where the name 'right whale' comes from, as they were the right whales to catch!"

For hundreds of years Bequia has wrested its living from the sea and Bequians are reputed to be the best sailors and best fisherman in the Caribbean. This is the last haven of the sailing fisherman although sadly, motors seem to be taking over. We always associate the Bequia boys with Tobago Cays where they dive deep to provide the yachtsmen with lobster.

Unlike most of the West Indian islands, whose populations are predominantly descendants of the Africans brought as slaves to work the sugar plantations, a substantial portion of Bequians are white. They are descended from Scottish migrants and also New Bedford Whalers, who came to the Grenadines pursuing their catch and made the huge Admiralty Bay their whaling base.

All through the Grenadines' anchorages we spent many a lively evening with fellow ARC competitors. Away from the bustle of Las Palmas and Barbados, and the freneticism of the race, we were able to appreciate the wide variety of personalities who were now relaxing West

Indian style. We not only enjoyed but came to admire many of these intrepid sailors: those who had little experience but lots of spunk, older couples who had been doggedly determined to complete the crossing on their own, and in particular a valiant Swede who was incapacitated by multiple sclerosis, but could contribute by steering, keeping watch and using his skills in navigation.

In Bequia we were able to buy glue to patch up our inflatable dinghy which had caused us endless problems by popping seams with startling and disturbing rapidity. We decided to go to the dock at Blue Lagoon in St. Vincent for the repair so everyone could still get ashore. With our 2.2 metre draft we had to come through the reef by the southerly unmarked channel. It turned out to be more than a little hazardous. Andy went up on the bow to peer into the depths ahead. He signalled 'to port, now dead ahead, to starboard, to port 10°'. Eventually we were in deep water again, clear of the many coral heads.

Much of the fine navigation in the Caribbean has to be 'eyeball'. So long as yachtsmen read the charts and keep a look-out on the bow, or even better from up the mast, they shouldn't come to grief. An unknown channel has to be entered when the sun is fairly high and behind to give the best visibility in the water. One learns to read the colours. Deep water looks navy blue, the blue becomes lighter over a sandy bottom until at about 2 metres it appears clear white, and we would be aground! Over a grassy or rocky bottom the water becomes greenish brown and rocks or coral heads that are close to the surface appear brown or black. It's just that last crucial 25 centimetres that is hard to estimate so is best avoided.

Few go hard and fast aground in the Caribbean although it's easy to become complacent with the sparkling water so inviting. Even experienced charter skippers have been known to get stuck on occasion and the bareboats more often. We spent several hours trying to tow a bareboat off the reef by Union Island, to no avail. It seemed such a crime that the beautiful 40 footer should end its days being pounded on the reef because someone either forgot to look at the chart or didn't keep a look out.

Although most boats have a depth-sounder a common error is forgetting that the reading gives only the depth below the transducer. On our boat this is forward of the mast. In a corally area this bears no relationship to the depths under the rest of the boat or even more important, to what lurks ahead or if relevant, behind.

The children loved the country atmosphere in Blue Lagoon and disappeared for the afternoon.

"We've had a great time on a farm," said Duncan when they finally returned.

"And we found a newborn lamb," added Colin.

"And we helped feed him," said Jason.

"And I love sugar cane!" grinned Jamie.

The next day we went to meet the hospitable local lady farmer. "I hope they can stay again." she said. "They are going to help me pick some vegetables for you."

The children staggered back laden with breadfruit, callaloo, peppers and, proudly carried by Jamie, more sugar cane. They had also been royally fed.

We had become used to having the Heukeloms as part of the family as they had been with us for a month, but now it was time for their flight. It had been a great visit for all and the boys enjoyed a pal and a third person for school.

As I was stowing the boat for sea Jamie asked,

"Can I have some sugar cane now?"

"Just one piece but I'm afraid the rest is going over the side."

"But why? I like it?" he complained.

"I know but there is nothing worse for rotting your teeth and then you would need lots of fillings in the holes."

"And that isn't very nice," added Colin.

"It's not fair!" To this day Jamie remains the one in the family with a very sweet tooth.

We had lingered longer than anticipated so Andy went into Kingstown to phone his sister Lyn in England who had planned to join us in Martinique.

"Stay on your LIAT flight one more stop", he had suggested, "and we'll meet you at The Hurricane Hole Hotel in Marigot Bay, St. Lucia."

It wasn't always so easy to change arrangements and several friends preferred not to have guests for that reason. Having taken time out to escape the rigours of routine of regular life themselves they resented having to meet the vacation deadlines of their friends.

In the early daylight hours a black squall approached off the north end of St. Vincent. I furled the genoa, we already had a reef in the mainsail, as one cannot predict the winds in a squall we always reduce canvas in advance. The wall of rain approached slowly, when it was about 300 metres away I could see the water whipping up, soon the heavens opened on *Bagheera*. It lasted fifteen minutes, and I was drenched. Then the skies

c

leared, the sun shone and it was perfect weather for Andy to take over the watch.

Marigot Bay was crowded but the same beautiful landlocked lagoon, its steep slopes verdant with palm, breadfruit, banana and mango. At the entrance, on the sandspit, the cluster of palms were silhouetted against the pink and mauve hues of the fading sunset.

We had barely set our anchor when Moses rowed over.

"Would you like a stalk of bananas, Ma'am".

"How much?"

"Just 10 'beewee'." That took us back. The local currency had always been know as BWI dollars or British West Indian dollars. Now most call it by its official name EC, Eastern Caribbean. "And I'll cut a fine large stalk to feed the lads!"

$5 didn't sound expensive, but it depended on the size.

"Why don't you bring a couple of stalks and the boys can choose?" I replied.

He returned with two huge stalks. We chose the less ripe and Andy strung it from the backstay.

"Daddy, isn't it upside down?" questioned Colin.

"No, bananas grow upwards, not downwards, and if you hang them this way they supposedly don't ripen all at once, although I think that's an old wife's tale!"

Alongside the string of fish tails from our Atlantic catches, it completed the setting for Lyn's arrival.

It was a relaxing three week cruise up to Antigua with a quick hop south to visit the elephant at the famed Pitons, two dramatic peaks that tower straight from the ocean floor. Due to the rapid drop-off, yachts drop a bow anchor then take a stern line ashore. The native boys were most persistent about taking our line and demanded $5 for the privilege.

"What do you think I had three sons for?" Andy called out laughing.

As was usual from our Mediterranean days, Duncan and Colin jumped into the dinghy. While Duncan manoeuvred the engine Colin paid out the line. To our dismay the locals continued to be both physically and verbally aggressive, grabbing our dinghy and trying to stop the boys tying our line round a palm tree when they reached the shore. Again times had changed, formerly one tied one's own line. Charging $5 was outrageous we thought when on a cruising budget and well able to do the job ourselves. Although forthright and aggressive we had always enjoyed the West Indians and it distressed us to see them so belligerent towards the children. However, to be fair, it is a typical result of advanced tourism, the locals demand the price that visiting bare-boat charterers will pay.

The marina at Rodney Bay was new to us. We needed to take on fuel and water, and do laundry. Andy was also interested to survey the acclaimed facilities and services.

"It's remarkable what they've done here," he commented on his return, "and I gather we shouldn't miss Activities Night at Gros Islets tonight."

"What activities are there?" I asked.

"It's an evening of fun I gather, a bland name but certainly not a bland event they tell me."

How right they were. The main 'drag' of Gros Islet fills with people dancing to West Indian music that blares from the most humungous speakers ever seen. The bars flourish and enticing aromas waft from the sidewalk barbecues; chicken legs or conch kebabs, but watch out for the hot sauce—AAAAAH!.

We ate and danced the night away. As a single woman Lyn was in great demand. It was noticeable that the only West Indian women around were the elderly or the pregnant.

It was a perfect sail for Lyn's first inter-island passage. We anchored at Fort de France, the capital of Martinique and a bustling French metropolis.

We were able to clear Customs and Immigration quickly using our British, rather than Canadian, passports as we were entering another Common Market country. Several yachtsmen had expressed concern over new visa requirements in the French islands. We were told that visas could be obtained on arrival if required and passed on the good news by radio the next morning.

"Is 'James Bond' still working in Immigration?" Andy asked before leaving.

"He's working at the Airport now."

"That's a pity. We would love to see him. Is he ever down here?"

"I can leave a message for him if you like."

"That would be great. Could you tell him Andy and Liza Copeland are here on *Bagheera*? He was at our wedding in 1973."

M. Le Breton, always known as 'James Bond', is a well remembered character amongst yachtsmen. He came aboard the next day and we reminisced about old times, particularly our wedding. Almost exactly 14 years before we had sailed across the Baie de Fort de France in the grand

72 foot yacht *Ticonderoga* and had been wed by a Swiss minister (in the pouring rain) whose only words in English were "You do everything you should!" Then the skies had cleared and we had an exhilarating sail whilst champagne and French delicacies were consumed in abundance. Designed by Hereshof *'Big Ty'* has beautiful lines and powerfully rides the waves. She held the record for the Transpac race from California to Hawaii for many years. We felt privileged to be married aboard her and most grateful to our friends for saving this day for us during the charter season.

Walking into town we passed the hotel where Andy and I had stayed for the week before our marriage. My wedding dress was in macrame, for weeks the islands had been out of the right kind of string. It arrived four days before the event and all I could remember of the hotel was sitting on starched white sheets frantically tying knots!

We took *Bagheera* round to sleepy Grand Anse D'Arlet to show Lyn the long, narrow colourful fishing boats and watched the nets being hauled up the sands. We had shark for dinner in a beach cafe. More than once as I turned round to take a photo, locals in the distance called out angrily and turned away. Many years ago I had read that in the Obea cult, which is widely observed alongside Christianity in the Caribbean, cameras were considered an 'Evil Eye', but we had never had a reaction before.

Although the anchorage is poor we wanted to stop at St.Pierre. Now a ghost town with a population of 6,000 this is the island's oldest city that at the turn of the century had 30,000 people and was acclaimed the Paris of the Caribbean. In 1902 Mount Pelée started rumbling and spitting out steam and although the wild life wisely left the area, city officials, needing numbers for the upcoming elections, down-played the warnings. At 8:00 AM on May 8TH, 1902 the volcano erupted and in three minutes the town was destroyed and its inhabitants calcified. Ironically the only survivor was a prisoner who was saved by the thick walls of his cell.

"Look at these scissors," Colin called over to me in the Musée Vulcanologique. "They are all stuck together."

"That's because of the heat," I replied. "It says here that the volcano belched forth clouds of burning ash that were over 20,000°C. that's why all the metal fused, just like the nails over here."

"And look as this food." Jamie pointed to the charred bread and rice.

"This huge church bell was just squashed and did you see the clocks, they stopped at 8 o'clock," said Duncan.

To the north of Martinique lies Dominica, whose national motto is

'Après Bondi, c'est la ter', which in French creole means 'After God, it is the land.' Dominica with its towering mountains, plunging gorges, dense lush rain forests with huge ferns and tangled vines is physically the most dramatic of the islands.

We had light winds for our sail across.

"Its strange," said Andy "the wind is almost southerly. I wonder what the anchorages are going to be like?"

With the normal easterly trade winds the west sides of the islands have the calm anchorages. Off Castries, the capital, it was rolly and uncomfortable so we moved up the coast to Portsmouth. Here unusually all the boats on anchor pointed out to sea, on a local westerly. I quickly took a photo to record this strange phenomenon which lasted two days.

The southern end of the bay was less rolly. There was a welcoming hotel closeby with great rum punch sundowner specials but getting ashore was reminiscent of Barbados, more than a little soggy. On the beach Andy noticed a hose going out to a swim platform.

"Yes it belongs to us," they said in the bar "and you're most welcome to go alongside and use as much water as you want."

"Ah, what bliss!" replied Lyn.

Not being able to bathe or shower everyday was the hardest part of cruising for our visitors. Swimming certainly helped so long as they towelled themselves off immediately. They soon learnt that letting the salt dry their skin meant any item of clothing felt horribly scratchy.

Next morning we went wild: hosing the boat and ourselves, washing clothing and anything else we could find. Then we filled every available container with the cool, pure, free mountain water. Only those who have lived with a limited water supply know how good it feels to be able to take an endless fresh water shower and how hard it is to pull yourself away.

After the 1979 hurricane the locals cleared Indian River of the debris, and they feel they should reap the benefit. We employed Christopher to take us up. He was thrilled to drive our inflatable. Our boys were entranced by the gnarled trees with their huge horizontal roots that intertwine along the banks and the overhanging vines where the river narrows. Christopher was most personable, and brought us bananas and coconuts for the trip. He was also informative; pointing out plants, butterflies and birds, telling the boys proudly that the sisserou and jacquot parrots are not found anywhere else in the world.

Dominica is the home of the last remnants of the Carib Indians, who came from South America over a thousand years ago. The fierce, cannibalistic Caribs wiped out the Arawak Indians and for two centuries succeeded in keeping the French and English at bay, including Christopher Columbus when he called at Dominica on his second voyage to the new world. The Caribs loved war for its own sake and in 1748 colonists agreed to let the Caribs keep the island. However the fertile land was irresistible, and gradually settlers moved in. Eventually some Caribs went back to South America, some were absorbed into the settler's culture while others went to live in a reserve on the windward coast. Their ancestors live there today and welcome visitors to their village.

We decided to tour the island to see the Caribs and go up into the steaming rain forest of the interior. Alec picked us up in his truck and instead of the rutted road we had suffered on a previous visit we found ourselves on an immaculate new road built by the Canadian government two years before. The Carib village is neat and colourful, over 300 are still fullbred they told us. They showed us their new community hall with pride.

"It's just like our Indian long houses." Colin said fascinated. He had just completed a term studying Northwest coast Indians on Correspondence.

"Yes, particularly in size," I replied "with a roof that is rather Polynesian."

They took us into the library and the boys joined the local children. They were quickly absorbed so the adults visited the gift shop. Lyn and I loved the dual toned woven baskets and I found one that was perfect for my scattered sewing supplies. Andy found the wife leaders. These loosely woven rattan tubes go over a finger, the man's at one end and the wife's on the other. When the wife tries to pull away the tube tightens and with the man being traditionally stronger he can lead his wife around. Andy bought several—for gifts he assured me!

The luxuriant rain forest was magnificent and the rain drops glistened as we hiked down the path to the Emerald Pool, having to push aside the huge leaves, twirled vines and dripping ferns. The boys couldn't resist diving into the brilliant green pool and climbing up the waterfall.

On the way back Alec picked us a bag of grapefruit. We love this West Indian variety that one can peel and eat like an orange.

When Colin and Andy went ashore to clear Customs later they met Alec again. He was carrying a box.

"I'm glad I've found you," he said. "This is for the boys, it flew into my car."

It was a small grey bird, a lesser antillian bullfinch we discovered later

153

from our reference book. Andy and I were concerned about keeping a wild bird on board. To our surprise, within no time, it was lying on its back on Colin's hand whilst he fed seeds into its beak. He finally put it in the cage with Malmsey, they both seemed quite content so we set sail.

In contrast to St. Lucia the eight island archipelago Iles des Saintes are small and dry. The people are fair-haired blue-eyed descendants of Breton and Norman sailors. Fishing is the main source of income, although tourism is rapidly on the increase. Several years ago there was some concern that, with a population of under 3,000, the islanders would suffer from inbreeding. It wasn't a problem for the French, they sent over some Naval ships and gave the sailors unlimited shoreleave!

We went ashore on Terre D'en Haut, the largest island. The only town, sleepy Bourg des Saintes, was as attractive as ever with its red roofs, balconied older wooden homes and profusion of flowers. We made straight for the bakery, the smell of fresh french bread being always irresistible. Years ago beautiful open style Breton fishing sailboats boats lined the waterfront but now boats are built to take large outboards.

The coastline is scalloped with coves, and white beaches abound. A favourite of ours is Grand Anse, one of the few accessible windward beaches of the Caribbean. Here the rollers bound in. We had a great time body surfing although had to be careful with the undertow.

"Look at all the holes in the sand," said Colin.

"Those are from the fairy crabs," informed Andy. "Let's see if we can entice some out, then we can have some crab races."

Try as we might they were too quick for us, nipping into their holes just as we thought we had them cornered.

To get to the beach we had taken the airport road, one of the three roads on the island. This passes a graveyard that has always charmed us for instead of gravestones they laid pink mouthed queen conch shells, adorned with vases of vibrantly coloured tropical flowers. Now there are also some huge white mausoleum tombs, waiting to be filled. Times were changing in the graveyard too.

We planned a quick stop in Deshaies Bay, at the north end of Guadeloupe and immediately went ashore to arrange dinner with Madame. This is a ritual. You sit down and order a pastis, and tentatively ask if dinner would be possible in your best French.

Madame always looks shocked, shakes her head and says "Impossible!" So you wait, order another pastis and try again. Eventually Madame breaks down. "Un repas léger seulement," she says finally and one always gets a superb three course French meal, with local fish, meat and vegetables, and her special dessert of pineapple marinated in wine and vanilla bean.

Later that afternoon we were surprised to see *Interlude* arrive. Last seen in Madeira Chuck and Gail Croft had crossed the Atlantic from Madeira to Antigua and were now heading south. Another boat to anchor was *Oyster Lady*, the boat we had ducked on the Atlantic crossing. We were able to exchange our photos.

Early next morning Lyn and I visited the capital of Guadeloupe Pointe-a-Pitre. There was no mistaking the arrival of the bus. It overflowed with passengers, music blared from the radio, the pigs squealed and chickens squawked. Everyone was in a market day mood. Lyn and I squeezed in and joined the happy throng.

Guadeloupe is shaped like a butterfly, the capital lies where the two wings meet. We've always been amused by the names of the islands because the mountainous one is called Basse Terre (low land) and the smaller low one is called Grande Terre (large land). Like Fort de France in Martinique, Pointe-a-Pitre is a lively town, the people have a French flair in dress and wonderful smells emanate from the many restaurants.

When we returned the boys told us their decision.

"We didn't think it fair to keep a wild bird that wasn't hurt," said Duncan. "So we took 'Porti' up the river and let him go."

"Did he seem alright?" I asked.

"He flew away," said Colin, "but he was such a nice little bird."

Lyn had been looking forward to seeing Antigua in particular, as she had been unable to visit whilst Andy had lived there from 1967-1973. The sight of Nelson's dockyard took her breath away. English Harbour was Britain's main naval station in the Lesser Antilles and the dockyard was built between 1723 and 1745. Nelson was stationed here. He was first under Sir Richard Hughes, (who supposedly had blinded himself in one eye whilst chasing a cockroach with a fork), then became commander himself.

The site is fascinating with the copper and lumber store, paymasters office, Admirals house, officers quarters and old mast house. Buildings have been tastefully restored to hold a museum, shops, yachting facilities and hotels. A favourite for us is the Admirals Inn. Its serene setting, with the tiny yellow bellies swooping down to gather a tiny morsel, belies the memorable boisterous evenings in days gone by.

A unique harbour, totally hidden from the sea and protected with its comparatively narrow entrance between Fort Barclay Point and the Pillars of Hercules, English Harbour continues to be the centre of yachting for in the West Indies. It also gathers boats from all over the world, especially in April/May for Antigua Race Week and is the base for some of the grandest classic vessels around. It was here that Andy came in 1967 to start Antigua Slipway then to run Carib Marine. He claims to have hired and fired half Antigua at that time but the locals always give him a royal welcome when we return.

"Hello Mr. 'Co-op-land'. Welcome back," was a frequent call as we set foot on shore.

It was a time of socialising with new friends, showing Simon and Jenny Collyer from England the joys of Caribbean sailing, diving and reminiscing with friends of 15-20 years ago. So many are still there or passing through regularly.

We anchored in the larger, breezier Falmouth Harbour, divided from English harbour by just a thin strip of land. Andy was one of the founder members of the Antigua Yacht Club and we dinghy raced again. One evening I took four year old Jamie with me on a 14 foot laser. He changed sides with enthusiasm for the tacking and gybing, and pulled up the centre board on the reaches and runs. We did rather well too. For once I had enough weight to compete with the men without hiking out for dear life.

The calm waters were ideal for windsurfing. We had splurged on buying a used board and sail in St.Lucia, but soon found out that knowing how to sail does not mean you can windsurf. People on the anchored yachts around were prolific with suggestions, as we inelegantly, yet again, cooled ourselves off! Duncan and Colin also went sailing. They had been loaned a small dinghy. One Sunday Duncan valiantly completed the open racing class course by himself. He was thrilled with his prize of a visor.

The longer one stays the harder it is to leave, but we were also delayed trying to sort out our insurance. Although becoming more popular by the year the Pacific is still considered off the established yachting track. Our insurance company finally agreed to our being insured but with the stipulation of three experienced adults on board for voyages.

"But what was a voyage?" we faxed back.

"A voyage is going to sea," they told us.

"But what if our anchor drags and we have to reset it? Do you consider this a voyage?"

If this was the case we technically had to have a third adult with us at all times, which would be extremely intrusive on family life. Although we thoroughly enjoy having our friends on board, having to have them was a different matter.

The insurance file grew fatter as the faxes whisked back and forth across the Atlantic. Finally it was decided that due to our clean record and offshore experience, we could be insured for trips up to 1000 nautical miles, with just the family aboard. This decision somewhat flummoxed us, in our memory most incidents happen as people approach land. However, as all but one leg in the Pacific would fit into this category, we agreed thankfully, despite the fact that they raised our deductible from $400 to $4000.

Now many of our cruising companions of the last two years were heading North to Florida whilst we would now be in a new small group heading South. We had a large beach barbecue on Green Island and Sunday afternoon visits to Shirley Heights, enjoying Roger the juggler and jump-ups to steel and reggae bands. Next day we waved goodbye to Steve and Andrea on *Severance*, Peter, Lydia, Anya and Ryan on *Blyss II*, both heading to Florida, and to Jo and Dennis Wallace from *Sweet Salera*, with whom we'd spent many an evening whilst cruising up the islands, off back to Europe—to name a few. No time to ponder, however, as Andy and I rushed back to Vancouver. His eldest daughter was getting married.

Vancouver was so welcoming, Steve and Alison's wedding very special, even the weather was perfect. It was a well timed trip too. Andy learnt that he hadn't missed much on the business scene and I realized that my work, friends and our lifestyle would still be there when we ultimately returned.

We were inundated with questions about the children, our travels and the boat. It had been almost two years since Andy left and the queries brought back memories of the difficult pre-cruising decisions, and reactions of family and friends to our plans. How wrong the morbid ones had been!

13. Venezuela and Curaçao

 It was a wrench leaving Antigua. We felt part of the community again and the children loved it, especially the dinghy sailing and having 'sleep-overs' with friends.

We left for Guadeloupe to sort out our dinghy problem, and anchored off Pointe-a-Pitre. The manufacturer had introduced a new seam welding process in the early eighties and has had problems ever since. Seams had popped on our dinghy with monotonous regularity and we had spend a fortune on adhesives, and hours in labour.

After much frustrating correspondence they finally told us that the dealer in Guadeloupe "would fix".

But on inspection the dealer instantly declared "cannot be fixed".

After much huffing and puffing a new dinghy was promised three days later. Why three days? The new dinghy had to be taken apart and re-glued.

Our days of waiting were used to advantage, getting several school assignments completed. Duncan made a Caribbean taped radio show, with music, local news and weather. We had just been given a recording of Harry Belafonte's calypsos which came in handy. He did a grand job but was frustrated by the clicking sound when we played it back. The Fisher Price tape recorder had given sterling service, even with a dunking or two, but was definitely on its last legs. We promised the boys to look for a new tape recorder in the duty-free zone in Panama.

Even Jamie had a part in Duncan's version of 'How the Sea is Salt' and we all studied our lines diligently. Unusually we had no cruising pals around this time for an audience, so we congratulated ourselves for an outstanding family performance!

The boys also enjoyed using our new hand-held radio. Since being in the Caribbean we had listened to many boats who had portable VHF radios and we quickly realised the advantages. With just one dinghy, part of the family was frequently getting stranded on the boat or the shore with no method of communication. It could also be substitute babysitter if Andy and I were both off *Bagheera*. Andy had found a used SMR handheld to buy in Vancouver.

"Are we going to use the call sign *Bagheera* mobile?" Duncan asked.

We had heard 'mobile' commonly used by yachts in Antigua.

"I think that sounds are bit ostentatious for us." I commented.

"How about another character from the 'Jungle Book'?"

After many suggestions the mongoose Rikki Tikki Tavi won the vote.

"*Bagheera, Bagheera* this is Rikki Tikki Tavi," Jamie chanted.

The boys found many excuses to go ashore to try out our new 'toy'.

Phillipe, the Beneteau dealer, had been most welcoming and very helpful with our dinghy problem, sending and receiving telexes to France. One evening he came on board for a drink. Looking around he startled us with the comment,

"I'm surprised that your boom is in one piece with your main sheet led like that."

"What do you mean?" inquired Andy. "That is how it came from Beneteau."

"There have been several booms broken here rigged like that," he continued. "You should spread the load out, have the blocks much farther apart."

So that the mainsail is easier to pull in, the mainsheet has a six to one purchase between the deck and the boom, through a series of pulleys. Three of these are attached to the boom. We had them close together.

"We've been really lucky then, with the strong winds in the Atlantic," I commented.

There is always something new to learn!

Finally the new dinghy was declared "fit for a hurricane". As we were making the exchange I heard Andy exclaim "Oh no!".

"What's wrong?" I responded alarmed.

"I can't believe it, the 'new' dinghy was built in the same year, even the same month as our old one. It will be just as bad, another of the same poor batch," he replied exasperatedly.

"But I have fixed," the most pleasant Guadeloupan assured us.

We enjoyed just two weeks with a perfectly inflated tender, then one morning we found it looking limp and forlorn. It was only half filled with air. More faxes rushed to and fro and finally the manufacturer admitted defeat, and said that a brand new 1987 dinghy would await us in Papeete, Tahiti. One has to admire a company that honours a warranty twice over. Cynically we wondered if they would give us a third if—heaven forbid—the situation repeated itself (they did!).

As we sailed down to La Blanquilla, an uninhabited islet which belongs to Venezuela, we began to realize the joys of a long distance radio. Having made the decision to sail across the Pacific we felt that for weather information and safety a high frequency (HF) radio was a necessity, and Peter, on *Blyss*, had shown us what fun it could be socially. We chose the Icom 735, a Ham radio, and Andy installed many yards of two inch copper strip crisscrossing the inside of the hull and grounded to the keel for the groundplane. We used the backstay for an antenna and apparently have a reasonable signal.

It opened up a new world. We were in contact with boats in transit through the Panama Canal and in the Galapagos Islands, and learnt about weather peculiarities, clearing and permit procedures as well as about the great sights ashore. We also kept in touch with *Blyss* and found out they had reached Puerto Rico. They were cruising with *Severance* and *Modus Vivendi*, who we had last seen in the early days, October '85, departing Lisbon to Madeira. Michel, Claudette and Caroline had enjoyed a year in Sint Maarten where Michel had worked as a tennis coach. They were on their way back to Quebec.

La Blanquilla is a gem. A flat island, visited by just a few fishermen, it has sparkling white sandy beaches, arched overhanging caves, and emerald green seas.

We couldn't wait to get into the water. After anchoring the diving bag was hauled out of the lazarette and masks, snorkels and flippers claimed. Even Jamie had his own gear now, and I had finally treated myself to a prescription mask. The difference was remarkable I could now actually see what everyone else was talking about.

"The fish seem so large here," called out Colin exhilarated, "and there are so many different types."

Huge black French angelfish, schools of red, feathery squirrel fish, brilliant blue tangs, foureye butterflyfish, several grumpy looking but friendly groupers, and long thin trumpetfish, to name a few, were gliding through the coral. The caves were teaming, especially with the hatchet fish lurking in the shadows. "Daddy, can we go and get our spear guns?" asked Duncan.

We had bought him a spear gun in Turkey. He had practised diligently in the West Indian islands, and was becoming skilled and very tenacious.

"Of course", Andy called back, "Lets get some fish for breakfast, lunch and dinner!"

Andy shot a pompano for breakfast, and they both shot delicious glasseye snapper for dinner, and that was just the beginning. Meanwhile Colin, Jamie and I swam to shore to look for shells, now Colin's passion. They were small but we found ten new types to identify. The beautiful white sands begged sandcastles; Jamies's had many volcanoes, Colin's was an intricate Greek village with stadium and race course.

We had anchored quite far out in the bay as we thought the dark patches in the water close in were coral, but there was none. Instead we found schools of green smelt that were so dense I could hardly see Jamie, who was holding my hand. He was fascinated by so many fish so close together and just wanted to stay playing in them, although they didn't tolerate us for long, moving out of our path in swarms. Ashore was scrubland, with many cacti. We saw signs of wild goats, wild burros and iguana tracks. It was a lovely introduction to Venezuela.

We put on the number two genoa for the next trip as we knew we would be 'on the wind' in 20 knots or more and this sail would be more efficient. This was the first time we had changed sails for several months and it seemed such an effort as we took our bed apart, moved several other items aside and found the sail we wanted. We store most of the spare sails under the forward berth. When I think of how many times we change sails in a race without thought I realised how truly we were in the cruising mode, although there are a few more helping hands when racing.

We set out for the duty free island of Margarita at midnight. The wind was blowing hard; we were close-hauled but our number two genoa and one reef in the mainsail was a perfect combination. The boat was well balanced for 'Felicity', our newly installed Aries windvane. Andy had been working her in on the trip down, with some frustration and frequent comments such as—"Just like a woman, illogical, unpredictable, can't be forced to do anything against her will"—with the inevitable response of "It sounds just like a man to me!"

Andy took the first watch and I retired to sleep in the main cabin. About two hours later he woke me.

"Liza, wake up, the forward cabin is awash," he said urgently.

What a disaster and all my fault! In my dozy state I had closed one of the levers above the retaining catch thus creating a small gap, but with constant water over the deck the cabin was drenched. I just couldn't believe how far the water penetrated, into all our best books, typewriter, Andy's clothes, all the linen and towels, and below our berth into the sails, lifejackets, school books and cans.

As I constantly manoeuvred soggy paper and linen around the boat for the next three days I thought it really was a huge penalty for such a small error. But Margarita was worth it.

It was fun to be back in a noisy, Spanish community again. We joined the evening amble in Pampatar, dined on delicious Spanish fare, and loved the markets in Porlamar. We were overwhelmed by the size, quality and abundance of the fruit and vegetables, and the variety of fresh meats and fish.

As the bolivar was rapidly falling Venezuela had become very reasonably priced, especially after the West Indies. The streets were lined with boutiques selling clothing imported from Europe, the Far East and the United States. I was tempted, but we settled for new shoes only. We also bought cases of 24 cans of beer for $2.95 and gin, a good name brand, was $2 a bottle at Crazy Pepe's. Needless to say we stocked up, particularly thinking of the fish we hoped to catch crossing the Pacific.

After our busy hot shopping expedition we stood at the water's edge admiring the pelicans perched jauntily on the gunnels of the colourful fishing boats, gently bobbing at anchor. They were awaiting the arrival of the new catch. We so much enjoyed these graceful yet clumsy birds who frequently made us jump, flopping in the water beside us with a big splash, whilst in pursuit of a fish. Distinctive with their great bill and food pouch hanging beneath, in flight they are incredibly beautiful, a diagonal single line of birds alternately flapping and gliding in unison. Although common in the Caribbean we enjoyed them particularly in Venezuela, where huge flocks are everywhere.

Before leaving the town of Porlamar we filled up with 100 litres of diesel, outboard fuel and used all the water we wanted (all piped from the mainland) for a total of $7; less than one fill up of just water in Antigua.

We left for Boco del Rio, motoring under 'full laundry', enjoying an Easter brunch with 20 centimetre long mangoes and succulent sweet pineapple, as well as the hoped for chocolates.

Being a Sunday this maze of lakes and mangroves which traverse the island was full of narrow, high bowed, Spanish-style pleasure boats, roaring around with 300 horsepower engines on their sterns. Everyone was in a friendly holiday spirit, waving as they passed, calling out words of greeting.

Andy and the boys went to explore in our dinghy and came back laden with shells. The boys were pleased with the bright orange fighting conchs, a new kind of crown conch and a shell that was half way between an olive and bubble called a marginella. They were especially excited at having seen their first wild parakeets. Andy had also located a dangerous, unmarked coral reef just outside the entrance.

That evening, relaxing with a cool Polar beer, we admired a spectacular pink mackerel sky, a sign we were easing out of the trade wind belt into a climate that was influenced by the continental land mass.

In contrast to Margarita Island the Peninsula de Araya, on the Venezuelan mainland, appeared a desert. It is famous for its salt pans and the huge piles of salt added to the desolate landscape. We headed to Cumana, and confidently made our way into the marina only to come to a sliding halt at the entrance. A fisherman came out to lead us in and we just managed to barrel our way through the muddy bar. It was about 1.9 metres, we needed an extra 0.3 metres. Our guide book stated the depth as 3.5 metres; Andy made a note to inform them!

Andy spent all the next morning trying to get the 'zarpe', or cruising permit. It only took us a short way down the coast to Puerto la Cruz. Afterwards some Canadians came over.

"Why didn't you get one for the whole coast?" they inquired.

"I asked but they didn't offer it to me," replied Andy. "Well at least I can tell others behind us." Patience with officialdom is often difficult, but the only way for a smooth transit.

The fingered inlet of Mochima is spectacular with its bright red soil contrasting with the green mangroves. A small village at the end of the four mile inlet was smothered in flowers. The restaurant on stilts served excellent tuna, which cost a remarkable $10 for eight of us, including ten beers. As we were leaving we spotted some brilliant green parrots and many nesting birds. It was so sheltered you could anchor anywhere.

After a cruise through the islands we were soon at the bustling town of Puerto La Cruz, where we could conveniently anchor right off the centre of the city. We stocked up at CaDa, the supermarket chain.

Andy and I headed for opposite ends of the store with our trolleys, finally meeting in the middle. We were both ecstatic.

"I can't believe the choice here," I enthused.

"I know," replied Andy, whose cart was as laden as mine. "To have all the North American foods (many made under licence in Venezuela) plus all the Spanish hams, chorizos, olives etc. is a wonderful combination."

"In addition to the fantastic produce and look at these thick fruit juices." We both decided we could eat here forever!

Bagheera needed to be hauled out for a bottom paint, so we pushed on to Carenero. We arrived Friday evening and were told we could haul out first thing on Monday morning. It was a perfect place to relax; the people were very friendly, as in all of Venezuela, and the lagoon great for windsurfing. Duncan was taken off waterskiing for the day by a local and was thrilled to be allowed to drive the speed boat.

Early evening we went by dinghy into the inner lake and saw one of our most magnificent sights of nature yet, flocks of scarlet ibis sauntering back to roost for the night. They formed an almost unreal luminous red blaze across the sky, then alighted in a favourite tree that was already crowded with great white and cattle egrets. Why they chose this tree and left the others empty was a mystery but the mass of red and white birds was spectacular.

We were up at 6:00 on Monday morning after another hot, humid, mosquito-laden night. Duncan and Andy in particular suffered. The humidity this year was as high as anyone could remember.

The haul out went well with the workmen painting the bottom whilst we attacked the waterline stripes. It was full speed ahead as we were only allowed two days without a government permit.

The workers arrived with scrapers in hand.

"No scrapers," Andy instructed. "We clean by water," he continued, holding up the hose.

The workers looked at each other sceptically, sharp scrapers still poised, you could tell they thought Andy quite mad. They hadn't come across copolymer antifouling before, a paint that self-cleans by gradually wearing off as the boat moves through the water. They were full of laughter when they saw hosing actually worked, it was a lot easier than scraping. Meanwhile I taped the whole waterline of the boat nine times, in various stages, so we could paint our blue and white stripes—and I used to think that once around our San Juan 24 footer took forever. A final hull polish and showers for all and *Bagheera* was ready to go back in the water, painted and shiny after the cheapest haul out yet, despite using extra labour. We had bought the paint in Antigua.

We left that night for Club Puerto Azul, hoping to leave the boat in the marina. We wanted to travel inland to Merida, up in the Andes mountains, a spectacular trip I had completed by bus years ago. The timing seemed perfect but we had picked a poor weekend. Carlos, the welcoming Port Captain, told us of labour unrest. There had been a referendum for a 40% across the board wage increase and there would be demonstrations this weekend at the Merida University, and no buses would get through.

We settled for a visit to the bustling, noisy Caracas and relaxing in the club; hard to take with beaches, swimming pools, television, live entertainment and the most wonderfully varied food at the cafeteria. We finally indulged in three meals a day here as we knew prices would be high in the Pacific.

"You mean we can have anything we want?" asked Duncan incredulously. Being used to our budget restraints this was too good to be true.

There was something for everyone—a variety of fruit plates, salads, several different cooked meats and fish, pasta dishes, creamy deserts, fruit filled yoghurts, icecreams galore and strong espresso coffee. The maximum we spent in a day for the whole family was $24! Fortunately our waistlines were saved by the one kilometre walk back to the boat.

The boys loved the amenities but they were also thrilled by the birds on the shore. A wood stork was their favourite. This very tame carrion eater was used to getting fed by the fishermen and lorded it over the pelicans.

Back on the dock we met the crew of another ARC boat *Braganza*, from New Zealand. Peter, Lance and Lezette had just flown out of Merida as the students had stopped all the buses.

"I know you," said Andy to Lezette. "You were one of the girls dressed as a mop at the 'fashion show' in Las Palmas!"

"Yes," said Duncan giggling, "she got us to pop your 'boobs' Daddy!"

We were thrilled that their planned route across the Pacific coincided with ours.

It had been a great stay at this magnificent yacht and country club and quite lived up to Andy's and my memories. It was here that we had first met when we were both taking part in the 1971 Sunfish Dinghy World Championships. Andy had been representing Antigua and I, the British Virgin Islands. The current port captain had been on the protest committee.

165

Andy and Jamie watching a wood stork and pelicans in Puerto Azul, Venezuela

We went to get our clearance documents in La Guaira and did a final shop. We met Lance in the supermarket and agreed to share a cab back to the boats. As our carts grew higher and higher, we realized this wouldn't be feasible. We ended up needing two taxis each, although both of us had spent under $200 apiece.

Los Roques is a renowned diving area, which has been likened to twenty Tobago Cays (in the Windwards) in one. Although very windy the diving was superb, with forests of the huge branched elkhorn and staghorn coral. Andy made a point of again carefully pointing out to the boys the mustard/brown fire coral, with white tips or edges, which stings when touched. This is easy to do as they commonly grow on top of the reef, close to the surface.

We whistled downwind to Curaçao, the middle of the Dutch ABC islands (Aruba and Bonaire being the others) being treated to a flock of flamingos on route. Typically Dutch in architecture we found Curaçao attractive but touristy. It was also very expensive. We moved on quickly, although had time to spend an evening with *Medium Dry*, a Dutch boat we first met in Menorca. We even had a letter for them which we had brought from Antigua.

14. The San Blas Islands and the Panama Canal

The 680 nautical mile trip to the San Blas Islands was quick, even though we made a detour to keep 50 nautical miles off the Colombian coast. At that time yachts were at risk from drug peddlers looking for vehicles to transport their cargoes north. With the strong wind 'up our chuff', huge following seas and the favourable equatorial current we had our fastest day yet—202 nautical miles in a twenty four hour period.

"This must be the best sailing ever," enthused Andy. "But, ironically, if we go on like this we will arrive at night. Unfortunately the area is very poorly charted and the islands are so low, they will be impossible to see."

"Oh, no! It's so much fun barrelling along like this. Do you want me to furl the genoa now?" I replied.

"Yes, we can always take it out again if we slow down too much."

The San Blas Archipelago comprises some 365 islands stretching about 100 nautical miles along the Caribbean Sea from the Colombian border to the Panamanian Province of Colon. We made our landfall in the Chichime Cays and were charmed by the small, white, sandy islets crowded by palms, and by the people who were wearing their striking traditional costumes. The Cuna Indians live now almost as they did before the European invasion at the beginning of the 16th century. About 25,000 in number, they are scattered across some forty of the islands and a strip on the mainland. Communities vary in size from densely populated villages to only a couple of dwellings which house an extended family, and such was our first encounter.

Ashore a lady approached us with a gift of a coconut. We were honoured; coconuts are like a currency in the islands. Although the land is communally-owned, coconut trees belong to individuals. We had already warned the boys not to pick them up in their usual fashion, as even those on the ground are spoken for.

The Cuna are bronze-hued and small in stature. The women have short black hair and long fringe bangs. Their dress is colourful with red and gold headscarf, long blue and gold sarong skirt, and mola blouses with big, puffy sleeves. Bracelets, ankle and knee bands are made out of tiny beads, mostly bright yellow and orange, and strung in geometric designs. Completing this distinctive dress are hammered silver or gold necklaces and nose rings. A black line is painted from forehead to nose tip for the final dramatic touch.

Their mola blouses, now of international acclaim and commanding high prices in ethnic stores, are works of art. The molas are made using several layers of different coloured cloth, maroon being a dominant colour. Designs are cut down from the top layer and they are intricately sewn in minute stitching. The designs represent many aspects of life from their ancient religion Shamanism, tribal myths, and wonders of the land to modern phenomena. Thus the universe, birds, animals, reptiles, jungle gods, medicine men, crucifixions, and aeroplanes are all incorporated symbolically. Front and back panels vary in pattern but retain the same theme. Molas are highly prized and can take many months to make. They last a long time with new sleeves added periodically, and become family heirlooms.

We sailed north to pick up friends, Carl and Elaine Schumacher, who were taking the twenty-five minute flight from Panama City.

As we approached the island of Porvenir, which seemed far too small to hold an airstrip, Andy called down,

"Liza, come up quickly."

Why are these calls always when one is grabbing a few peaceful moments in the head?!

"I'm disoriented," said Andy with uncharacteristic hesitation in navigation.

"That must be Porvenir but an entire island has been left off the chart. Just stand by while I try to sort this out."

He came back up in a couple of minutes.

Colin in the San Blas Islands.

"Well the Satnav agrees with me on our position. Another island must have been formed."

As we cruised the islands for the next ten days, we realised that the charts, which were from surveys two centuries ago, were far from accurate. Reefs had grown, sand banks formed and yes, whole islands had been created or had disappeared.

To our surprise, as we were anchoring, our friends arrived alongside in a dugout canoe. They had arrived an hour early at 7:30 AM as during the rainy season (May-November), weather conditions are more predictable at dawn, so the tiny aircraft can leave well ahead of schedule. All inter-island transportation is by these canoes, called cayucos. Picturesque when sailing along with their spritsail rig, they are the mainstay of the Cuna lifestyle used for fishing, collecting vegetables and water from the mainland, as well as keeping their social life active. They are skilfully carved from mango wood and ideal for this predominantly calm water area, out of the hurricane zone and behind a substantial barrier reef.

Carl and Elaine's 'chauffeur' had suggested a visit to the nearby islands of Wichub Walla and Nalunega and although a little touristy due to a hotel we were delighted with our first Cuna villages. It was a passage back in time with the simple bamboo-walled, palm-frond roofed dwellings on the sands. Inside, the cabins were spacious and cool but spartan. A few clothes hung from the rafters and hammocks acted as chair or bed. Cooking was by wood fire although we noticed the occasional gas stove, the ovens used mainly for baking bread. The islands were immaculate, no sign of garbage anywhere, with sandy paths freshly swept.

Molas were strung up for sale everywhere; designs, quality and price varied considerably. There were also some fascinating handicrafts.

"Look at this medicine man's 'spell stick'", exclaimed Andy. "It's got such character and the wood is so smooth."

Jamie was watching the other children.

"Look, Mummy, at that spinning game they're playing." It was so simple, made from seed pods and gave never-ending amusement. Delighted, he picked out a set of the large, shiny dark brown pods.

Duncan and Colin had been eyeing the little green parakeets to be seen everywhere.

"Couldn't we have another bird?" they begged. "They are so pretty and so tame."

"It wouldn't be fair," we argued. "There just isn't room in the cage for two, and they might not get on."

They settled on choosing their own bracelets and molas.

Beads were strung and we soon had our own designs up our arms or around our ankles. Single panel molas ranged from about $10 to $50 although in the outer islands we found prices cheaper with generally the whole blouse, thus two molas, for the same price. "Have you found a mola you like?" I asked Colin.

"It's so hard, with so many. But look at these. Don't you think the designs look like the Haida's ravens and fish? They have drawn them in just the same geometric way." The Haida are a British Columbian Indian tribe famous for their art.

The women were charmingly aggressive in persuading us to buy their wares, adding words of Spanish into their Chibchan to be more convincing and throwing persuasive smiles. Elaine and I took time choosing our designs, enjoying their vibrant interchange and frequent laughter.

We had quite a following armada as we came in to anchor off Islas Ammon that night, the dugout canoes full to overflowing with women and children displaying their wares. They sold Jamie and Colin boars' tooth necklaces and one with barracuda teeth to Duncan. They were delighted with half of a 14 pound tuna we had just caught, apparently they seldom catch pelagic species, and loaded us with mangoes.

It is a remarkable chain to cruise. Whenever we sailed close to the villages, we were frequently followed by flotillas of canoes, all offering molas, necklaces, shells and carvings and occasionally bread and eggs. Although initially reserved in the outer islands, the natives soon relaxed, and loved to come on board. Often Jamie disappeared ashore whilst Duncan and Colin were completing school. To our amusement, he had no problems in communicating with the local children. He spoke in English, the Cuna answered in Chibchan, and there was complete understanding on both sides. Everyday he returned with gifts of carvings, paddles, or shells, and his fingers were yellow from eating the wild mangoes.

Elaine was a big hit in the islands. The girls loved her bright red nail polish and were ecstatic when she produced a bottle and painted their nails too. We laughed as they left, they could hardly paddle for gazing at their hands. From then on, whenever we arrived at a village or passed a canoe, cries of "Elaine, Elaine," sounded over the water and they would frantically paddle over, the ladies holding up their hands!

A few days after our arrival, Carl spotted a sail on the horizon. It was *Braganza*. With minimal charts they were creeping in and had randomly chosen the channel right by our current anchorage. Andy roared over in the dinghy. On their present heading, they would pass right over the shallow reef. It was a great reunion and we stayed here, by the outer reef, for a memorable couple of days. At 6:30 the next morning there was a knock on the hull. Dozily Andy peered out of the forward hatch and found the local Shaman, or medicine man, alongside in his canoe.

"Any niños want to come fishing?" he called out in Spanish. "I'm off to catch barracuda."

"Yes, I would," called Duncan, leaping out of his berth enthusiastically—most uncharacteristic for him at this hour.

We watched them depart, paddling in the sparkling turquoise sea. The palm trees waving gently in the breeze behind. They returned late afternoon. Duncan was elated having learnt several new fishing techniques and helped to land a bumper catch.

Andy talked to the shaman in Spanish about being a medicine man. As a race the Cuna seemed very healthy, despite a limited diet of fish, coconut, mangoes, with some crops such as yams, corn and plantains grown on the mainland. He told us that they use plants for their medicines and have no need for western doctors.

One interesting medical phenomena however is their high rate of albinoism. The Cuna have the highest proportion of Albino births in the world (about 7 per 1,000) and we saw several. Immediately noticed by the first Europeans it gave rise to the myth that a tribe of 'white' Indians lived in this area.

The reefs were beautiful and the sea life abundant. We caught giant crab and lobster in abundance, and made great stews from conch. The conditions were perfect for our windsurfing skills and Lezette, the ultimate extrovert, held court surrounded by canoes, Cuna ladies and molas galore. The ladies finally persuaded her to go ashore to be dressed-up, but her howls of laughter turned to howls of pain as they insisted on inserting a nose ring!

We enjoyed these people; attractive, clean and fun, they have a most enviable uncluttered lifestyle. The women spend their days stitching outside their homes, talking and laughing with the other women, or paddling several kilometres to the rivers, where they wash and bathe, whilst the children play. We joined the ladies from Rio Sidra to collect fresh water. We took plastic containers, they used gourds, and we equally enjoyed a bath in the delicious cool river. We could barely tear Elaine away.

"Such bliss, such bliss," she drooled. "I don't remember fresh water feeling so good!"

Like all our guests, she greatly missed daily showers. I must admit in the hot, humid conditions, the sea was just too warm to be refreshing.

The Cuna men go fishing, cultivate their crops on the mainland and trade, or they might go visiting, an important Cuna pastime. One reason is the practice of a matrilocal extended family system. When a man marries, he moves in with his wife's family, so he may have family and relatives on many different islands. The girl chooses her man but he has the final say of approval. The Cuna are forbidden to marry whites or even non-Cuna Indians. Traditionally they have maintained their racial purity by ordering strangers off the island before sundown!

Historically, the Cuna have had the reputation of being the most fierce and determined of all Central American Indian tribes, and were never conquered by the white invaders. They have struggled hard to retain their independence and traditional ways of life. As recently as 1920, Panamanian forces with modern weapons tried to subdue the Cuna but were beaten back with bows, arrows and other primitive weapons. Now they are fighting a new battle. With large numbers of the men, and also some of the women, commuting to Panama City for employment (they are renowned for their hard work), the beginnings of television in the islands, and the influx of tourists, even cruise ships, it is becoming harder to maintain their society's rules and structure. Inevitably, modern influences are creeping into their simple lifestyle which has previously survived such a long test of time.

Politically, the Cuna have representation on the Panamanian National Assembly. Now a separate territory within Panama, each well-populated island has a chief and meeting house. The chiefs meet when the need arises. The Panamanian Government leaves them much to their own devices, having realised that the Cuna operate an enviable social system with few of the problems of our modern society.

We will never forget the San Blas islands. They are magical, and we feel privileged that our family has had the experience of being with such a unique people who are so fiercely proud of their culture.

It was an overnight trip to Christobel in Colon. We motored, as there wasn't a breath of wind, leaving a glowing trail of phosphorescence in our wake. As I came on my early morning watch, I glanced at the chart Andy had laid out of the Panama Canal.

"What the heck?" I muttered to myself.

My instinct was to turn the chart upsidedown but the compass rose clearly pointed to north at the top. My confusion was that it showed the Caribbean on the left side and the Pacific on the right. This was too much at 4:30 in the morning! Taking a closer look I realized that at this point the central American isthmus lies east to west and the canal runs through it, from the Caribbean to the Pacific, north-west to south-east.

We moored stern-to at the Yacht club to arrange for our canal transit. Almost immediately Bob and Betsy Baillie were hailing us. As Andy and I came up on deck they chorused, "Oh, we recognise you!"

Bob, a New Zealander, and Betsy, from Bermuda, had both lived in Vancouver and we had many friends in common. They knew all the requirements for transitting the canal. That afternoon Andy made arrangements for the boat to be measured and he completed the canal paperwork. To our relief, special days had been allocated to yachts only; we hadn't fancied being sandwiched between large ships when surged around by the huge volumes of water rushing into the locks.

The chores were dispensed with easily. Finding the luxury of a washing machine we did nine loads and laid the washing out to dry on the grass. Luck was with us, it stayed sunny all day; previously, we had been having loud thunderstorms with heavy rains in the afternoons.

Having been told that goods were cheaper on this side of the peninsula, a taxi took us to Reyes, a well-stocked supermarket. Prices were still a shock after Venezuela but about the same as Canada.

Elaine was amazed by the quantities.

"I just can't believe all this food!" she said incredulously, after we had filled the fifth cart. After the tenth she was aghast.

Although I planned to stock up further in Panama City, my thoughts were on our next voyages. We knew supplies were limited in the Galapagos Islands, so I had to plan for about four months to reach Tahiti. How relaxed we all were compared to the flurry of activity before the Atlantic crossing. We had learnt that there is a substitution for every-thing—well almost everything—Andy still had his phobia about running out of toilet paper!

As promised, we took the boys to the 'Free Zone'. They bought duty free tape machines and Duncan asked for a piano keyboard for his birthday. Only the brave went out by foot into Colon, and then in groups, the city having a bad reputation for mugging. Carl, Elaine, Pete and Lezette, who ventured a short distance to make overseas phone calls, were turned back by concerned police. Three days later we were ready to transit the Panama Canal with the four required 100 foot (30 metre) lines in place (we understand 150 foot (46 metre) lines are required now). Our extra line handler, a lad from the local American base, and our pilot arrived on board early. Nine boats were scheduled to go through the canal together, including Bob and Betsy on *Belair*, *Braganza* and another Canadian boat, the beautiful 70 foot schooner *Archangel*.

The trip up to the locks was more like a river than a canal. As we motored along Duncan read out from the information we had been given.

"We go up three locks one right after the other on this side, that takes us up 26 metres, and then we go across a man-made lake called Lake Gatún. There are three locks down to the Pacific on the other side, one separate and two together. Altogether the canal is 81.6 kilometres long."

"And each transit of the canal takes 192,000 litres of water from the lake to the ocean," our American lad continued.

"Wow, that's an awful lot of showers!" said Colin incredulously.

We laughed. Only a water-conscious boat kid would make such a comment.

On entering the first concrete chamber we were rafted in pairs. Lines from the bow and stern were passed up to men on shore and fastened. The huge steel gates closed silently behind us and the valves opened. Immediately the water started teeming in, swirling around us and rapidly buoying us up. We gazed, mesmerised, but as line-handlers we also had to attend to our jobs. As the water level rose we had to keep tension on the lines. All went well until the boat next to us delayed in taking in the slack. Suddenly we were both whirled close to the wall on our side. For a moment we envisioned being crushed against the concrete but Andy quickly threw the engine in reverse and drove us back to the middle. It was over in a flash except for our shattered nerves.

It took about ten minutes for the water to reach the level of the next lock. The gates in front opened, then men on shore pulled our lines, walking us through to the next chamber. As we passed some officials, our Pilot had a few terse words. He was not pleased that the locks had been filled at the speed for big ships, instead of the slower rate recommended for small boats. He told us the turbulence is always worst in the first lock because of the force from the fall above (all from gravity) and from the mix of fresh water meeting the salt.

The next two locks were 'plain sailing' and then we were in a lake full of islands, the former hilltops of days gone by. Dead trees jut up through the water and long coarse stems of green leafed water hyacinths float on the surface. To the west of the locks is the huge earth Gatún Dam, one of the largest in the world. The lake would be a lovely area to cruise but we were scheduled to stay overnight only. We thought we might have a party with some of the other boats but it had been a long day. Instead we listened to the noisy monkeys and other jungle life, then soon 'crashed' on deck as it was a hot and humid night.

Another pilot joined us early the next morning and we completed the 35 kilometre trip along the former Chargres River valley, then entered the 13 kilometre Gaillard Cut. The Cut had been the hardest part of the canal to build. Moving the soft volcanic material was like digging a bag of grain; as soon as a hole was dug more rock and earth tumbled in. Dredgers still work constantly here, because of the earthslides, to keep the channel clear and 13 metres deep. There was a delay after we entered Miguel Lock, the first of the easy 'down' locks. Our pilot couldn't understand it; then suddenly we realised *Braganza* wasn't in sight. Just as we became convinced they must have had engine troubles, they rushed in at full speed.

"Sam flew overboard," was passed down the line of yachts. Sam was their new pet, a San Blas parrot.

"Oh, no!" mourned the boys.

"It's all right," came down later. "They managed to scoop him up."

We were all relieved, Sam was a such an endearing bird. But what a moment to choose to go swimming!

We were lowered 9.3 metres; then after motoring across the man-made Miraflores Lake, two chambers lowered us to the level of the Pacific. As the Pacific has a tidal rise and fall of 3.8 metres this height varies. A fascinating sight was watching a huge ship beside us. As we disappeared down it became larger and larger, towering over us, as it went up.

The canal is considered to be one of the great engineering wonders of our age. The problem was the hard rock base. It was too expensive to bore through it, so most of the canal had to be constructed above sea level. In addition it is the world's only multi-lock canal that can handle two way traffic.

Before the opening of the Canal, a ship sailing from New York City to San Francisco had to travel more than 11,000 nautical miles. The Canal shortens the journey by over 4,300 nautical and eliminates the feared rounding of Cape Horn. Construction of a canal had been considered as far back as 1534, when Charles I of Spain ordered a survey. Frenchman Ferdinand de Lesseps was the first to start digging, but the project was finally abandoned by the French as too costly and dangerous. In 1902, after much negotiation, the American Congress gave President Roosevelt permission to build the canal providing the United States would have permanent control of the canal zone. The greatest obstacle

The Panama Canal

to building the canal was in fact a medical rather than an engineering or financial one. The Isthmus of Panama was one of the most disease ridden areas of the world and the first two years of canal building were mostly devoted to clearing brush and draining swamps where mosquitoes swarmed. By 1906 they had wiped out yellow fever and eliminated rats that carried bubonic plague in the Canal Zone. By 1913 the rate of deaths caused by malaria had dramatically declined.

Our transit of the canal was unbelievably inexpensive compared to our experience of the Corinth Canal in Greece. We paid $95 US for the transit, the pilots and the boat measurement. Several months later, to our surprise, we received a rebate making the total fee only $35. I recently read that the highest canal toll was $120,439.20, paid by the Star Princess on October 5, 1990. The lowest toll was 36¢, paid by author and adventurer Richard Halliburton for swimming the canal in 1928.

Once clear of the canal we headed for Balboa.

"Look at the bridge ahead," called out Colin from the bow.

"That's the Bridge of the Americas," volunteered our American lad again. "It joins the North and South American continents."

It was symbolically bathed in sunlight.

We tied to a mooring at the Balboa Yacht Club on the outskirts of Panama City to collect mail, complete a final top up on victuals and to try to get our video camera repaired.

It was almost time for Carl and Elaine's departure so we all piled into their Panama City hotel room for the night, the children watching the Wizard of Oz and persuading Andy to go across the road for a McDonald's takeout—while we went for a delicious seafood 'zarzuela' dinner. The next morning we went on a tour and saw the attractive ruins of the old colonial city, beautiful homes, bustling commercial streets, the zoo, and most interestingly, the Museum of Anthropology. It was fascinating to see how little the Cuna lifestyle has changed over the centuries.

Our thoughts turned to the Pacific but we had one complication to attend to. In our mail was a letter from a skin specialist I had visited while back in Vancouver. I had a mole on the top of my left arm that had discoloured, distorted in shape and bled. A biopsy showed it to be malignant, and instructions were given to have a centimetre all around removed as soon as possible.

The Canadian and British Consulates recommended doctors. A Turk, educated in Eastern block countries and the United States, completed the surgery at the hospital with no fuss, although I was somewhat taken aback at the $500 fee. What he was more bothered about was preventative surgery for the children, particularly hauling out their appendices. I was aghast at the suggestion at the time although, when talking to the surgeon on the *Young Endeavour* during the Tall Ships events in Australia, she said it had been suggested for their trip from England to Australia. Instead we settled on a prescription for antibiotics that would contain an acute attack long enough to seek help.

There was time for a quick trip to the nearby island of Toboga, known as the 'island of flowers'. For us it was the island of showers, so *Braganza* and *Bagheera* joined *Belair* for 'dark and stormies', potent dark rum and ginger beer concoctions but our conversation was far from gloomy. It was an elated discussion about exploring our next ocean; first to the famed Galapagos Islands and then to idyllic French Polynesia, where the sun would always shine.

Back in Panama we completed the last chores: a final stock up at the market of sacks of potatoes and onions, crates of fruit and vegetables, and a last post of mail, including my latest newsletter which I had finished in the small hours.

The boys, with Jason Heukelom, find their first queen conch
shells off Mayreau

Lyn, Andy's sister, in the Castries market, St. Lucia

Marigot Bay, St. Lucia

Ticonderoga – the yacht on which Andy and I were married in 1973

Looking down over English Harbour and Falmouth from Shirley Heights

The renovated Copper and Lumber Store, now a hotel, in the Dockyard, English Harbour

THE SAN BLAS ISLANDS

Jamie with his new Cuna friends

Liza is given a Cuna bracelet

THE GALAPAGOS ISLANDS

With a giant tortoise in the Darwin Institute

Duncan 'talking' with a sea lion on Floreana

A land iguana

Bluefooted boobies

A sea iguana

Bora Bora – Polynesian style with Kristin and Erin from *Nimbus*

Hide-and-go-seek on board – Jamie in our Tongan basket

Colin and Jamie with lobster and war club carved for them in
Ongea Levu in the Lau Group, FIJI

The Chief in Mbengga Island, FIJI. He tried to trade his wife for me!

Ile des Pins, NEW CALEDONIA

AUSTRALIA

Bagheera's crew with Lisa Roote and Mike Oswald during the Tall Ships events in Hobart, Tasmania

Guayas, from Ecuador, sailing past the Sydney Opera House during the Tall Ships Parade

We also bought a bimini sun cover for the cockpit. I had been wanting one for a while, now the situation was urgent and a power boat shop had the ideal design in stock. What a difference it has made to our comfort, besides protecting us from the harmful rays.

Lisa Roote arrived from Vancouver to sail with us as far as Tahiti. It was the only time we needed extra crew for insurance coverage, as the Galapagos to Marqueses voyage was over 1,000 nautical miles. We left for Galapagos on Tuesday morning, May 9th with *Braganza*, although sadly Lezette had departed to fly back to South Africa. *Belair* was two days ahead.

15. Galapagos

> "Both in space and time, we seem to be brought somewhat near to that great fact— that mystery of mysteries—the first appearance of new beings on this earth."
> —Charles Darwin, The Voyage of the Beagle

Although the Galapagos Islands were discovered by the Bishop of Panama in 1535, it was Charles Darwin, a naturalist who travelled around the globe in HMS *Beagle* in 1835, who created the legendary magic. His stories of wondrous wildlife were further heightened when his observations of the finches, their beaks in particular, resulted in his theory of evolution by natural selection. A theory that overturned the whole train of previous scientific thought.

It was a slow eight days sailing to the Galapagos. The winds were light initially and 'on the nose' when they filled in. A new radio acquaintance had informed us of a strong north-westerly set to the current and our course was adjusted accordingly. With our Satnav navigational system this would have become apparent but we were concerned for our friends on *Braganza* who, with overcast skies for five days, were unable to take an accurate sextant fix to establish their position. As we were well out of VHF radio range we couldn't inform them. Although they had spent time and money on repairs to their HF radio in Panama, it still wasn't working.

We frequently talked to *Belair*. They always seemed to have more wind than us and one night while on watch I became inspired. It was the start of 'An Ode to Bob and Betsy Baillie from Bermuda on *Belair* by *Bagheera*!' As we travelled across the Pacific together many a memorable experience was shared and it wasn't hard to accumulate verses along the way. The boys loved giving suggestions and singing 'Bob and Betsy Baillie from Bermuda hail . . . '

We were still two days away from our landfall for Duncan's eleventh birthday on June 15th, but we did have some entertainment managing to land a huge Dorado fish—huge for us anyway. It was 1.25 metres long and became our diet for the next two days. It was not the regular birthday he had requested in Turkey but when we reached the islands we had a birthday party with some other 'boat kids'. We used a tortoise theme for the cake and games and his request was satisfied.

We crossed the equator on June 16th, with Andy claiming his rights as King Neptune. He was the only one who had visited the southern hemisphere previously, although that had been to the Antarctic and he had never been ashore! As King Neptune, he dispensed copious quantities of shaving cream over us all and fed us some revolting concoction—producing the anticipated hysterics. Ugh!

As we drew closer to the islands a host of swooping, inquisitive birds greeted us. There were boobies and tropicbirds, noddies and fairy terns. One large frigate bird stayed with us for several hours.

"It's almost as though he is our pilot and responsible for our safe landfall," I said, my sentiments in harmony with the anticipated magic of the islands.

"More like he is waiting for food!" commented Andy. "The frigates always prefer to steal than catch their own fish."

Land had been sighted before he finally whirled around the boat, cried his farewell, and was out of sight.

We arrived at Santa Cruz Island, at 3:00 AM local time on June 17th, having already gained an hour. As the wind died and the current increased, we resorted to motoring and to our amazement as we entered Academy Bay, Bob and Betsy were waving from *Belair*. Bob came over in their dinghy.

"How fantastic of you to come out at this hour," we whispered. "I wanted to help you put down a stern anchor," he replied. "It's really necessary as the anchorage is so crowded with yachts and local boats."

Unfortunately, we did not have a visa to cruise the islands. Traditionally these were difficult to obtain, but recently people had applied through their local aquarium societies, or through Ecuadorian Consulates, and several friends received the permit in about four months. I kicked myself as I could have applied when back in Vancouver in March, having been family members of the active Vancouver Aquarium for years. However, the new officials were sympathetic and immediately gave us six days in Academy Bay and suggested we visit some other islands by local boat.

Andy and the boys returned with a black, wrinkled, dragonlike marine iguana in the dinghy, and put him in the washing tub for a good look.

"These iguanas are endemic," Andy informed us. "That is, they are only found here and they are the only truly marine lizard in the world."

"What do they eat?" asked Colin.

"They forage for marine algae at low tide and the adults swim offshore and graze at the bottom, as deep as 12 metres, I believe," Andy continued.

"Are these the lizards that are solar panels?" asked Duncan.

"Yes, that's right. They bask in the sun until their body temperatures are almost 38 degrees celsius before they enter the water to feed; because the water is cold here, they lose their body temperature very quickly."

"But I thought the Equator was supposed to be hot, jungles and stuff, so the water should be hot," responded Colin.

"Well, it generally is, but the Galapagos Islands are affected by the cold Humbolt current for part of the year, which comes up from the south. That is what makes the animal and plant life special here, they have all had to adapt to this unique environment."

After a good visit Duncan popped him back into the ocean. An introduction to the Galapagos wild life had begun, but there were other important introductions to be made. Within no time a dinghy arrived alongside with two children on board.

"There are lots of children on boats here," they told the boys. "Do you want to come with us to the beach this afternoon?"

"Oh, can we?" they turned to us.

"Of course," I replied, and they disappeared for the afternoon in a huge inflatable.

Bob and Betsy were amazed by the ease of it all.

"One of the wonderful characteristics of 'boat kids' is the immediate acceptance of each other," I told them, as I was to tell so many others in our travels. "It doesn't matter about age or sex, it's just great to see kids, and the older ones always take care of the younger ones."

The fabled animal of the Galapagos is the giant tortoise.

Having poured over pictures in books during the trip, the boys were dying to see them. With only five days of school left

I agreed with them completely. We needed all this time to explore.

Beyond the small town of Puerto Ayora is the Charles Darwin Research Station that was established in 1964 by the Charles Darwin Foundation, under the auspices of UNESCO and the International Union for the Conservation of Nature. Its three objectives are scientific, educational and protective, and it is a delightful, accessible place in which to see and learn about the giant tortoises.

These reptiles appeared some 80 million years ago and became extinct in the rest of the world about 100,000 years ago. Today the one other similar species lives half way round the world in Aldabra, part of the Seychelles.

In a wild setting full of cacti we saw several species of Darwin's finches before arriving at the tortoises.

"Wow, they're HUGE," exclaimed Duncan, the first to reach the open pens.

For those of us used to the small pet variety, the tortoises were unbelievably massive with dome-shaped shells up to 1 metre wide, and weighing as much as 230 kilograms. But they were docile and friendly.

As the boys went over to them they lifted up their heads.

"Look," cried Colin delighted "this one likes me rubbing his neck, but it feels really leathery!"

"And they like to eat these yellow flowers," said Jamie, holding a bunch he had picked close-by. He had noticed some others tearing them off enthusiastically.

Slowly and awkwardly they raised themselves up on their legs and ponderously ambled along. Although they can move faster it wasn't hard to understand how their numbers had been so reduced by the buc-caneers, whalers and sealers of the 17th, 18th and 19th centuries. Not only did they stay alive without food and water for over a year on board the ships, but they were easy to catch. Of the estimated 250,000 original tortoise population, only about 15,000 are left.

In the next pen we came across a different type, a saddle back. The dome-shaped tortoises had short legs and neck as they live in humid environments such as Santa Cruz, where the vegetation is low and abundant. The saddle backs live on islands with uneven soil and no low grass, so have longer necks and a curved shell to allow them to reach up higher for food.

It is due to the work at the Darwin Institute that nine of the original thirteen species are not endangered. Only one of a tenth species, called Lonesome George, is known to be alive, although scientists have scoured the islands and zoos fruitlessly for a Pinta female.

The station has a tortoise breeding house where tortoises are raised, as the eggs and young are at risk from the feral dogs, rats and pigs. Over 900 have been repatriated into the wild. We looked into the hatchery;

the tortoises were tiny, making it impossible to believe they could grow so large.

As we were about to leave, Bob and Betsy arrived, so the boys enthusiastically showed them around.

"They're so friendly, look at their lovely smiles," said Jamie as he leaned over one of the largest, ready to give him a hug. How nonchalant a four year old can be!

Walking back along the barren shore, the black rocks were so littered with marine iguanas and bright red Sally Lightfoot crabs that we had to be careful not to step on them. Colin found some new shells and was thrilled with a shark's vertebrae. Perfect for a necklace!

Early next morning a local boat, or panga, took us up to Plaza Sur, an island off the coast renowned for its bird and animal life. About halfway there, we saw a sail on the horizon.

"I wonder if that's Pete and Lance," said Colin wistfully.

We had been concerned about their non-arrival. The sail came closer and closer.

"I really do think it's them," said Andy finally.

"Maybe they will come right by us," I said hopefully.

We were in luck; quite by chance, we passed very close.

Suddenly they realised who was waving and shouting, and frantically waved back. We were relieved; we thought they had been pushed so far off course by the current, that they had missed the islands altogether.

Plaza Sur is a small 1 x 0.2 kilometre dry island that looks like a tilted table top, gradually rising from the beach to cliffs on the south side. We landed at the jetty, after our captain had persuaded the sea lions to move. Hundreds of bulls and cows were sprawled over the rocks sunning themselves, with many of the pups having enormous fun playing at the water's edge. In contrast were the slow-moving, yellow, prehistoric-looking, land iguanas that wandered towards us through the grass as we walked up the path.

"They are just like mini-dinosaurs," said Colin delighted.

"And they grunt just like Daddy when he's asleep," giggled Jamie.

The island is covered with tree-sized opuntia, the prickly pear cactus, attractive with bright russet bark and prickly green paddles. These paddles are a source of food for both the finches and land iguanas, and we watched fascinated as the pink-tongued iguanas stood on their hind legs to reach a succulent morsel. Although as Duncan remarked, "you would think they would get pierced by all those spines." Not such a tender morsel after all!

Hundreds of birds wheeled, soared and cried as we peered down over the rocky cliffs: red-billed tropicbirds, shearwaters, and the blue-footed boobies, whose feet are a brilliant blue. The indigenous (except for a few that have strayed to the mainland) orange-eyed swallow-tailed gulls were incredibly tame and we had a fleeting glimpse of a male frigate bird puff up his huge heart-shaped red balloon to attract the ladies.

Our guide told us that 58 resident bird species have been found on the islands of which 28 are endemic. In particular he mentioned the waved albatross whose entire population of over 12,000 birds breeds on the single island of Hood (Espanola). There are two native flightless seabirds, the Galapagos penguin and the flightless cormorant. The rarest bird is the lava gull, with only 400 pairs still alive.

We were amazed by the lack of fear in the birds and animals. Being able to get so close gave us not only a feeling of oneness with nature but a very personal appreciation of the glories of this special environment.

Our guide led us back along the path that was marked with wooden pegs. As in all the islands, keeping to the paths was strictly reinforced.

Once back at the charter boat, we donned our snorkelling gear and hopped over the side. The sea lions were delighted; darting back and forth, wheeling and arching between us and skimming through our legs. Although apprehensive at first Jamie loved the experience, clinging to my back as I dove down, and quite happy to watch by himself when I had to rest, quite out of breath. The sea lions seemed as excited as the boys; they obviously loved to play whether with crabs, shells, seaweed or us. We even noticed one grab a marine iguana's tail and spin it around for fun.

Squalls and heavy rain greeted us the next morning, so a planned tour of Santa Cruz Island was put off. We had been surprised how cool it had been, considering we were on the Equator, but apparently it was typical. From January to early May is the hot wet season with temperatures around 28°c. The cool or dry season has an average temperature of 18°c, although the interior can be hotter. In May the cool Humbolt current brings the garua, a bank of cloud. The other current that affects the Galapagos, El Nio, comes from the north in December and often brings heavy rains.

Instead we spent the day on school and chores; Andy did his least favourite maintenance job, an oil change, I waded through tons of laundry in the huge washing tubs provided at the friendly, attractive Galapagos Hotel, and Lisa and Duncan did a sterling job of hauling fuel and water out to the boat in jerry cans which was hot, hard labour. That evening we ate out, prices were very reasonable, and Pete and Lance entertained us with Sam's antics on the trip, a true boat character.

The group of us, including Tom and Nellie from *L'Affaire*, took a tour bus to go inland; it was an unexpectedly fascinating day. In contrast to the barren volcanic shoreline, the interior has lush, green countryside, with fruit and vegetables grown in abundance.

Our first stop was at the Gemelos, where we gazed down into the enormous twin pits that were formed when the earth's surface had collapsed into subterranean cavities. They were full of Darwin's finches and the striking red and black vermilion fly catchers. We learnt that the Galapagos archipelago is formed mainly of lava from a succession of underwater volcanic eruptions, and the long tube at Bellavista, formed by the rushing lava, was impressively huge and very eerie. After a filling lunch in Santa Rosa, with half a chicken per person, it was time for the highlight; a horse-riding trip into the interior to find giant tortoises in the wild.

"I can't ride on one of those wooden saddles," Andy muttered to me when we arrived at the horses.

"Why not?" I replied. "The locals seem fine."

"They just aren't built for the human anatomy, especially not mine!"

He was even more emphatic when he returned three hours later!

Three giant tortoises were found, which was unusual, and everyone was extremely happy. One in particular was huge and reputed to be two hundred years old. Duncan's head seemed tiny as he peered from behind its shell for the photo.

Our six days were up and we departed south to spend a couple of extra days that were permitted at the island of Floreana. As Andy pulled up the anchor at 5:00 AM I was touched to find a bag of buns on the deck from Pete and Lance, to help us on our way.

Floreana is a home of the pale pink flamingos. We watched them all standing on one spindly leg in the still, cool haze of dawn, and identified several other birds: yellow warblers, vermilion flycatchers, common gallinule, and thought we glimpsed a short-eared owl.

Like so many before us we had been touched by the magic of the islands. If only we could have stayed longer, but our time was up. The boys had a last swim with the sea lions and Duncan had a final chat with them on the beach. We took a long exploring ride in the dinghy and watched fascinated as the blue footed boobies performed their ritualistic mating dance, bobbing backwards and forwards with their wings held high and throwing sticks at each other! Our last dive was on the volcanic

Duncan with the giant tortoise reputed to be 200 years old

crater, Devils Crown, eyeing the many nurse and white-tipped sharks and noting the different markings and colours of the reef fish compared to the Caribbean.

The children spent the afternoon with their friends, roaring around the bay on a surfboard towed by a huge dinghy, then disappeared to watch a video aboard another yacht. We had tea on board *Jeshun*, prepared by Julia an interesting South African, now living in Australia, one of the few single-handers we encountered and the only woman.

I wrote some last minute postcards and gave them to friends that we joined for a sundowner. They were going round Post Office Bay where a post box barrel has been used for centuries by fisherman and trading vessels alike. You post your letters unstamped and collect others to deliver, if you can. My cards all arrived in record time, far sooner than those sent by regular mail!

It was a long, peaceful night's sleep, and early next morning we weighed anchor for what would be our longest voyage at sea. It would be at least a 3,000 nautical-mile trip to the Marquesas, our first landfall in French Polynesia.

The South Pacific

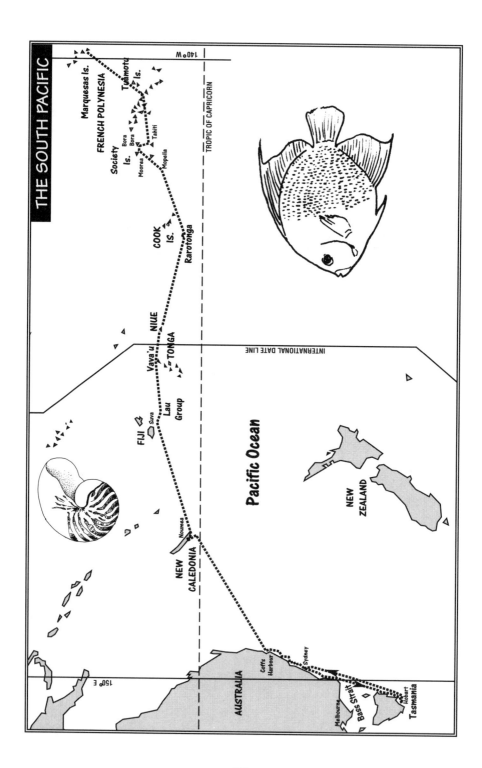

THE SOUTH PACIFIC

Marquesas Is.

FRENCH POLYNESIA

Tuamotu Is.

Society Is.

Bora Bora

Moorea

Tahiti

Mopelia

COOK IS.

Rarotonga

NIUE

Vava'u

TONGA

Lau Group

FIJI

Suva

Nouméa

NEW CALEDONIA

Pacific Ocean

NEW ZEALAND

AUSTRALIA

Coffs Harbour

Sydney

Melbourne

Bass Strait

Hobart

Tasmania

140°W

TROPIC OF CAPRICORN

INTERNATIONAL DATE LINE

150° E

16. French Polynesia

The Longest Passage and The Marquesas

HIVA OA, OA POU, NUKA HIVA

We left Floreana with very different emotions compared to leaving the Canaries for the Atlantic crossing. Then it was our first ocean crossing for many years, and our first with children aboard. We had been charged with nervous tension as well as exhilaration, the culmination of many weeks of anticipation and preparation.

Setting off from the Galapagos Islands was so matter of fact, so low key that when the reality of the long trip ahead hit me on my first night watch it was like a dull ache, at first hard to identify. Then the chill of apprehension prickled through my body, and with it the anxiety of being all alone crossing this, the largest of oceans. Worst of all was the panic of claustrophobia as I thought of our small living area below. On deck the dark, eerie swells loomed as effective as a prison cell to physical and emotional escape.

Fortunately my night watch was soon over and I fell into an exhausted deep sleep. I awoke next morning to the soothing sound of the ocean rippling against the hull. An ideal 10-15 knot wind had filled in, giving us a fast comfortable ride in calm seas. It was to be the perfect trip and my doubts were buried forever.

One of the highlights of the day, which dispelled any fears of isolation, was our radio schedule at 8:00 AM. Established initially with *Belair*, several other boats joined us, and we all checked in with our position, the well-being of the crew and the number and size of fish caught. Then it was chit-chat time, jokes or riddles of the day, and activities on board; *Archangel* even had a mid-ocean fancy dress ball! It provided our contact with the world and we all hovered round the radio at the chart table stimulated by the interaction.

We also enjoyed the entertainment from a choice of radio stations. The BBC World Service is particularly varied and informative, (and clear in most parts of the world with their many relay stations), and we could receive from Canada, Australia, the United States and even propaganda programmes on radio Moscow, when reception was good.

The only problem was that the cord on the ear phones wasn't long enough to reach from the HF radio to the cockpit. One night I came up on deck for my watch to find Andy with a self-satisfied grin. Able to use all of the cockpit cushions just for himself he looked wonderfully comfortable and had the earphones in place.

"That looks great," I enthused. "Night watches are going to fly by, now we can keep watch and listen to the radio at the same time. How did you manage it?"

"I used some electrical cord, but mind the connection, it needs to be kept straight."

"What's on?"

"I'm listening to the BBC now but I think this programme will come to an end soon. You'll have to listen for other frequencies and I've written down the frequencies and times for Voice of America. They're on the chart table."

I was in luck. On the hour 'Top of the Pops in the Sixties' came on. They played all my old favourites, and I danced the night away!

Two boats, who had left a day later, had gained on us initially, but on reaching the same wind pattern had stayed exactly 50 nautical miles astern. They were becoming quite frustrated. The boats were the 55 foot American *Godspeed* and the 70 foot Canadian *Archangel*. Finally Michael Davies on *Archangel* could contain himself no longer.

"Who is this 38-foot yacht with a 50-foot waterline!," he boomed in chit-chat time. (One of the variables of hull speed is related to waterline length.)

"It's our secret weapon!" Andy replied.

"Surely you're not motoring?"

"Good heavens no, we're only carrying 150 litres of diesel."

"Well what sails have you got up?"

"You're getting closer."

"You're not flying a spinnaker, I can't believe it. You racing freaks!"

"Well we do like to go fast," Andy admitted. "But this is a great wind for our 'chute. We don't have to play it, we just pin it in and don't touch the sheets all day, but it sure helps our speed."

"Do you fly it at night too?"

"No, we learned our lesson there; for some reason the winds are really fluky at night at the moment."

On our second evening, after a perfect red sunset and the breeze steady as a rock, we decided to leave the spinnaker up. What a disaster! On one collapse the spinnaker performed a spinning top act around the genoa, which was furled on the forestay. To make matters worse we found that the protective sun strip on the genoa, seemed to act like glue to the lightweight nylon spinnaker, and we were hours pulling and yanking, unwinding and winding up. Of course it was a pitch-black night, so we only had light from a flashlight and spreader lights on the mast. It did have to happen on my watch, just when I had gone to the head. You can guess who was not too impressed!

As a fleet we caught few fish but daily lost several lures. We used heavier line than in the Atlantic, but boats with lines up to 250 pound test had the same problem.

We concluded that all the interested fish were very large, borne out by those who did manage to land some on board. Our significant catches were a 1.3 metre dorado (mahi mahi), and a fat tuna which we decided weighed over 40 pounds as it broke our scale and seemed to weigh more than Jamie!

A day out of Hiva Oa the wind became light and later died completely. The boys had been finishing their last art assignments and with their work completed and organized in envelopes to be sent back to the Correspondence Branch in British Columbia, all was ready for the year end ritual.

"Which books can go over the side Mummy?" said Colin.

"I've made a pile for each of you," I replied smiling.

It was time for the satisfying activity of tearing up and throwing over the side all the old worksheets and previous work that had already been marked and returned.

Archangel was rapidly catching us up, having started her engine, and Duncan thought he would throw his books out to port so she might run over them. Within no time Michael was on the radio.

"*Bagheera, Bagheera*, this is *Archangel*."

"Go ahead *Archangel*." Duncan replied.

"I guess school must be out?"

"That's right!"

"Well Duncan you didn't do very well on the Math assignment, but your story looked great!"

They caught us up in no time. The boys were thrilled that Michael's son had dressed up as a clown, and we all watched the perfect green flash together as the sun disappeared. Then *Archangel* roared off and was soon over the horizon herself.

The next afternoon we made our landfall in French Polynesia. Logging just under 3,000 nautical miles we had taken nineteen days, averaging over 150 nautical miles a day. It was July 14th, French Bastille day, but it was quite quiet in the harbour, the big celebrations being in Tahiti during the month-long Tiurai Festival.

To celebrate our arrival, *Archangel* invited us for dinner and wonders of all wonders, HOT showers with FRESH water. We had only been able to have salt water ones during the trip. It is great to have friends with water-makers, that can fill one's tanks as well. It was a relaxing evening and WONDERFUL to sleep the night through, in a calm anchorage, with not a worry in the world—at least not until we picked up our mail and had to cope with the realities of life again.

French Polynesia is an overseas Territory of France and consists of five archipelagos: The Marquesas, the Tuamotus, the Societies, the Gambiers and the Australs. The Marquesas are spectacular, high, rugged islands to the north-east of the group, only six of the ten are populated. With no protective barrier reefs there are few calm anchorages and, as coastal plains have not formed, most of the population is found in the narrow, but fertile, river valleys.

It is generally assumed that the Polynesians were originally seafaring people from Southeast Asia. The Marquesas were probably populated by migrants from Samoa in about AD 300. Some settled permanently whilst others continued north to Hawaii or south to Easter Island. They sailed in large double hulled canoes which could carry fifty to a hundred people, with food, plants and live animals. Although it has been postulated that the Polynesians could have arrived from South America there is little evidence to support this theory except the existence of the New World sweet potato throughout Polynesia and the observations of Thor Heyerdahl, who sailed by raft with the prevailing easterly winds from Peru to the Tuamotus.

The first European recorded in the islands was Mendana who landed on July 21, 1595 whilst voyaging from Peru. The Spanish worked hard to keep this discovery from the English. Sadly from this time on, through shootings, opium, introduced diseases, and the Marquesans' cannibalistic ways their numbers rapidly dwindled. From an estimated 50,000 at the end of the 19th century the population had fallen to about 20,000 when the islands were annexed by the French in 1842. Those who survived adopted Roman Catholicism and much of their cultural heritage was annihilated. There are about 7,000 Marquesans today.

The crew from *Archangel* and I hitched a ride into Atuona to clear in with Customs and Immigration. I filled out the usual stack of forms and was given an allowance of fourteen official days (twenty unofficial) to reach Papeete where the required bond would have to paid. Atuona was made forever famous when Paul Gauguin went to live there in 1902 and we were shown how to get to his grave. On the way we looked in the few stores, they were expensive and the only fruit we could find to buy were apples, nectarines and plums, hardly the tropical fare that we expected.

The children went up river whilst we had a day of chores: hours of scrubbing the three week pile of laundry on a convenient rock by a fresh water tap, and loading cans of fuel we purchased from a copra boat, which was awkward and tiring in the surge.

Then we headed off to find the children.

"There they are," I said to Andy after a few minutes walk down the road.

Colin started running and everyone was waving. We waved back then Andy suddenly stopped.

"My God. Look at the kid who's being carried, it must be Jamie, his face is covered in blood," he cried in alarm, already speeding down the road.

"It's alright," said one of the older children. "It's actually just a small cut but it's right between his eyes and won't stop bleeding."

Jamie clung to me terrified but it was only a small wound and when I applied pressure it soon stopped bleeding. As I cleaned up his face my heart rate started slowing down, together with my vivid imagination that had been working overtime.

"What happened?" we finally asked.

"One of the children threw a stone and it bounced off a rock," they said. "It really wasn't anyone's fault." And people worry about us going to sea!

Back at the bay Andy noticed some strange looking fish. They were crawling along the rocks and we watched them browsing on weed then skip from rock to rock, obviously happy out of the water. It seemed that it was only with reluctance that they slithered back into the sea and became fish again.

"Are they mud skippers?" whispered Duncan.

"I think so," replied Andy, "but they look different from any I've seen before. Maybe you can look them up. I think when we get to Tahiti we might have to buy some more reference books. That was fascinating."

With *Archangel* we headed around to Puamau on the north-east coast. We went to every corner of the bay but there was a huge surge. Finally we anchored behind some rocks on the east side and managed to get some protection. We donned our diving gear and almost immediately Andy came up with a large hump-back cowrie. It was broad and heavy, chocolate brown with a tall speckled back. It felt so smooth and looked so shiny, a fitting first of the many dramatic shells we were to find in the South Pacific.

We were a conspicuous group walking into the trailing village with the *Archangel* crew.

Lisa, soon to start photography school, was ecstatic.

"It is so beautiful with the steep hills and long sandy bay. And look a dugout canoe is just landing in the surf. This is too much!"

Our cameras were out in a flash, although after Galapagos everyone was running low on film.

The locals were full of welcoming greetings as they told us the way to the Mayor's home, so we could pay our respects. We climbed up and up before finally reaching his yellow painted home. He came outside to greet us, proudly decked in his beekeeping hat.

His grandchildren were eager to show us around and took us up to shady clearings of ancient worship to see the abandoned stone sculptured, thick lipped, Tikis. In ancient times the Marquesans were considered to have one of the most refined art styles in the Pacific and Tikis were carved in wood as well as stone, and could be in miniature or like these, two metres high and massive. Now they command little respect and the local children stood on their heads posing and pointing for us to take photos.

On our way down we gorged on the local mangoes the children called 'pommes' and later were invited to join the village party, part of the Bastille fiesta, which was being held that evening. We decided to return to the boats for a siesta, so as to be in fine form for the dancing. On the way the girls practised the Polynesian hip wriggle and the boys the knee shaking tamure, much to the local children's amusement.

What a lively evening it was. The tall golden skinned locals were

Puamau Bay, Hiva Oa

dressed in their brightly coloured finery, with fragrant flower leis adorning their long dark hair. Everyone danced the night away, with the local people full of encouragement. One man even grabbed one of Michael's son's knees from behind to get him into the required rhythm. The young girls performed with the most sensuous of hip swaying but it was the Mama of the restaurant who stole the night. She tied a bright pink sash around her very large 'derrière', which accentuated her hips that were gyrating at unbelievable speed, to everyones' clapping and cheering. With a big smile she beckoned four year old Jamie to join her and he launched into the newly learnt tamure and danced up a storm.

"I could never have believed his small knees could have moved so fast," I commented to Andy in amazement.

"He's certainly going to sleep well," said Andy. "I wonder if he will make it back to the boat, he's become awfully heavy to carry."

It was just before midnight when we left, laden with a huge bag of pawpaws, soursop, mangoes, grapefruit, and bananas. It had been a wonderful introduction to the friendliness and exuberance of the local people and a treasure for our memories, as later in the Society Islands we found the French Polynesians led more of a western consumer lifestyle, with dancing a chore for tourists.

The next morning Betsy burst forth loud and clear on the VHF radio.

"*Bagheera, Bagheera*, this is *Belair*."

"Where are you, *Belair*? This is *Bagheera*."

"Only 10 miles to go, where are you going to be tonight? We will try to clear in quickly and then come and join you."

"Terrific, we are going round to Hanamenu Bay. *Archangel* will be there too. Try to hitch a ride in a truck into Atuona, it's a long walk."

"Thanks for the tip, hope to see you later in Hanamenu. *Belair* clear."

"*Bagheera* standing by."

They made it round by late afternoon. It was fun to share the exhilaration of completing this long leg. It had certainly brought into perspective the vastness of the Pacific Ocean, which is over double the size of the Atlantic, and could hold all the land masses of the world with room to spare.

"Lobster, lobster," called out Duncan as he approached in the dinghy. He excitedly held it up for our inspection, our first from the Pacific.

"Where did you find it?"

"Over on the far side of the bay and I caught it by hand!"

It provided a fitting dinner with which to welcome the Belairs. Betsy had celebrated a birthday on the trip and I was able to give her the cross-stitch picture I had sewn as a memento of her Galapagos visit. It was but one of the many pleasurable and satisfying projects one could accomplish on the boat, and particularly during passage making, for which there seems little time in one's regular lifestyle.

While I had a boat cleanout the following day Andy and the boys went ashore to explore. They came back full of enthusiasm.

"Look, we caught all these fresh water shrimp," Duncan enthused.

"We found the waterfall you said was in your guide book," said Colin. "It's lovely with hibiscus and lilies."

"And HUGE shiny leaves," added Jamie.

"So we've come back for the water cans and I thought you might want to bring the laundry ashore," said Andy.

We collected water, did the laundry and laid it on the rocks to dry, then lazed in the deliciously icy fresh water. It was hard to tear ourselves away.

Two days later Lisa and Colin complained of unbearably itchy skin. Tiny welts were beginning to appear. No problems were reported on *Archangel* or *Belair*.

"Must be a *Bagheera* disease." quipped Michael on the radio.

By radio time next morning almost everyone had been smitten by the *Bagheera* disease. Despite no sensation of being bitten at the pool itself the tiny insects, aptly named no-see-ums or no-nos, had devoured a veritable feast. If measured by the complaints they should have been satiated for weeks.

We had departed south whilst *Belair* and *Archangel* went north. Hanavave's Bay of Virgins in Fatu Hiva has the reputation of being one of the most beautiful anchorages in the Pacific. It was in Fatu Hiva that Thor Heyerdahl spent most of 1936. Infuriatingly, as we headed south overnight, the wind built until we were pounding into big seas. Andy did not want to beat another forty miles in 30 knot winds and we finally turned round. I was disappointed, and a little irritated as he slept the next afternoon, thinking back on his arguments that the trip would have been a waste of time.

However Oa Pou, with its jagged volcanic plugs soaring up from the ocean bed, was also spectacular and we went ashore to the pretty flowered village of Hakahau in search of pamplemousse. Since being given them on fiesta night, we had become addicted to these Pacific grapefruit, which are huge, sweet and incredibly succulent. There was fruit everywhere but everyone laughed when we wanted to buy some. Finally we were directed to a house which was surrounded by fruit trees and we picked our own at a steep $1 each but they were worth it. We also found a market gardener selling his produce, which was very fresh and quite varied as he used the different climates of the higher slopes.

Nuka Hiva is the largest and most populous of the Marquesas and several yachts had gathered for a barbecue.

As soon as we arrived Bob and Betsy came over and introduced us to their new crew member Barbara.

"We're having chicken tonight," Betsy told us. "Don't worry we've bought enough for you too."

"How much do I owe you?" I asked.

"Not much. It seems crazy but a 5 pound (2.3 kilogram) box of American chicken legs only costs $6. There are about eleven legs and thighs to a box. It's the cheapest food around. Everything else costs a fortune."

L'Affaire, who had also joined our radio net since Galapagos, had just arrived as had single handed Julia in her self-built, *Jeshan*. A couple from a 24 footer, appropriately named the *Little Boat*, also joined us. With only about 6 inches of freeboard in the centre we were all concerned for this boat's seaworthiness, but heard subsequently that they arrived safely in New Zealand. A novel but uncomfortable way to travel, shown by the girls legs which were a mass of saltwater sores, from constant immersion as the cockpit was frequently awash.

We had a cake to celebrate Michael's birthday, but were sad that this was also a farewell. Michael was due back in Kingston, Ontario, to run his Whig-Standard Newspaper. We were to hear from him frequently via his letters to Jamie, and our mutual exchange at Christmas.

Almost one year later we spoke to him on the radio when *Archangel* was in Fiji and *Bagheera* was in Sydney, Australia. It wasn't until January 1991, three and a half years later, that we met again. *Archangel* was entering as *Bagheera* was leaving Durban, South Africa. Finally in Hout Bay, near Capetown, we were together for a couple of weeks and it was just like old times with *Belair* on the dock beside us.

People frequently ask "What was the highlight of your trip?"' We always reply that the special camaraderie we experienced with so many of our fellow travellers comes very high on our list.

17. French Polynesia

The Tuamotu and Society Islands

MAKEMO, KAUEHI
TAHITI, MOOREA, BORA BORA, MOPELIA

The sixty-nine islands of the Tuamotus form the largest group of atolls in the world and lie almost in two parallel lines. I've heard them described romantically as two chains of silver bracelets and, in direct contrast, as a recipe for disaster! With unpredictable currents, poor visibility due to the low elevation of the islands, frequent line squalls, and the difficulties in locating and navigating through the narrow passes, this area presents a particular challenge for sailors.

SatNav and the more recent Global Positioning System (GPS) electronic navigational aids have helped to alleviate some of these predicaments, but when land is finally sighted, one always seems to close the shore much too rapidly for comfort. Once inside the atolls, however, their rings of shimmering sands are just like shiny silver bracelets surrounding lagoons, themselves jewels of aquamarine.

Our landfall was at Makemo and we arrived after four days of varied weather. The only unusual event was a freak wave one night. Lisa was in the cockpit on watch at the time.

"I couldn't believe it," she told us. "The sea was absolutely calm then suddenly we were way over on our side. For a moment I thought I would end up swimming!"

"Were you wearing your lifeharness?" Andy asked her.

"Oh yes," she replied. "I wouldn't dare disobey the Captain's orders!

I have to admit though I would never have thought it necessary in that kind of sea and there was almost no wind."

"Unfortunately many people have thought that way and ended up in trouble when they were on deck alone. That's why we stick to the rule, but I agree you certainly wouldn't have expected a wave like that in these conditions."

I had explained to the boys that generally an atoll is a coral reef in the shape of a ring or horseshoe, enclosing a lagoon. Andy had drawn diagrams to show how islands submerge with the fringing reef continuing to grow up to the surface of the ocean. They were intrigued and couldn't wait to arrive. Unfortunately Makemo is a large atoll and the boys were soon expressing their disappointment.

"This doesn't look like your diagram at all Daddy," complained Duncan.

"It's just like being on the ocean. We can't even see ahead and where's the rest of the atoll?" added Colin.

It wasn't quite how we had imagined it either. We had expected calm protected waters not the swell which was causing such an unpleasant hobby horsing motion when at anchor.

Our thoughts were diverted by the three other yachts in the anchorage. Early on the boys had noted their Canadian ensigns. One was from Vancouver, one from nearby Victoria, and one was an American boat but, the boys discovered later, the owner's wife was from Vancouver!

"We've seen so few Canadians, how come so many are here?" asked Duncan surprised.

"This is the beginning of the next 'milk run'," I explained. "Just as we were with a group coming across the Atlantic and up through the Caribbean, now we will be meeting a lot of Canadians and Americans who have left the west coast to sail the South Pacific."

"Good. Do you think there will be some kids?"

"I'm sure we'll come across some in the Society Islands as many yachts make their landfall in Tahiti."

We recognized Gord and Nancy on *Beaumaris*, and now that school was over, I could enjoy being a regular person and go over for a morning coffee.

"It's lovely ashore here," they told us. "Considering it is all sand the undergrowth is surprisingly green and lush. But why don't you try one of the smaller atolls next. Kauehi is spectacular."

The dinghy had hardly touched the beach before we started picking up new Pacific shells: purple and yellow drupes, more cone shells that needed specific identification, and giant clams. We found the Gendarmerie and followed the instructions from Hiva Oa to clear in with the police. The one and only gendarme was most relaxed and just asked us to sign the yacht visitor's book. He watched amused as I thumbed through and was pleased that we found a couple of familiar names.

It is impossible to ignore the aroma of newly baked French bread. As we were negotiating the purchase of several of the long crispy baguettes that had been baked in half an oil drum, the local Medic approached to see if we needed a hand. He invited us back for coffee and while we talked, his son, Kim, and Jamie had a fine play. Kim spoke in French, Jamie in English, but as usual there was no communication barrier at all. Herve's English was good and he laughed at their interchange.

Herve was from France, and had also lived in New Caledonia. He worked as a relief Medical officer around the islands. He was full of information and had many concerns, in particular about the French Nuclear Testing programme that began in the early '60's, when France had transferred its nuclear programme from Algeria to Moruroa, in the southern Tuamotus. He told us that almost a hundred nuclear explosions, forty-one in the atmosphere, had taken place.

The future of the islands was an additional worry. Before the testing trade was reasonably well balanced he told us, but twenty years later, imports were twenty times higher than exports. Other than tourism, which had dwindled in recent years due to the artificially high Pacific Franc, the economy was now dominated by French Government spending. Most imports came from France, and exports, such as coconut oil (copra), cultured pearls and some vanilla, were meagre.

"How do the local people feel?" we asked.

"I think that with so much agitation from other nations to have the nuclear testing stopped, the local people have become more aware of the dangers," Herve replied. "The problem is that although they fear the dangers they worry about what will happen to the islands economically if the testing stops. They know it generates huge influxes of capital, spending and employment, and they are now used to a consumer lifestyle and don't want to go back to living on fish and coconuts."

"What a distressing situation," said Andy, "in such paradise."

It was a quick overnight passage to Kauehi, with the wind on the beam. At a distance the reef islands, known as motus, were quite confusing, but we found the pass easily and had an uneventful entry into the lagoon, with the current against us as the tide was on the ebb. Some atolls have very narrow, shallow passes, and with currents reaching over 6 knots going in or out, there have been some very anxious moments and not a few disasters.

Once inside the lagoon it was magical, with brilliant turquoise water, sparkling white sands, and palm trees laden with coconuts. Some locals came to greet us, apologizing that their chief was in Papeete for the celebrations and could not welcome us himself. Ashore in the small village of Tearivero, we were greeted with smiles and a little girl gave us a gift of shell necklaces.

Wandering through we were struck by the prefabricated homes and later learned that these were given as an incentive to keep people working the copra on the islands as the towns were becoming overcrowded. Brightly coloured 'pereu' material hung in all the windows. Copra is still the main income producing agricultural product. The meat is dried and the oil extracted to make cosmetics, soap and cooking oils. Coconut meal is used for cattle feed. Husks were everywhere.

Most homes had solar panels on the roofs, that were also provided by the government. Later we met several yachtsmen who had made excellent deals on solar panels during their stay in the French Polynesia.

We explored further in the dinghy and rounding a long peninsula of leaning palm trees, came across a mini lagoon surrounded by sandy islets.

"Look," said Colin excitedly, "it's the perfect atoll, just as I thought it would be."

The diving was spectacular, with the clumps of coral each supporting its own community of brightly coloured fish. Being so close to the surface the bright colours of the tangs, angelfish, triggerfish, parrotfish and timid butterflyfish flash in the sunlight as they dart to and fro. Small giant clams are embedded in the coral, displaying their frilled mantles of greens, blues and yellows.

"I don't know if it's my imagination but all these fish seem bigger than their Caribbean cousins," I commented to Andy.

"I think you're right," he replied. "This is certainly the perfect area for snorkelling."

Later Andy was peering over the side. "I'm sure there are shells at the end of those trails," he commented. "I think I'll just go and check them out."

We were in about eight metres and after a couple of dives he came up triumphant.

"Look what I've found." It was about 10 centimetres long, and twirled with dark markings. "I think it's an auger. Do you want to look it up?"

. "Where did you find it?" called the boys.

"Just at the end of one of these trails. Do you see they are everywhere right by the boat?"

We were all in the water in no time, first diving at one end of the trail and if having no success then at the other. The shells were just under the surface. Soon we had collected a pile and noticed that we had four different species. I reached for the shell books and we all pored over them.

"They are all augers as you thought," I said. "This heavy one is a marlinspike and the other three are a crenulata, a subulata and a dimidiata."

"How are we going to remember those names?" moaned Colin.

"I know, it's going to be difficult as these are the Latin names but the good side is that we are finding some of the more unusual varieties. Only the common ones have been given English names," I replied.

The shells were laid out and with much discussion and deliberation the best examples were chosen. We were increasingly aware of conservation during our travels. Knowing there were huge numbers of these varieties we weren't concerned about taking our few samples, but those that were not chosen were carefully put back in their familiar habitat.

The next afternoon *Belair* arrived. I had hoped to prepare them fish. There were grouper and snapper for the asking, but the locals informed us that these were not safe to eat. Ciguatera has become a major problem in the islands and it would appear very little reef seafood is now safe for consumption.

Ciguatera is a disease that starts when the reef is damaged, causing the micro algae, dinoflagellate, to dramatically multiply. It is then passed up the food chain to the larger fish. The toxin accumulates in the human body, thus the fish that is eaten just before the symptoms of itching, tingling and vomiting develop may not be as dangerous as those eaten previously, where no symptoms were evident. This has led to confused information, and except for extreme cases, we felt most locals really did not know which fish were safe to eat and which were not.

It is devastating to the local people, fish being a major part of their diet, and there is much speculation that the recent increase in ciguatera has been caused by the nuclear testing. Herve had told us that about 80% of his clinics were related to ciguatera poisoning and it was one of his major concerns.

As always it was great to see the Belairs and the following day we revelled in the perfect South Pacific experience. It was a spectacular day and we visited ashore, dove in the crystal clear water, windsurfed, and found many new shells. Duncan was thrilled to find a colony of spider conch and Colin found the small yellow money cowries and the gold ringers that are a special species native to French Polynesia.

Having learnt our lesson with gritty sandy barbecues in the dark we collected our wood early. Andy produced 'spider conch à la *Bagheera*', and several creative salads came from the galley of *Belair*.

We finished with the final rays of the sun, then launched with gusto into campfire songs, while Duncan kept the blaze of the fire high. The evening ended with land hermit crab races.

"I've chosen a winner," declared Duncan. "He was really difficult to catch."

"So was mine," added Colin.

We drew a circular course in the sand. Andy did the countdown and the crabs were let go in the centre. The boys did everything they could to encourage *Bagheera's* fine looking representatives but budge they would not, and *Belair* won with no contest!

As always we checked around the deck, the anchor and the dinghy, and did a quick clearing up job below before climbing into a blissful berth. We were just dozing off when Bob's voice boomed out on the radio.

"*Bagheera*, what's happened? We can hardly see you. You must have dragged."

We leapt out of bed and found our anchor had dragged several hundred metres. It seemed impossible, particularly as it was so calm.

"What do you think caused it?" I asked.

"I don't know," replied Andy, "unless the anchor hooked a lump of coral."

When I woke next morning, I was shivering.

"How can I be so cold?" I complained to Andy. I opened up the forward hatch.

"You won't believe it," I exclaimed.

"What? Surely we haven't dragged again."

"No we're fine but its wet and grey. Visibility is so poor I can barely make out a palm tree. What's happened to our paradise of yesterday?" I mourned.

We left late morning for Tahiti. It was our wettest, most uncomfortable trip in the South Pacific. There was apparently a narrow band of poor weather and, just our luck, *Bagheera* and *Belair* were right in the middle of it. With winds gusting over 35 knots and seas from three directions we had to give Otto van Helm a rest and hand steer.

"I hope this isn't an omen for what we are to find in the Society Islands," I commented.

Tales of Tahiti, the enchanting paradise of love and eternal sunshine, were brought back by the first explorers, Wallis, Bouganville and Cook over two centuries ago. They were followed with more eloquent accounts by a host of famous writers such as Rupert Brooke, Somerset Maugham and Robert Louis Stevenson. All waxed poetic about the luxurious vegetation, the fragrance of the gardenia (tiara Tahiti) and the beauty of the Polynesian women who performed 'droll and wanton' tricks.

A famous story during Wallis' visit in 1767 tells how the Tahitian women lured the sailors ashore to exchange love for nails. This worked well until the ships started falling apart and severe restrictions had to be placed on shore parties, food and water only!

Sadly, like so many of our friends, we had our illusions quickly shattered. Although, like Maui, Tahiti consists of two ancient volcanoes that are joined by a low isthmus, and is impressive at first sight, onshore it has little of the grandeur of the Marquesas and the people had little of the Polynesian charm we had experienced previously. In Papeete we were back to big city life, and it wasn't appealing.

It was particularly the officials who alienated the yachtsmen and it was hard to find a boat where someone wasn't fuming about an unreasonable request regarding the amount of the bond (supposedly the price of an airfare to your country of origin, in case you had to be deported) or the visa requirements. Services were also irritating. An example was the Visa credit card office. All four people in front of me were refused cash withdrawals due to insufficient funds, and predictably I was too. All of us were in credit. The issue was critical. We needed the money for our bonds. Fortunately the Mastercard agents were a little more accommodating.

Above all, the prices were horrendous for food, even in the markets, and a case of beer was an exorbitant $37. It quite devastated the customary spontaneous yacht social life. You become rather discriminating about entertaining at that price! Later we learned that it was cheaper if you took your bottles to be filled at the brewery.

We anchored in the 'low rent zone' with a line ashore from the stern as it was much cheaper than going stern-to the quay. The location was similar but it necessitated making the short trip ashore by dinghy. After doing this several times a day I became convinced that high tide, such as it was, was always around lunchtime. I mentioned this rather sceptically to Andy who gave me one of those withering looks, so I decided to make my enquiries elsewhere!

My observations had been right. In Tahiti high tide is always between noon and 2:00 PM and again around midnight. Low tides are at dawn and dusk. I couldn't find a concrete explanation of this at the time. Someone said the US Pilot claimed it was due to the water surfing over the reefs with the sea breeze that fills in during the morning, while a Frenchman told us it was caused by the unique positioning of the sun and moon in relation to Tahiti's position on the globe. A week ago, while I was thinking about writing this chapter, I mentioned the phenomenon to my husband again, and received another withering look! Two days later he returned from work smugly clutching a magazine. A complete explanation was in the latest issue of Ocean Navigator!

It explained that high tides often rotate through oceans around a central 'amphidromic' point, one of which is close to Tahiti. Apparently the level here is unaffected by lunar tides. Instead high tides radiate from this location and the level is only affected by the small solar tide. As the tide only varies from one to two feet it is not a significant practical issue, but it is a unique phenomenon. Interestingly the traditional term of 'sun tide' wasn't so wrong.

Having had our fill of dusty, noisy Papeete we decided to go to Maeve beach for a couple of days for the boys to swim. They invited the children from *Godspeed* to join us. By the time we arrived it was blowing 40 knots, and with a bay full of boats with dragging anchors we decided to return to the calm Papeete harbour.

"But Daddy we're not going back to the same spot are we?" Colin asked.

"It does seem an anticlimax I must agree. How about we anchor in the harbour for the night and then we can go diving too."

Cheers greeted his decision. The diving went well and is remembered for our first orange Mitra mitra shells.

It was a quiet peaceful evening. At 3:30 AM there was a shattering explosion. We leapt up on deck to find what appeared to be a whole block ablaze, right where we had been anchored stern-to the shore. Was it perhaps a gas explosion or a bomb, we questioned?

Next morning I went to investigate, first to *Godspeed*, where they were picking up huge, jagged chunks of glass off the deck. I was horrified, shuddering to think what might have happened to Colin or to their daughter, Jamie, who had been sleeping in our cockpit if we had returned to moor beside them. Another boat had the glass of their compass shattered, as were most of the windows in cars along the street. Thank goodness we had returned our rental car two days before.

It was a bomb. It had exploded in an apartment, and the force had devastated much of the building. There were even several window frames dangling in the trees to which we had tied our lines. The occupant was apparently the lawyer of one of the rival gangs, there being frequent conflicts between the Tahitians and Chinese, descendants of the cotton plantation labourers.

We cleared out next day, at least I should say tried to leave, for the officials suddenly decided that Jamie and I needed visas. My British passport was being renewed. Although they had accepted this on entry they refused to let us clear out with extended cruising time, despite specific official documentation. With our Canadian passports we needed visas. They would have cost, with photos, $75 each. The officials would not change their minds and Andy and I decided that French Polynesia wasn't worth it.

With three days of grace until our allowed month was up, we left for Moorea, twice as old as Tahiti and twice as beautiful. We relaxed again in turquoise seas by white sand beaches, which had been almost non-existent in Tahiti. Surrounded by jagged peaks Opunohu Bay is outstandingly beautiful. At its head rises Mt. Mouaroa with its shark's tooth spire which has been immortalized as 'Bali Hai' in the film South Pacific.

We walked to Papetoai, pleasantly surprised by the lack of tourist development, and visited the red-roofed, octagonal Protestant church. A local told us that it was built on the site of the temple of Oro, the war god, in 1822, and is the oldest church that has been constantly in use in the islands. Shopping was relaxed and many prices more favourable than those in Papeete. Our negative feelings towards the Societies were starting to fade. This was indeed living up to our expectations.

After a brilliant orange sunrise, highlighting the peaks of Raiatea and Tahaa, we entered the pass at Bora Bora. The ultimate South Pacific vision was before us. With its twin basalt peaks towering a sheer 700 metres, surrounded by the whiter than white motus of the reef, Bora Bora is an unforgettable sight. The waters are such a brilliant turquoise that the sky and even the clouds that linger at the peaks seem to reflect their tones.

There were several yachts ahead. A group was moored off the Yacht Club with others around the corner, at the Oa Oa Hotel. Duncan had the binoculars.

"I can see one Canadian flag," he commented.

Opunohu Bay, Moorea

"Oh, I see," said Andy "can I have a look?"

He gazed through the binoculars. "That boat looks very familiar. I can just about make out the name. It looks like *Nimbus*."

"I remember them. It's the Seller family. They often came to the Royal Vancouver Yacht Club Easter cruises and they have two daughters just about the same ages as Duncan and Colin." I replied.

David, Linda, Kristin and Erin piled on deck as we approached. What excitement there was at this unexpected meeting.

"Great to see you," called out Dave. "We thought you were still in the Caribbean." We discovered frequently during our travels that mail and news take a while to circulate.

Alas, there were no mooring buoys free for us and with depths over 25 metres we decided to go further up the lagoon and anchor off the sands by the Bora Bora Hotel. Soon the radio was humming between *Nimbus* and *Bagheera* and within no time Karen from *Cool Change* was on the air.

"It's my daughter Shannon's eleventh birthday party tomorrow," she told us. "I gather from the conversation you have children aboard. I hope they will be able to come."

"Fantastic," I replied. "Just tell me what time you are planning it and where, and we'll be there."

It was the start of an extremely social week with a group of yachtsmen who were all entranced by the beautiful setting, with its clear, calm waters and facilities ashore. Many were reluctant to head out into the ocean for the next long trip.

Interestingly most of us were beyond our visa limits by this time, but although the authorities patrolled they seemed very relaxed. Ironically the only boat we knew who ran into problems was one that paid the required $90 in stamp duty for a visa extension, only to be turned down and instructed to leave immediately. After considerable 'discussions', phone calls to Papeete and their daughter in tears, they were finally allowed to stay.

Suddenly the weather changed and we had gusts up to 35 knots and teeming rain.

"What can you expect when two British Columbian boats get together," we joked with *Nimbus*.

In the lulls we went snorkelling and introduced the Seller family to many of our Pacific underwater discoveries. We made sea urchin and shark backbone necklaces, concocted a creamy clam chowder from giant clams, identified more shells and ate quantities of Linda's moist banana bread.

Then one morning there was *Braganza* under full sail tacking up the lagoon.

Jamie gave us a running commentary.

"They're coming towards us. Oh, now they're going away again. Now they're coming back. They're almost here!"

Pete and Lance anchored and leapt in the dinghy right away. "Do you realize its been three months?" said Pete.

"Three months since the Galapagos Islands?" I replied. "It's unbelievable."

We all relaxed for a few more days, exploring ashore and the boys played with some children they had met in Moorea who were now staying in the lavish Bora Bora hotel. One night we were thoroughly spoilt by Tom on *L'Affaire* and taken there for dinner. It always amazes me the elegance we sailors attain when we've had our clothes crammed into small lockers and skirts around our waists to get ashore in the breaking waves. But immaculate we all were, and Nellie and I felt wonderful in the fragrant leis and bougainvillaea wreaths that Tom had organized.

We gorged on fresh foods from the huge, exotic buffet—caviar, smoked salmon and lobster, and finished with mountains of strawberries and home-made ice cream. The dancing was very sophisticated with the dancers in fine costumes. It was an evening of luxury and so nice to be pampered!

We left on the August 25th with American *Onskan*, another Beneteau First 38s, and *Nimbus*. As we sailed through the channel we threw our leis overboard, the traditional gesture that we would be back again. On the horizon *Belair* and *Archangel*, now with Michael's eldest son and daughter-in-law aboard, were just arriving.

We were heading for Mopelia, 120 nautical miles away, the last and most westerly atoll of French Polynesia. The wind was easterly, with a touch of north, blowing 10-15 knots initially but reducing, and we had a very rolly sea.

With a boost from the engine, as the wind petered out during the starry night, we arrived at 10:30 AM. As we headed round to the north-west side we passed a rusty wreck.

"I wonder what a ship was doing here?"

"I was told about it in Bora Bora," replied Andy. "Apparently it was one of the German raiders. In the First World War they disguised their warships as neutral merchant ships and ravaged the Allied shipping. I believe it was doing repairs and went up on the reef in a storm."

The pass is unmarked but we knew it was between the wreck and some wooded motus. At a distance the only indication of its existence was disturbed water caused by the strong current that was flowing out of the lagoon. It was a good time to enter, Andy had calculated, but with five knots surging against us in the very narrow pass it was still scary being on the helm, particularly when inexplicably a preventer line got caught on the mainsail. Suddenly the depth sounder flashed down to 2.3 metres and the keel brushed the bottom before we were out of the strong current and catapulted into the deep lagoon. It took a while for the adrenaline to calm down.

It was a beautiful atoll, about 4 by 6 nautical miles, and we could see all the way around. A dinghy was on its way over. It was Ray from *Tantivy III*, another Vancouver boat. He gave us the run down.

"There's no permanent population with a chief or officials," he informed us, "just Michel up this end and two others at the other end, on copra contracts."

We anchored close to Ray, quickly putting our shell bag over the stern where the odour was a little more bearable, and were soon ashore exploring with Chris and Sarah from *Onskan*. Michel was very friendly, cut us green coconuts to drink and a stalk of bananas. A cutlass (machete) was an indispensable tool here.

Andy asked if we could buy any lobsters.

"No buy," replied Michel with a big smile. "Let's go get some, MAINTENANT!"

We went back to the pass where two more boats were hovering outside. The tide had turned now and they needed to pluck up courage quickly. *Solmar* soon entered the pass with one person up the mast at the spreaders for increased visibility. A multi-national boat, *Solmar* was constructed of steel and built in New Zealand. Jo and Leisa were originally from Mozambique, but had moved to South Africa when many Portuguese had left after the Communist takeover. Their boat was registered in Sri Lanka! American *Horizon* followed behind.

Michel strode along the barrier reef whilst we tottered behind; it was very rough walking in the sharp uneven coral and our feet kept slipping in our plastic reef shoes.

Finally Jamie and I gave up and joined Ray and Sarah on a nearby island. It was almost a mini Galapagos in bird life. The baby frigate birds were pure white, fluffy and amazingly tame, only giving a token snarl when they were actually stroked, although the adults were somewhat more reticent, keeping a distant 6 metres away. White terns frequently bobbed down at us and brown terns ran around our feet.

A couple of times we came across serene tropicbirds, sitting on the ground unperturbed guarding their rosy pink eggs. Some were pure white, some patterned with black but all had huge, dominant beady eyes that watched us, as we crept by, fascinated but trying not to intrude. In the trees were brown boobies, some still sitting on their nests. There seemed to be a wide time span for breeding here, with some fledgling frigates already gaining their dark upper wings, while others were only just hatching.

The wind had increased again and it was beautifully cool as we walked through the verdant green undergrowth, with the palms swaying against the brilliant blue sky.

Meanwhile the reef party had been unbelievably successful. It was the first time we had seen these leather lobsters caught, and a hazardous business it was too, requiring a quick stretch and grab over the edge of the outer reef, as the wave receded, meanwhile having to be safely back out of harms way when the next ocean swell pounded in. With the reef dropping off thousands of metres, and the downwards suction of the swells, one would have no chance.

Michel was extremely skilled, however, and in no time the lobster party was returning with a bulging bag.

"How was it?" I called out. "Are there enough lobsters for all the boats?"

"How will thirty-four go round?" replied Andy grinning.

Everyone gathered for the barbecue. Not only were there succulent lobsters but Michel provided entertainment as well. *Horizon* produced a guitar and Michel sung the night away, first with fiery then haunting Polynesian songs, before launching into his world wide repertoire. He was a talented musician and told us he planned to go around the world singing when the final two years of the copra contract were completed.

The next day we went back to the reef, as Michel insisted it was his turn to entertain us, and came back laden with goods: seaweed for a 'salade de mer', octopus and parrot fish. All eager to learn we watched carefully as he stripped the multi-lobed leaves off the stalks of the green seaweed and drew out the salt by marinating them in vinegar for an hour. Having drained the liquid off he added coconut milk and chopped onion.

Michel instructed us to beat the octopus until the upper side was almost white, then he cut it up and cooked it with a little water over a fire of coconut husks. When cooked to his satisfaction he stirred in coconut milk and explained that the octopus would be ready when it turned pink. Finally he barbecued the parrot fish, basting them with oil, soy, garlic and ginger sauce. Every dish was delicious, Polynesian with a definite French flourish, and we finished with a lemon cake which Duncan had decided spontaneously to make on the boat.

Michel obviously loved the varied company of the international sailors, there were twenty-eight in 1986 he told us, but not many this year. We started a yacht visitors' book for him with addresses, rhymes and photos, and he promised to look us all up during his world tour. We are still hoping to hear from him . . .

18. The Cook Islands and Niue

When the wind had died en route to Mopelia *Nimbus* had decided that, as they would not reach the atoll in time to enter the pass in daylight, they should bear away for the Cook islands. Dave was never to hear the end of it from his family when we mentioned that we had motored.

It was early days in their offshore cruising and Linda moaned,

"You didn't even give us that option!"

We found the Cook Islanders to be very friendly people. The harbour had just re-opened after two years of rebuilding and it was a novelty to see so many boats in the harbour. There were fourteen of us along the wall, most of whom had met somewhere along the line, and they included a variety of nationalities, although Americans and Canadians dominated.

Raratonga is the largest of the Cook Islands and was never visited by Cook himself. The other fourteen islands are spread out over nearly two million square kilometres of ocean and vary widely in form. Most are inaccessible by yacht.

Dave came over in the dinghy on our arrival and helped us tie our lines to the wall.

"You can get ashore either with a plank or ferry by dinghy," he told us.

"Which do you recommend?"

"We are using both. The plank is convenient, but can get quite precarious, especially after a sundowner! The dinghy is better for the children but at low tide it's hard to climb up the seawall."

"Where did you get your plank?"

"Oh, there are plenty on the shore," Dave assured us.

"Sounds good. We'll go for both too."

"Anything else we should know?"

"Yes, the harbour becomes untenable with a northerly wind and everyone has to move out. The only problem is that the officials in Tonga are very unhappy if you don't have your clearing out papers from here."

"So we all have to hang around offshore waiting for the wind to change if we have to clear out of here in a hurry, rather than heading straight off?"

"That's right."

Onskan had been close behind us from Mopelia. When the wind had finally died we had motored and she had dropped behind.

"I wonder why Chris doesn't start the engine?" said Andy.

As they entered the harbour we went out in the dinghy to give them a hand.

"At least the engine didn't choose to die as we were coming out of the pass at Mopelia!" said Chris as we took a stern line to pull him in.

"Hopefully I'll be able to get it fixed here."

"I'm sure you can," replied Andy. "The facilities look good."

After clearing in with the officials and a quick trip to the bank, the supermarket and the laundromat, the main chores which can take days in some places, were done. Only fuel and water were left to arrange. These were quickly solved. Wayne from *Velella* arranged a fuel truck to service all the boats, and we found we could fill up with running water from the shore.

"Great," I said to Andy when I heard the news. "How wonderful to have a week with the pressure water turned on."

"Does that mean we can actually let the water run when we clean our teeth?" enquired Colin.

"I don't know if we should be that extravagant!" replied Andy with a twinkle in his eye.

As we walked into town Duncan noticed another rusty wreck offshore. It was apparently the hull of the *Yankee*, a brigantine that had been owned by Irving Johnson, a famous sailor, adventurer and writer for National Geographic. In 1964, several years after they had sold the boat, the wind had changed while charterers caroused below.

"It was supposedly quite a party with several bar girls, and no-one noticed they were dragging until they were completely wrecked on the reef," a shopkeeper told us.

Strung out along the shore with the green slopes of Maungatea soaring behind, the town of Avarua has a sleepy 19th century air. On the shore outrigger canoes were pulled up under the old ironwood trees and, along with baskets made with cowrie shells, models of the canoes made some of the most attractive souvenirs. We were back to reasonable prices and good shops, although we were distressed by the video stores. It appeared that movies were one of the main forms of entertainment but the choices on the shelves were some of the worst, most violent films ever made, an unfortunate aspect of our culture to share.

Since our arrival the boys had been more than envious of the motor scooters that the Sellers, along with several others, had rented.

"That looks so much fun," said Duncan. "Are we going to rent them too?"

"It certainly would be great to see the island," I replied, "but how are we going to manage five on two scooters?"

"Jamie can come on the back with me," suggested Duncan hopefully.

"Not really, I think it will have to be a car, but we'll have to check out the prices first."

"Oh no, that's so boring!" Colin added to the discussion.

Normally renting a car caused great excitement!

Today, however, while the Sellers departed by scooter, we could easily take the bus a third of the way round the island to see Piri Puruto III perform. Piri is the self-proclaimed Master of Disaster–The Warrior–The Greatest Coconut Tree Climber–The Magnificent Traditional Firemaker. Grand names and without doubt Piri is brash, but a great entertainer and informative also.

He told us about the 'fantastic' coconut that could provide food and drinks, housing, furniture, matting, rope, baskets, clothing, as well as the oil that is manufactured into soap, candles and cosmetics. This information was delivered with a repertoire of stories that even included recipes for nursing mums.

Then he was the tree climber and soared up a 37 metre palm at breakneck speed using a piece of hibiscus bark, twisted in a figure of eight around his feet, for grip.

"Seventeen seconds," called out an amazed Duncan, who was the official time keeper.

Piri's twelve year old son followed him up, somewhat more cautiously. He was in training, we were told.

Piri finished with a flourishing demonstration of making instant fire with a stick and bark and gave us the tip that the smoke from the burning husks is an effective mosquito repellent.

The boys were full of comments at the bus stop. As we waited and waited it dawned on me that I hadn't checked on the bus schedule, but it was only 5:00 PM. Finally a New Zealand family stopped.

"The last bus was at 4:00 PM you know. Do want a ride into town?"

They gave us a tour on the way, typical of Cook Island hospitality.

"I can't believe the buses stop so early," I said to Andy later. "You know the last time we were stranded was in the Med.

Do you realize that was well over a year ago."

"And if we had kept to our original plan we would now be back in Vancouver." he replied.

Our seven day visit passed quickly. There was dinghy racing at the sailing club and the boys preparing sheets of photographs as they had been asked to talk about our travels to the local Cub group. We explored the lush twisting valleys by car and toured on the oldest road in Polynesia, the Ara Metua, whose coral foundation was laid a thousand years ago. Along the way we bought fresh produce from the many market gardens. We also did the usual boat hopping, met several holidaying New Zealand families and particularly enjoyed the local people who loved to chat and come aboard. Sadly many seemed to get instantly seasick.

"They seem to have lost the genes of their seafaring ancestors!" commented Andy after he had rapidly escorted another group ashore.

One evening we went to a Polynesian show, put on by some visiting children from New Zealand schools. The performances varied from gentle Tongan themes to the vibrant dances of the Maori's. The dancers were full of vigour and confidence but it was the youngest children's group that stole the show. They acted out a moving Maori myth that ended with a small boy snoring most convincingly through the microphone!

We went to another children's performance at the Tamure Hotel where local flower decked children enthusiastically swayed their hips and shook their knees.

The audience was invited to dance too and the tiniest girl was the first to request a partner, charmingly asking 1.95 metre Chris, from *Onskan*, for "the pleasure."

After the show, while we were waiting outside for the rest of our group, several of the local mothers with their children gathered around us.

Dancers seen in the Tamure Hotel, Raratonga (photo Air New Zealand)

Finally one sidled up to me shyly saying, "You have three fine sons and we have many beautiful daughters."

I smiled and replied, "But my sons are only eleven, eight and four."

"Just the time to start making the arrangements," was the response!

Experiencing a Polynesian church service is a must the guide book told us. On Sunday morning we dressed up in our finery and joined the throngs entering the whitewashed Cook Islands Christian Church, built in 1855. The congregation sat in the middle of the church, behind the ladies of the choir who were all in white with broadbrimmed hats, and in front of the men, also dressed in their best attire.

Regular hymns were transformed. The women have remarkably strong, high singing voices and the men harmonized to perfection. "But where are the instruments?" I whispered to Andy.

I had been trying to peer around without looking too obvious to find the source of the rhythmic plucking sounds. It was only later in the day, when we came across a small group spontaneously singing, that we realized these 'instruments' were actually men's voices. They rocked back and forth as they produced this unusual accompaniment.

We talked daily on the radio to *Belair*. They had just reached a northern atoll, Suvarov, after a wet trip with strong winds on the nose, but like all atolls it was a picturesque setting. A local family had visited them with a gift of fish in a handwoven basket. The forecast for us was south-westerly winds but light, as we were the other side of the high pressure system.

Nimbus left for Niue and Dave reported almost no wind but big 2 metre swells. We decided to leave also, after a last visit to provision. Piri gave me a ride into town on the back of his scooter, at breakneck coconut climbing speed.

The autohelm was set, and we immediately settled into our watch system. Before I dozed off in the forward cabin, I commented to Andy how relaxed and outgoing we had found the local people to be.

"Absolutely delightful," Andy agreed, "but aren't they fortunate that aid from New Zealand pays for 50% of their government budget."

The next morning the wind clocked round to the south-east and we were able to throw up the spinnaker during daylight hours. "Rolling and flopping along," entered Andy in our log book.

I noted later, "*Nimbus* disappeared over the horizon in a cloud of exhaust smoke."

"Are the girls organizing you, Dave?" Andy quipped over the VHF radio.

"That's right!" was the reply. "But I have to agree it's far more comfortable." *Nimbus* was heavier and slower than *Bagheera* in light airs, and the motion in these seas was unpleasant.

That night Duncan caught a strange fish from the deep.

"It looks just like the espada we had in Madeira," I commented. Duncan did his research.

"It's called a snake mackerel, and they weren't identified until Thor Heyerdahl's Kon Tiki expedition."

It was very long, black and ugly. The flesh was delicious but unlike the espada there were large bones just under the skin.

It was during this trip that Andy and I developed a new watch system, not that it was radically altered but it made a huge difference in making night watches pass more quickly. Our secret? We changed watch on the half hour. On *Bagheera* we write in the log on the hour. We found that the half hour before writing in the log flies by: getting dressed, getting oriented and making tea. Similarly the last half hour rapidly disappears with writing in the log, plotting a last position, clearing up and getting ready for bed. It's magic! Three hours turns into two.

Five days later, just as *Bagheera* was arriving at Niue's open roadstead anchorage by the town of Alofi, we saw the huge back of a whale. There was a humpback and calf and we were able to drift quite close to them. Ray from *Tantivy* told us they had been around for two days.

"Watch for the chasms when you are anchoring," he warned as he left in his dinghy, heading off to talk to *Nimbus* on the radio.

Niue is an uplifted atoll, in fact twice uplifted, and the double terracing stands out quite plainly. It is renowned for the beauty of its deep chasms in the coral ashore, but these extend into the ocean bed too. Not only would the anchor go too deep if it went into one of these coral crevices, it could easily foul.

We had just finished anchoring satisfactorily when Colin called out, "Look, look. The whales are coming this way!"

Andy threw the bag of snorkelling gear in the dinghy and we rushed off to meet them. With the mother and baby was a third middle sized humpback whale.

"Can we go diving with them?" the boys asked, tremendously excited.

"Yes we can," said Andy, "but we must all stay close together."

Diving within about 3 metres of a whale is a wondrous experience for anyone but particularly awesome when you are only eleven, eight and four years old.

"It was just as though we'd climbed into the killer whale pool at the aquarium at home," Colin explained to Kristin and Erin later.

"And look at all the sea snakes here," said Duncan.

"I know they're really neat," said Kristin, "but is it safe to swim with them?"

"We thought they might be poisonous, like a cobra," added Erin.

"Actually they're very poisonous," said Andy, "and their venom is several times more potent than a cobra's, but they won't attack you unless you really bother them."

We saw sea snakes throughout the rest of the South Pacific and watched them for hours. Most were about a metre long and blue or yellowish in colour, with bands that were sometimes dark and sometimes faded depending on when they had changed their skins. They find their food along the sandy or coral bottom and are constantly moving or burrowing into a gobi fish hole. Then they come to the surface to breathe and their small heads pop up out of the water. Like land snakes they love to bask in the sun and also lay their eggs ashore.

The only known attacks on humans by sea snakes have been ones when they were aggravated in the extreme, usually when being captured. Their mouths are too small to bite humans, except fingers or ears, but some, particularly a large beige variety, are very inquisitive and seem to want to touch one with the tip of their tongues, much too close to the venom for comfort! We had been told that one way to get rid of them was to stay absolutely still, but for children snorkelling this was hardly a realistic solution. Instead we found guiding them away with a speargun or stick seemed to work.

That evening I organized presents and party ideas as Colin's ninth birthday was only a day away. The Nimbus' and Bagheera's had discussed touring the island by rental car and Colin requested that this be a birthday trip. At 8:00 AM the Sellers rowed over for breakfast, singing 'Happy Birthday' Polynesian style, accompanied by Kristin on the ukulele. It was a delightful start to a great day.

First stop was Avaiki Cave, a magical place with different levels of stalactites and stalagmites dripping like candles in muted hues of misty green, yellow and mauve. As we climbed round pillars, under arches and through tunnels to motionless, clear pools, we could hear the muffled roar of the pounding ocean below.

The children could have stayed all day.

"It's so pretty here," cried Erin. "Just like a Disney movie."

Matapa Chasm was the old bathing place for the Royalty. It was a sharp rocky climb down to the long inland channel, with the water almost fresh at its inner end. Did the Royalty have rush mats laid down for them, we wondered? There were beautiful butterflies everywhere and Andy found an old vanilla orchid plantation, and gave us all a supply of beans.

Whilst in 'town' we had been told of a man with an extensive shell collection. Disappointingly he was not at home but at his bush garden. Apparently most people have their bush gardens as the land can only be used once in seven years. We thought the gardens colourful and neat considering the lack of soil but in the centre of the island the forest was lush and green with huge crow's-nest ferns and an abundance of poinsettia. We saw several birds: white long-tailed terns, parakeets, swamp hens and owls that were rather like our barn owl.

There were few people around but we passed one group of boys playing cricket. As they waved enthusiastically we noticed that they all had long plaits down their backs.

"I've read about that," I commented. "I believe they have a hair cutting ceremony when they are teenagers which symbolizes their manhood."

"That's right," said Linda "and the girls have a similar ear piercing one."

After picking up Wayne and Ginney who had just arrived on *Velella*, we headed around the south of the island to Togo Chasm. It is a rough walk over the old coral rock, and we were glad that some of the roughest parts had been cemented. What a contrast to the rounded forms of the weeping limestone on the lee side of the island.

At the end of the path was a steep drop and a rope.

"Can we go down it?" questioned Duncan.

"Yes, if you can get up again!"

He was down in a flash. The rest of us were a little more reticent but at the bottom we found a different world; a white sand, palm-treed oasis with a clear green pool.

The Niue Hotel kindly let us shower off, (it had been a very dusty day), before serving a special birthday dinner. The boys had been concerned about their birthday parties before we left but as usual in our travels Colin had been able to spend it with other children and special friends.

It was time to start the school year. Duncan was now in grade six, Colin in grade four, and Jamie just beginning kindergarten. It was the first time there had been three children for school and I could see that life was going to be busy, and finding space for us all a challenge.

"I think we are going to have to use the chart table at times," I commented tentatively to Andy.

"But that is my office and workshop!" was the predictable reply.

Andy generally did the inevitable boat maintenance during school time. Fortunately Jamie did not have too many fine motor projects but I filed away the problem for future thought on night watches.

Colin had developed a large blood blister above his stomach. Before we left we decided it should be checked, so made an appointment at the local hospital. They recommended he have it removed; the charge was $8. Niue is totally dependent on official aid from New Zealand, and the sample was sent there to be analyzed. We received the benign results on our arrival in Australia. Now our only reminder is Colin's perfect 'cockroach' scar.

During a last shop we stopped at the Post Office as we had started an album for stamps connected with sea life.

Thinking the boys were Americans, the post-master said to them,

"Now remember to tell your friends to write Savage Island on the address when they write to you here," he said with a twinkle.

"Savage Island?"

"Yep, when Captain Cook came here he thought us pretty unfriendly, savages no less, after the friendly Tongans."

"And you have to put that in the address?" I asked.

"Only from the United States I'm told," he replied laughing.

Unlike Captain Cook we had found the Niuans most friendly, but were disturbed by the number of empty homes. With free entry into New Zealand and the chance of higher paying jobs (over 80% of the Niue workforce is government employed) the population of Niue has fallen below 2,500, whilst over 10,000 Niuans reside in New Zealand.

As we departed Jamie gave a sigh. "It's so sad we have to leave. It was such a nice place."

He was still clutching his varnished wood plaque carved in the shape of the island, which he had been given by a girl in the liquor store, of all places. It was the first souvenir he asked for, when we started unpacking at home.

19. The Kingdom of Tonga

Vava'u

There were light winds for the trip to the Kingdom of Tonga and realizing we would arrive at night I furled the genoa and slipped in behind *Nimbus*, who had radar. Andy was on the 4:30 to 7:30 PM watch so it was his turn to cook dinner. Jamie and I were reading a story in the cockpit and enjoying the last rays of the sun.

"Could you throw these peelings over the side?" he called up. "You know I can't believe how much garbage has accumulated in such a short time."

"It's horrifying," I replied. "Everything these days seems to come double wrapped, hermetically sealed or in plastic containers. It piles up in no-time at all. I didn't have time to unwrap the shopping before we left but as it's such a short trip I thought I would keep it until Tonga."

We had been disgusted by the litter in the oceans and on the beaches during our travels. The Mediterranean was particularly bad. During the summer tourist months the beaches are cleaned but in the winter, on the north coast of Menorca for example, it was solid plastic.

Those on shore litter, big ships empty their garbage into the oceans, and it is only too easy for boaters to throw their rubbish overboard too. It is soon out of sight and out of mind, except for those in their wake or for the fish below. One evening in the Tobago Cays in the Caribbean we had watched incensed as a rapid succession of beer cans were tossed

225

overboard during a party on a large yacht. Finally Steve from *Severance* could stand it no longer. He roared off in the dinghy, methodically collected every one and presented them with a full garbage bag. Without doubt they got the message.

In fact we dispensed with most garbage overboard, unless we were close to land, but not without some preparation. Biodegradables go over the side, including cut up paper and cardboard. Cans are pierced at both ends, and bottles filled with water, so that they sink immediately. Plastics are the real problem as most float and if possible we keep them until we can put them in a garbage container on shore. If not we cut the plastic into small pieces. We used to throw these straight over the side but having heard of birds and turtles that have died through ingested plastic we now put them in a perforated garbage bag with a couple of rocks so they sink to the deep. Batteries, paints, used lube oil spray cans, etc. never went into the sea.

We arrived at Vava'a, the northern Tongan group of islands, at dawn and made our landfall at Neiafu. The 228 nautical mile trip had taken a couple of days in time, but three in date. We had just crossed the International Dateline and Tonga is the first country to herald the new day.

Mr. Aisea Sikaleti greeted us as we were pulling into the dock. As he took our lines he told us, "It's Saturday, you know, so the officials aren't working, but don't worry Captain, I'll drive you and find them."

He returned with Andy, some officials and quantities of pawpaws— and insisted we go to his feast that night!

It sounded touristy but fun, the price was reasonable, and *Nimbus* and our friends Skip and Denise from *Endymion* decided to come too.

The children were immediately taken with the handicrafts displayed, wanting to buy feather and bead headdresses and grass skirts, worn by both girls and boys. Andy and I were especially attracted by the coarse woven two-tone baskets and ended up by buying an unusual octagonal one. Prices were minimal and as the evening wore on we were showered with gifts. The traditional dancing, accompanied by guitar and banjo, was more sedate here. Tongan dances are stories that are acted by the dancers and told by the singers. The girls and the men, who performed a mock fight in their story, were very personable and their obvious enjoyment was infectious.

Dinner was cooked in the traditional way, underground in an umu oven, with the food in layers. The pig was at the bottom, then various types of fish, octopus, lobster and clams cooked in leaves. These were served with taro, breadfruit, coconut cream in cooked papaya, raw fish salad in giant clam shells, and quantities of water melon. This magnificent feast was laid out on palm fronds and we did it justice.

"I'm so glad Aisea persuaded us to come," exclaimed Andy after yet another helping. "All the food is so succulent and full of flavour."

"And there's so much of it," I replied.

We were lucky. The next week when friends went, there were twice as many people and the quantities were sparse.

With the cooking done it was time for the big mamas to join in the dancing and fun was had by all, although Jamie could hardly move his legs next morning.

Although a small area (about 60 by 60 nautical miles), Vava'u abounds with tiny islands with excellent anchorages, and quite reminded us of our local Pacific northwest Gulf Islands. We enjoyed exploring them with the *Nimbus* family and sharing several barbecues.

The famous Coral Gardens were lovely with colours of muted blues, mauves, greens and yellows. Types and shapes of coral where also varied, although I missed the forests of staghorn and elkhorn.

Mariner's Cave is at the north end of Nuapapu Island, and we finally found it by watching for a patch of deep, dark water with a lone coconut high above. The cave's story was told around the world by Will Mariner and the cave named after him. You reach the cave by swimming through an underwater tunnel. Apparently a young noble, who feared his evil king's intentions, hid his sweetheart here, coming back with food and water in the black of night. Finally, after he had rapidly built an ocean going canoe, he managed to spirit her away. A very spooky, dark place, I must say, for the maiden to spend her days alone.

Andy is a strong underwater swimmer and he volunteered to be the pioneer of the group.

"Its fantastic!" he called out on surfacing. Without any hesitation Duncan and Colin were in after him.

He took them through one at a time and came back for the Seller family and myself. We were a little more reticent, but his enthusiasm won the day and I went after him. It was an uncomfortably long time underwater, and as I felt a moment's panic, my thoughts flashing back to Krka Falls in Yugoslavia when I'd gasped for breath. Andy yanked me firmly by the hand and we came up inside the gloomy cave.

The cave is never exposed to light. The colours of the smooth, loamy rock are muted, and we found delicate, intricate, pale pink coral.

In contrast Swallow's Cave could be entered by dinghy. Its unusual jagged entrance was spoilt for us by the graffiti on the walls, but just to the right of the caves, in denuded trees, were a colony of fruit bats. They were a perfect subject for the poem Duncan had to write for English. He looked up some information and combined it with our observations and experiences.

The Fruit Bat

His name is a Flying Fox,
But he's not like the fox you know.
His graceful wings are four feet wide,
And at each end they have a toe.
All through the day he hangs upsidedown,
In a crowded tree, which is like a town.
At night he goes out to look for food,
What kind of food, depends on his mood.
We were fascinated, as we sat,
By this flying mammal, the fruit bat.

by Duncan Copeland
Grade 6

We found several new varieties of shells and our reference books were in constant use. The boys by now were quite sophisticated with their research and knowledge. Latin names such as Lambis chiragra, Terebellum terebellum and Conus nussatella readily reeled off their tongues as they avidly discussed new finds.

Some interesting arguments also ensued.

"You know there are six classes of shells?"

"No there are not, there are seven."

"Well my book definitely says six."

At the final count half our books said six and half seven!

They all included the bivalves or Pelecypods, with two shells, the Gastropods or snails, the Cephalopods, like squid, octopus and the nautilus, the Scaphopods or tusk shells, the Amphineura or chitons, eight plated shells that cling onto rocks, and the Monoplacophora a deep sea primitive group which until recently was only known from fossils. The seventh class mentioned in some books is the Aplacophora that consists of shell free animals possessing worm-shaped bodies.

"It seems that the solution to the mystery is that there are really six classes of shells but seven classes of mollusks," I concluded.

Although many of us have the vision of wandering along beautiful sandy beaches, finding endless specimens of perfect shells for the taking, this is far from the reality. It's easy to forget that although we are looking for shells, where we find them (except for sunbleached, sea battered ones) is dictated by the habits of the animal inside, the mollusk.

Few mollusks like sun and few like to be out of the water for extended periods, if at all. Learning about the ways of the mollusk greatly increases one's chances of collecting a wide variety. So as well as analysing the characteristics of new finds for identification we all became engrossed in learning about the mollusks themselves.

Daily the comments flowed:

"Did you know that flamingo tongues are often found on fan coral?"

"Conchs camouflage themselves with a brown periostracum and scavenge along the sand. We should be diving for them in shallow water and it says that muddy sand holds more nutrients and better, bigger shells."

"And helmets are carnivores, they bury themselves by day. Just a hump sticks up."

"When's low tide? We'll find many more gastropods at the bottom of the intertidal zone."

"We must turn more rocks over. Cowries are underneath, and we should feel under the coral too."

"Only if there are no sea cucumbers or nudibranchs around. They are so slimy. Ugh!"

"Remember to turn the rocks back again. This book keeps reminding us that the mollusks that are protected and in the shade don't want to be left exposed in the sun."

"Murex's like mangrove oysters. We should look as we haven't got many varieties."

"Yuck, the mud around the mangroves always stinks!"

As the flow continued so did our collection.

There was only one problem with this—cleaning—and the problem with the problem was that it all fell on me!

Many shells can be boiled to kill the animal inside and then the animal can be pulled out. Unfortunately it is not quite so simple for most varieties. Augers, for example, have long bodies that always seem to break off as they are removed. The shiny side of conch shells will frequently crack when heated (or frozen) and cowries have such a narrow slit that the bodies just won't slide through. I developed several techniques with various instruments. In particular I found that curling an animal round when removing it from the shell, if that is how it lived naturally, greatly increased the chances of getting it out whole. Vigorous shakes after filling the shell with sea water could also work wonders.

When all else failed we resorted to the mesh bag over the stern. The theory is that the organisms in the sea will eat away what is left in the shell in no time at all. We soon learnt that no time at all could be weeks and during that time the stench became unbearable. Never anchor downwind of a boat with a shell bag over the side! There were also the catastrophes such as motoring away with the bag trailing in the water and treasured specimens lost.

Cleaning the growth on the outside was another matter. Generally a short soak in bleach and a stiff brush is sufficient but shiny surfaces must be sealed with Vaseline. I learnt later that keeping shiny shells such as cowries in paraffin kills the mollusk and seems to enhance the shiny finish. For the most part I left shells that needed the more toxic muriatic acid and a sharp pick until we got home.

When cleaned to our satisfaction we give our shells a coating of baby oil and alcohol, usually gin in our case. The oil brings out the translucent colour, and gives a natural look. The alcohol helps it penetrate so the effect lasts longer. I oil our shells about once a year.

Cleaning aside, shell collecting became a marvellous family activity. It is not only interesting and varied, as we searched both the shores and underwater, but always rewarding, and something the whole family enjoyed doing together. It stimulated much thought and knowledge, and the boys took great pride in their individual collections. Now that we are home we have some spectacular displays and many stories to go with them.

We did however observe strict rules regarding conservation, only taking the minimum, and were careful about safety. We were horrified to hear that Aisea's four year old son had died from being poisoned by a cone. We insisted the boys used their tongs to examine specimens and made sure they knew to keep the barbed harpoon-like proboscis away from their bodies as it ejects the toxin like a dart.

We also wore plastic reef shoes in case of stone fish when walking along the shore. These sedentary hunters lie on the bottom waiting for small fish and marine animals, and blend in completely with the rocks and weed. They are much feared by people because they are covered with extremely poisonous spines. The poison is so potent it can lead to a rapid agonizing death.

David on *Nimbus* had read in the Almanac that there would be an eclipse of the sun one afternoon. Everyone gathered on *Bagheera* to make

Eclipse of the sun in Vava'u with the Seller family from *Nimbus*

viewers. When I had my films developed in Raratonga I found my camera was defective due to sand and water damage. I had several black negatives returned. Although we try to keep camera equipment protected this is a problem on a boat as is film deterioration due to the heat and humidity.

We cut up cardboard boxes and covered the viewing slits with several thicknesses of negatives. It was a memorable sight; everyone looking through their viewers, Dave through his sextant, all commenting on the sun's progress.

"This is the second eclipse we have seen," Jamie told the *Nimbus* girls. "The first was of the moon. I remember I kept on pointing out the moon for weeks afterwards!"

On Sunday Linda, the children and myself decided to go to another service, this time at the small Methodist church on Hunga Island. The local people welcomed us warmly. Only about twenty-five sang but the volume was remarkable. In contrast to Raratonga the women wore no hats and they were almost all dressed in black, with the traditional Tongan pandanus-leaf mat skirt, or ta'ovala fasted with a waistband. These are very bulky and accentuate size, considered a measure of beauty. The men mostly wore a white shirt and tie, black jacket, and traditional black or maroon skirt, (although some also had a pandanus mat secured with a coconut-fibre cord), with rubber or leather thongs or barefeet. It was a curious mix of their traditional dress with the western styles that were insisted on by the missionaries.

As we headed back to the boat we were called discreetly from one of the houses.

"Would we like to buy a tapa?" they asked.

Linda and I looked at each other and nodded.

We were intrigued and went inside but were surprised as Tonga had very strict rules for Sundays: no work, no sports and particularly no trade. In fact I had been rather apprehensive on the previous Sunday when Andy had started hammering on the foredeck, while fixing a problem with the anchor windlass.

Tapa cloth plays a major part in everyday life in Tonga. It is used for decorations, partitions, bedding, for special gifts and worn as a costume in traditional dancing.

Tapas are made from the paper of the mulberry tree, which is stripped and the white inner bark beaten into long pieces of cloth. When there is enough for the required size (up to 150 metre lengths for special occasions) the women take it to their homes to be slept on, to flatten the cloth and smooth out the creases. After the pieces have been glued together with arrowroot or tapioca they are ready for the design. This takes great skill as a relief of the pattern has to be made beforehand using the ribs of palm leaves sewn to a base of a young coconut shoot. Raw sap is used to make an impression and the pattern completed using brushes. Natural dyes are used and boiled to produce different shades of brown, tan and black.

The ladies carefully laid out their tapa across the rush mats in the house. It was a lovely cloth, about 2 metres by 3 metres, and was of the Tongan Royal family with the road up to the palace, the surrounding trees, the royal crest and sacred birds.

Linda and I could already envision it adorning a wall in our Vancouver homes. "How much?" we asked.

"$50," they answered with no hesitation.

Our money was back at our boats so we said we would return later, which also gave us time to discuss the matter between ourselves and with our husbands!

Meanwhile the ladies insisted on giving us some food and we left with steaming fish cooked in banana leaves, baked paw paw as a vegetable, and their version of tapioca pudding, tapioca, or cassava, in coconut milk.

We lunched on *Nimbus* and decided we would like to share the tapa cloth and, after consulting with other boats, decided we would offer $40.

Linda and I returned to find a bargaining committee. We offered our price but one of the men countered,

"No, we want a generator."

"But a generator is worth hundreds of dollars and we wouldn't carry an extra," Linda explained calmly.

"Well other boats have given us generators for tapa cloths," he insisted.

Linda and I felt it was time to leave but the ladies wanted to sell, and they were happy with our price. The men laughed as we left. They knew they were being outrageous but why not try? Unfortunately some yachts have given very extravagant items when bargaining, particularly charterers on short visits, which causes dissatisfaction on all sides in future negotiations.

We rushed back to the boat as *Bagheera* was leaving for the Tongan Ha'apai Group to the south. It was hard to say farewell to *Nimbus*, we had all so much enjoyed each other's company, but they were heading to New Zealand so could afford to linger, whilst we had to move quickly to make Australia before the cyclone season.

Linda gave us the mementoes she had composed for our visitors book and we finally tore ourselves away. The pass was negotiated uneventfully and we started to beat into the southerly wind, then motorsailed as the breeze was light. We had been having engine problems. Andy went below to do a routine check and found oil oozing from the rear seal. Regretfully it seemed more sensible to ease sheets and head straight for Fiji.

20. Fiji and New Caledonia

Lau Group, Suva and Mbengga Island
Noumea and the Ile des Pins

T ime for your watch, Andy."

It was 7:20 AM, the morning after our Tongan departure. I checked around below, put away the cruising guide for Fiji which I had been studying, plotted our position, and returned to the deck for a last 360 degree search of the horizon, before handing over–and made a last check on the dinghy.

We had set out with the plan of just an overnight trip down to the Ha'apai group and the winds were light so we decided to tow the dinghy. This saved us the work of hauling it on deck, where it had to be deflated and secured. The next day it would have to be inflated again and launched.

As I glanced astern I realized something was wrong. The dinghy was dragging on one side, and as Andy came on deck it started slewing sideways as the port pontoon deflated. We both groaned in horror, surely not another dinghy collapse. We had just got this dinghy in Papeete, our third under warranty.

Obviously it was going to have to come on board. With difficulty we hauled it along the starboard side of *Bagheera*. Andy climbed down into the dinghy to rig the bridle and attach the outboard to our hoisting pulley system at the stern of *Bagheera*. Fortunately this went off without a hitch; I was not at all happy with Andy off *Bagheera* in the middle of the ocean.

Once back on board Andy rigged a spinnaker halyard, and started winching the dinghy up, with Duncan tailing.

It was a heavy job, with the dinghy jerking due to the lumpy seas, and bumping into the topsides. Finally we had it as high as the lifelines at which point we usually just heave it on board.

"Pull it in Liza, pull it in," Andy shouted.

I was irritated, what did he think I was trying to do, but try as I might it was just too heavy. Andy looked annoyed, cleated the halyard and came aft. He had a go, then looked up puzzled.

"Good grief, the pontoon must have water in it," he deduced.

The port pontoon weighed a ton, and was half full of water. There were five half-oval holes through the underside.

We inspected them, mystified.

"They must have been made by a fish," Andy finally concluded. "From the shape I bet it was a marlin. He must have mistaken the dinghy skidding over the surface for a school of fish."

Suddenly it came to Andy that he had heard a similar story in the Raratonga sailing club. He had pooh-poohed it at the time!

It took almost three days to sail the 236 nautical miles to the Lau group in Fiji. The winds were light and we didn't want to use our engine, but it was agony only moving at 3 knots. Our friends Tim and Leisa, on the Camper and Nicholson 75-foot *Mustang*, took only twenty-four hours to cover the same distance.

With light winds forecast to continue, we decided to stop at Ongea Levu, and try to do some repairs. The Lau Islands are about half way between Tonga and Suva, the capital of Fiji. They are seldom visited by yachtsmen as one is required to clear in with the officials in Suva first, and then beat back 200 nautical miles into wind.

As we did not have permission, we anchored just inside the lagoon and started unloading the aft head so Andy could access the engine.

Within minutes the boys shouted down,

"There's a sail and it's coming towards us really fast."

Soon a traditional outrigger canoe (a proa) was alongside. We invited the two men on board and explained our predicament. They asked to take a look at the engine, agreed there was a problem, then cordially extended an invitation from the chief to visit their village.

"We'll race you there," said one of the Fijians. "But you must follow us in for the last part because it gets very shallow and there are many coral heads."

"Okay we will, thank you," replied Andy.

"Does anyone want to come with us?" said the other.

"Yes I do," replied Duncan at once, and quickly hopped on board.

We sailed in tandem across the pale green lagoon, with its curiously worn tiny islands, some like mushrooms and others, Jamie thought, like the shells we had been collecting. The two men showed us the best anchorage and departed to inform the village.

Duncan returned a hour later, full of chatter.

"It's was really fun ashore," he reported, "they have lots of fish and there are shells everywhere. All the ladies were really nice and gave me this fruit. They all wanted to talk but of course I couldn't understand a word! Look at this olive shell isn't it huge?"

He held it up for inspection. Apricot coloured on the inside with a brown zigzag pattern on the shiny back. It was about 9 centimetres long and indeed a prize.

"That must be an orange-mouthed olive," I said. "What a beautiful specimen for our collection. Well done."

He had returned in a power boat with another Andy, who claimed to run the post office and the radio. He asked us to write down our names and boat details, presumably, we thought, to radio Suva. Then, after asking for some fuel, he took Duncan off fishing. They returned after dark. I was becoming concerned, as generally activities end at dusk in the tropics.

The three men were delighted to come on board for coffee, and chocolate cake was a great hit. They had brought us a huge (10 POUND?) giant clam and five fish for our supper.

Early next morning we went ashore to pay our respects to the chief and bring the traditional gift of kava, the root of the pepper plant which is pounded with water into a drink. We had purchased it in the market in Neiafu, as we had heard the Tongan kava was of particularly high quality and greatly desired by the Fijians.

We were showered us with gifts of shells, fruit and fish as we walked up the long, white sand inlet. The tide was out and there were hundreds of crabs running over our toes, with a huge, bright pink claw perched awkwardly on their backs.

"What a perfect, sheltered setting," I said to Andy, "and the colours of the sea, sand and hibiscus flowers are so vivid. I'm so glad we stopped here; at last we'll get to see a traditional Polynesian or Melanesian village."

"I know how you feel," he agreed. "The San Blas Islands spoilt us for the South Pacific in some ways."

The village was set back from the shore and we were almost there before I realized.

"Oh no!" I exclaimed.

"What's wrong, Mummy?" asked Jamie worried.

"It's okay Jamie, I've just realized the whole village is made out of corrugated iron!"

Only the chief's house was made out of palm in the traditional way. Maintenance we learned was the issue. A palm frond roof requires intensive manual labour and only lasts three to five years, although those made of pandanus lasts ten to fifteen. Corrugated iron, of course, lasts an eternity but to us was so ugly in comparison, although great care had been taken to build Polynesian style, with curves in both walls and ceilings,

The chief was already at his bush garden but had left word that the kava ceremony would be at 4:00 PM.

Back on board it was a day of entertaining. The villagers were fascinated by our yacht and equipment, and soon two newly baked loaves, more chocolate cake and gallons of juice were consumed amidst much chatter and laughter. In turn they brought paw paw and coconuts; the water not too sweet, just perfect for drinking while the flesh was still soft for eating.

While we went to the chief's house for the kava ceremony the boys disappeared with the village children. We had heard a great deal about the tranquillizing kava, or yanggona, which numbs the tongue and lips and eventually the whole body. These ceremonies are the centre of formal life for Fijians, and many Tongans and Samoans as well.

We joined the circle round the central carved bowl and were sincerely welcomed in Fijian. Following tradition we explained the reason for our visit, (although in English) and then the kava could be pulped into powder, put into a cloth and squeezed out with water. Finally deemed ready it was given to the chief in a coconut husk to sample. As guests of honour Andy and I were next. We followed the chiefs example, one clap before taking the bowl and three claps after draining it and handing it back.

More men arrived, smartly dressed in sarongs and shirts, among them the minister and the school teacher with whom we could converse.

"Can you come and teach tomorrow at my school?" asked the teacher on hearing I taught our children.

"Of course," I replied. "What would you like me to teach?"

"If you could tell us about your travels, that would be marvellous and maybe you have some pictures."

"That's not a problem. I have a large wall map and the boys have a sheets of pictures they put together in the Cook Islands."

"If they could come to the school too, they could talk to some of my pupils in English. The children here really need to be able to speak English to do well in life."

"I'm sure the boys would love to come as they have met so many of the children already."

"I hate to ask, but do you have English books you no longer require?"

"Lots," Andy interjected, jumping at this unexpected chance to lighten the boat.

The rounds of kava continued. Up to this point we had known what to expect, but a predicament was developing for Andy that he wasn't quite sure how to deal with. It was particularly Andy's problem not mine: he was expected to imbibe on every round of kava, whereas I, being a woman, was not. He moved around restlessly as we sat on the ground, and finally muttered to me, "How do we tactfully leave, I'm bursting!"

A few minutes later a mass of children's laughing faces arrived at the door, ours amongst them. Andy leapt to his feet.

"We must take the children home, it is getting late!" he gasped. It was all of 6:30 PM. He still had to wait another half hour while the villagers escorted us back up the inlet to our dinghy!

We had learned a lesson: a gift of one bundle of kava root is quite enough.

"What did the kava taste like?" asked Duncan.

"Well," said Andy, "to be generous, it is rather like peppery tea, but it is awfully muddy."

"Why do they drink it then?"

"It's rather like us drinking wine and beer. They like the effect."

"Did you feel anything?" I asked. "I don't think I really did except my lips tingled a bit."

"No I didn't feel much either. They say if you have a lot it feels as though your body and legs aren't attached any longer and they go in opposite directions."

"How awkward!"

We had another full day with more entertaining on the boat, a visit to the outer reef,(where Jamie was ecstatic to find 'my very own Tiger Cowrie'), and teaching at the school.

The village woodcarver and his wife were especially hospitable, and the boys returned with them after several hours.

"Look what Seleli made us," called out Colin excitedly.

He held up a huge lobster carved out of wood while Duncan and Jamie proudly displayed their war clubs.

"Seleli took us out to choose the wood," Duncan told us, "then we helped him cut it down and he carved these for us back at his house."

Fiji had just suffered two military coups, due to the conflicts between the Fijians and Indians (who had been brought in originally to work the sugar plantations), and there were many rumours about the current situation in Suva. We had hoped to hear on the radio from those ahead of us, particularly *Endymion* or *Mustang*, but for some reason we had heard from no-one after they had made their landfalls. We had learned, however, that a curfew existed between 5:00 PM and 8:00 AM and that one should not arrive in the harbour between these hours. We furled the genoa to slow down.

We had done it again; after a 200 nautical mile trip taking almost two days we had arrived in Suva on the day of rest when no officials were working. It became a bonus day. We cleaned up the boat, completed more school and had several visitors, not quite legal, but they all stayed in their dinghies. We found the other boats had suffered radio troubles or had transmitted, but for some reason propagation was poor. No mystery after all and *Nimbus* and *Belair* were most relieved when we came up on the radio next morning, loud and clear.

It took one and a half days to clear in and by the time we left Fiji I calculated they had 38 official sheets on us for their filing system. We laughed; whereas the French left behind fashionable clothing and excellent cuisine in their colonies, a major British heritage is a preoccupation with paperwork.

Due to the coups the customs and immigration officials were being painfully thorough. The military also came on board. With huge guns, hobnailed boots and stern expressions we could tell this could be a lengthy visit.

"Have you any firearms on board?" was one of their first questions.

"No, we don't carry guns," Andy replied.

"Oh yes we do!," cried Jamie, jumping up and running to his cabin. The officials leapt to attention, grabbed their guns and looked at Andy angrily. Before anything could be said Jamie rushed out.

"Here you are." Proudly he held up his new, bright green plastic water pistol.

The Fijians love children and the three men laughed until tears rolled down their cheeks. There were no more official questions. Instead we had a long discussion about the current crisis, and the sad conflict of two races, who live side by side with such different aspirations and expectations in life.

Later the Navy visited *Bagheera*.

"Where have you come from?"

"From Vava'u in Tonga," Andy replied, "but we stopped at the Lau Islands for two days as we had engine problems."

"Where abouts?"

"In Ongea Levu. A man named Andy, who runs the radio there, took our details and passed them on to Suva we understand."

"I'm glad you told me."

No more was heard about our stop. Later, however, a yacht arrived who had left Raratonga on a northerly wind without clearance papers. He was not allowed to stay in Tonga but called in at the Lau Group. In Suva he claimed he had sailed straight from Raratonga. When the lie was uncovered he was severely reprimanded and told to leave immediately.

There were many boats at the Royal Suva Yacht Club. The boys joined the children while Andy and I quizzed other boaters about the best places to visit.

"We've just stayed here," was a frequent comment. "Quite honestly we are islanded out, they're so much the same and we like the company here."

What happened to the free spirit, the need to get away from the herd, the desire to escape city life? Although none of us were tired of the islands I could understand however. We personally like to alternate between socializing with the large groups that gather by the towns and having time to ourselves, or with just a few boats, in remote areas. With children we could never be bored, but I can imagine that life could be quite lonely in paradise for a couple.

The Perkin's agents informed us we needed a new rear seal on the engine.

"I'm sorry to say it's one of those things where the part costs peanuts but the labour to access and replace it is considerably more," we were told.

"No doubt a Friday afternoon assembly job," Andy moaned. "Anyway it has to be fixed."

Mustang and several other yachts were enjoying a stay at the

Tradewinds Hotel. As we could go stern-to the hotel's gardens, this seemed an ideal spot to stay while the engine was hauled away.

The hotel was actually closed and New Zealanders David and Jo Natzki were managing the renovation. Colin and their younger daughter Kate instantly became pals and soon Colin was taking her for a spin in the dinghy.

Duncan, as 'Captain of dinghies', soon brought this to our attention.

"I really don't think it's safe that Colin goes off like that," he told us.

"Oh why?" asked Andy, "I know he isn't as proficient as you, but he knows how to run the outboard and there's no wind."

"But," replied Duncan, "he doesn't even know how to change the spark plugs."

Duncan had learned how to do this two weeks before!

There was many a memorable party and another successful introduction of Hallowe'en. The children, with some local Fijians, took great trouble with their costumes. With many American boats, including *Onskan*, and *Belair*, they more than filled their bags.

The adults continued into the night with many a trick: we had songs from *Belair* and a bagpipe player, I sang a final rendering of our Ode to Bob and Betsy Baillie from Bermuda on *Belair* (not forgetting Barbara too), Dave rendered a poem about *Bagheera*, and Charles on American *Rhinoceros* turned an orange into a 'peach'—you can use your imaginations on that one, we did!

The engine was repaired and replaced efficiently. The life raft was serviced, not only very inexpensively but Andy was able to see it inflated and checked through everything himself including the bottle of carbon dioxide. He became friendly with the Indian owner of the shop and we were invited to meet his family.

"If only more people had been like me and married a Fijian," he told us, "there would be none of the problems today. Sadly mixed marriages are very uncommon."

We also purchased an electric anchor windlass, a bargain we couldn't resist. Due to the coups there had been several devaluations and the chandler anxious to sell up and leave the islands. Not only would it save Andy's back hauling up the anchor itself but would facilitate bringing the dinghy on deck, and the even more arduous task of grinding Andy up the mast.

Mbengga Island is famous for its firewalkers, we saw none but loved the people. We went ashore with our kava at Ndakuni village. Many children greeted us along the beach giving and helping us find shells—blood mouthed conchs, murex, large cowries and then a perfect Chambered Nautilus that had floated in over the reef.

The chief was in church. We stopped to listen to the last vibrant hymn then he came out to welcome us. To our surprise he invited us to lunch; it was Scottish Pilchards (fish) from a can and noodle soup.

'Hundreds' of children returned to the boat and enthusiastically helped me make a huge cake. It rose high above our largest roasting pan. When two local girls helped wash up they counted over 45 cups and glasses.

Then they took the cake ashore.

"I think the chief liked it better than the kava," Colin confided to me later. "He had FIVE HUGE pieces."

The next day the chief arrived at *Bagheera*.

"What good timing," I told him. "I'm just taking another cake out of the oven."

He sniffed the air. "Brownies?," he asked, "my favourite!"

The chief had served as a Scout for the Australian army during the second world war. He spoke good English, had a splendid sense of humour and was a great raconteur—especially with vivid, gory stories about his army days in Papua New Guinea. Today, other than bringing his wife and grandsons to see our boat, he had a particular request. Would we be able to take several of the ladies of the village down to the south end for their special gathering? We readily agreed. Mbengga, like many other Fijian communities, had given up sailing craft in favour of outboard engines. Since the coups, however, there had been little fuel available.

Andy rose early, an hour before they were due to arrive. Fortunately he happened to glance to the shore.

"Good God, they are coming already. Liza, Duncan, Colin, Jamie get up quickly."

Twenty-two ladies climbed aboard, with a beaming chief who was tickled pink when we offered him the helm. Soon the ladies started to sing. They were beautiful, mellow, religious songs, harmonized to perfection. It was pure magic.

"Do you think I will offend them if I ask if I can tape them?" I whispered to Andy.

"I'm sure they wouldn't mind."

I held up the tape recorder, they laughed and nodded.

Finally in a pause I asked if they sang other non-religious songs. The chiefs wife understood and her face lit up.

"War songs?"

"Wonderful," I nodded and she vibrantly led us into battle.

Back at the Tradewinds we had just one more day with *Belair*. Having talked almost every day across the entire Pacific, and shared many experiences, this was the end of our cruising together. They would soon be heading to New Zealand whilst we were going to New Caledonia and on to Australia.

It was a day of shopping, organizing and visiting—with drinks on one boat, dinner on the next and a movie on another. Meanwhile the children were off doing their own rounds. We had a final breakfast party on board *Bagheera* before sadly leaving hospitable Fiji. We were delighted, however, that *Onskan*, *Velella*, and *Endymion* were all headed the same way.

New Caledonia was sighted at dawn on our sixth day out, 624 nautical miles later. We decided to drop our hook at Port Boise, a stunning anchorage with high, brick-red hills and bright-green dense foliage at the water's edge. Walking ashore I commented on the numbers of plants.

"Yes, there seem more varieties of trees and shrubs in this small area than in the entire Marquesas," replied Andy.

The Yacht Club in Noumea provides good docks and facilities and we pulled in beside *Lady Meg*, a familiar Royal Vancouver Yacht Club boat. They were bursting with local knowledge. When we took the efficient 'transport en commune' into town we knew exactly what we wanted to visit. What we hadn't appreciated was just how beautiful the many flamboyant trees would be, now that they were in full red bloom.

Having spent so much time under the water we found the Noumea Aquarium very informative. With a constant flow of water from the ocean they were able to have the tanks teeming with reef fish, sponges, gorgonians, sea snakes and coral. In one section the ultraviolet lighting produced glowing colours that could not normally be seen in the wild.

"Mummy have you seen the chambered nautilus?" asked Colin. "I'm sure there was one here when we came in."

"No I haven't, let's ask the attendant."

There was just one chambered nautilus and when the attendant gently pushed him to the front, he furiously started puffing himself back into the corner. Colin was thrilled to have seen him in action.

"You see lots of pictures of nautilus' and we have the shells, but I just couldn't think of them alive." Colin explained.

The New Caledonia Museum had displays of round, high-roofed huts, canoes and fishing methods, as well as carvings, masks and lapita pottery. There was much to interest the boys, but unfortunately the labels we were beyond our French.

After testing the huts out in the museum, Jamie was thrilled that we rented a car and drove across the southern end of the island to Yate, to sleep in similar huts ourselves.

About 145,000 people live in New Caledonia of which about 43% are Melanesian, 38% European and 12% Polynesian. The island has been inhabited for over three thousand years; the locals are called Kanaks. Recently, during the 1969-73 nickel boom, both the European and Polynesian populations dramatically increased. But, whereas the French, many of whom were on inflated French government salaries, were extremely affluent, the Kanaks, particularly on the north-east coast of Grande Terre, lived in poverty. Inevitably there were conflicts, with some violent incidents in the years before we arrived. There was a heavy military presence everywhere and travel in the north was restricted. A referendum, regarding New Caledonia's independence from France was imminent.

As we pulled into the dock in town to clear out with Customs and Immigration, the crew from *Endymion* took our lines. They had stopped at the Ile des Pins on their way and couldn't have been more positive. We had discussed a visit but Andy had not particularly wanted to beat into wind for a couple of days, in an area where navigation was tricky.

"Andy you have to go, it's as beautiful as Bora Bora," persuaded Denise.

That clinched it. With a strong sea breeze and the build up of short, sharp waves we stopped early at Ile Quere, en route, remembered only because poor Duncan was attacked by a swarm of bees.

We left at 5:00 the following morning in broad daylight, an indication we were now in higher latitudes. We hoped for and found a light breeze. By the time the wind had filled in, it had clocked round to the north, and we were able to sail our desired course.

In mid-afternoon *Bagheera* arrived at huge Kuto Bay. Bordered by brilliant white sands that were icing sugar fine, it was hard to keep the boys off the beach to complete school. Denise was right, it was another paradise, with the palm trees blending with the pines and a profusion of flowers.

The atmosphere ashore was superbly relaxing, except when the odd car or motorbike roared by with mufflers discarded. We explored an abandoned church then piled into the old ruined cells of the prison.

"They're so small," I commented. "How uncomfortable and very claustrophobic they must have been."

"Especially in the windless, sultry, humid seasons," added Andy.

It was a relief to get back to the wide sweeping bay, with its refreshing breeze and far horizon.

We had talked to *Onskan* on the radio. Our enthusiasm had persuaded them to come and join us, but they only had small scale charts. We talked them in, then Andy roared off in the dinghy to help them navigate through the last wriggle through the reef. We visited for drinks and they came to dinner on *Bagheera* to eat a huge grouper found by Duncan. South Pacific style we were all in pereus: cool, colourful lengths of material that even the boys like to wear, wrapped in a variety of ways.

We awoke next morning to rain and squalls. The forecast was for south-westerly winds and we decided that Kanumera Bay, around the corner, would be more sheltered. A huge black cloud was approaching from the south but we decided to 'go for it'. What a wonderful shower. And then, as so often happens, it passed far too quickly and we were left well lathered in shampoo but with no water to rinse. This time we didn't have to wait long, it was soon pouring with rain again.

Kanumera was another lovely bay, smaller in size but with an attractive craggy rock joined by a sandspit to the shore. We were to remember it well as that night, while aboard *Onskan* for a octopus and grouper dinner, the anchor chain started jerking. Another huge storm was approaching.

We rushed back to *Bagheera* to prepare for the onslaught, and it BLEW, pushing 50 knots in several of the gusts. Ahead another Beneteau 38 started to drag; that craggy rock was directly astern. The wind had changed so we were now on a lee shore and the anchorage felt worryingly confined.

We had just donned our oilskins when the rain came teeming down, reducing visibility to zero. I couldn't believe how cold it was; within minutes I was shaking violently, my teeth chattering. As a precaution Andy started the engine, it would take some of the strain off the anchor in the strongest gusts and would be prepared for action if our anchor didn't hold. We did not have far to drag before we would be up on the rocks.

An hour later, as quickly as it had come, the storm had gone. The wind swung back, the seas became calm and the stars appeared.

All was well, but it was a vivid reminder that we were running on overtime. The cyclone season can start at the end of October and although no weather reports had been worrying us yet, we felt it was time to head out of the tropics and complete the 900 nautical miles south to Australia.

Australia

Duncan with his latest catch, a tuna

21. Australian Landfall

Coffs Harbour, New South Wales—Hobart, Tasmania

Since Tonga we had been listening to Keri Keri radio on a regular basis, broadcast from close by Opua in New Zealand. John and Marlene run a volunteer, informative, personal service, geared primarily for yachts on their way to New Zealand for the cyclone season. They give an excellent weather forecast, at a speed which can be written down, and check in with vessels morning and/or evening.

There are a few others around the world who devote their time like this to yachtsmen. How grateful we are to them for their dedication, enthusiasm and helpfulness with any issue, whether big or small. They all intuitively know that an ordinarily minor concern can be a major problem for a small vessel.

As we headed south-west to Australia, we were frustrated to be moving out of radio range. It was harder to receive Keri-Keri and as they couldn't hear our transmission we had to contact another yacht to relay our information. We had already started listening to an Australian service, Penta Comstat, run by Derek and Janine, who relay the local forecast regarding the unpredictable weather systems along the Australian east coast. Even if the meteorologists weren't quite correct, at least, we felt, we had a fighting chance of being in the right place at the right time. It was also comforting to know that someone on the shore knew our position and would be concerned if we stopped checking in without prior notice.

Bagheera made good progress until a day out when the wind died completely. Although the ocean swells played havoc with our sea legs, we again noticed sea life that is usually hidden. In the Atlantic it had been a pod of whales. On this occasion the boys saw tiny swimming crabs, lively arthropods, jelly fish and blue sea snails.

"What are those feathery things?" asked Jamie.

"Can I get the net out?" Duncan asked.

He soon had the net unlashed and had several curious multi- fingered organisms to view in the bucket.

"They are glaucous nudibranchs," said Colin bringing up his new underwater guide from Noumea. "Aren't they strange?"

"And look they are feeding on the Portuguese-man-o'-war jelly fish," added Andy.

Then a school of false killer whales came by to check us out; it all seemed so peaceful until Penta Comstat told us that a cold front was approaching.

"Gale force winds," said Janine, "Nor'west to forty gusting fifty ahead of a front associated with a deep depression crossing the Tasman Sea."

"Oh hell!" moaned Andy. "We had better reduce sail."

We changed down to our number three small jib and put a third reef in the mainsail. The winds were north-westerly so we altered course to go with them, soon furling the genoa with a steady 30 knots and gusts up to 50, then 60 knots.

"It's unbelievable," I yelled down to Andy who was at the chart table plotting our position, "the wind is blowing the tops off the waves, it sounds just like machine gun bullets on the mainsail and it really stings one's face."

"Are you okay?"

"Fine, but it's really cold and wet, I hope it doesn't get up any more."

This front had caused a lot of damage to some Australian coastal communities and it continued to be vicious. Then the lightning started. The flashes were constant and one continued right into the boat, snaking violently around on the cockpit floor. I let out a piercing scream. Andy rushed up the companionway, one leg in and one out of his oilskins, just as I realized it was the flashlight that had fallen down as the boat lurched in the squall and turned itself on!

The winds eased a little but it was a wild night with confused seas, and both Andy and I were up most of the time. Lulled by the calm we had both foregone our habitual daytime sleep, in favour of a gleaming vessel for our imminent arrival. We both regretted it, feeling weary and taking turns at the now unfamiliar task of steering at sea.

Next morning all was calm with a steady 15 knots, blue skies and a rising barometer. It's Sod's Law that these situations always occur at night. Duncan offered to stay on watch so we could both sleep. This was unusual practice, as generally one of us was awake when the children were on watch, but by this time Duncan had earned our respect as a responsible seaman. After ensuring he was in his life-harness and clipped on, Andy and I gratefully climbed into our berth. He didn't disturb us for five hours.

The wind died completely as *Bagheera* approached Coffs Harbour, New South Wales, giving perfect conditions for our Australian landfall. Our anchor was down at ten minutes past midnight on November 22nd but we had done it again—it was Sunday, of course!

In fact it made no difference. We were invited into the dock mid-morning and the officials were extremely pleasant. Australia has strict immigration and health laws, allowing little fresh or even canned food (in particular meat) into their country. Knowing the rules I had these supplies down to a minimum, just a couple of cans of ham and half a dozen eggs.

"No worries," said Eric, "just show me the empty tins and the shells tomorrow."

We had to say goodbye to Fred, our philodendron, a plant we had nursed from Portugal. And then there was our current budgerigar, Malmseyboo.

When we were in Fiji the children had thoroughly researched the brochures in the Australian Consulate, whilst I was procuring our visas. They were very worried as the texts indicated in no uncertain terms, that foreign birds and animals could not be taken into Australia. Such was their concern and upset, that I had ended up talking to the head of the Australian Wildlife Division in Canberra. After all a budgerigar was an Australian species, I ventured, and I obtained not only his absolute assurance that we could take in our pet, but that if anyone gave us trouble they should phone him personally.

With these words from the top I was confident, and it was enough for the officials in Coffs Harbour. They decreed they would seal the cage, and its door was duly covered with officialdom. The fact that we removed the bottom of the cage for cleaning was studiously ignored by both parties. Of course we had no intention of letting our budgie into the bush. After our previous disasters we always clipped its wings. We really loved our personal interaction with our pet, enjoying his many endearing habits—such as sitting on our shoulders, nibbling our ears and trying to chew the pages of our books—and able to tolerate the 'inevitable' ones!

We were informed we could move to the marina so asked Colin and Jamie to walk round and alert Wayne and Ginney on *Velella*, who had arrived a couple of days before. By the time *Bagheera* reached the berth there was a great welcoming party, but Colin and Jamie were already bottoms-up on the dock, fishing with other children.

Wayne and Ginney climbed aboard.

"Icy, cold, Foster beer. Fantastic!" I sang, as they handed me a package. "What's this magazine?"

"It's the official 'Tall Ships' publication," Wayne replied. "And guess what? You are in it too, a picture and a write-up."

"I don't believe it!"

Little did we realize how many people were to read this issue and subsequently recognize us as we travelled down the coast.

Aussie John Gardner, on *Time*, came over with many helpful suggestions, including telling us there was an open Sunday market on up the road.

"Obviously all your food has been taken," he said, "no banks are open today so why don't I lend you a hundred dollars?"

"That's very kind of you," I replied, "but are you sure, fifty would be fine."

"No take a hundred. You might not get to the bank tomorrow and it will tide you over. Why doesn't Duncan come over with me now?" It was our first taste of Australian spontaneous helpfulness and generosity which we were to experience frequently over the next twenty months.

On Monday morning Eric from Customs arrived to take us to town. On the way back with our groceries he drove us up through the Eucalyptus trees and banana plantations to the local lookout. As we were surveying the coast and the town a loud hiss moved up the hillside, and when almost unbearable, it faded away again. They were the loudest cicadas we have ever heard.

We had our first introduction to the extreme Australian climate as we came out of the laundromat one day.

"Don't worry," I said to the boys as we struggled with the heavy bags, "It's just the air from the outlet for the dryers."

A few minutes later Jamie asked "Is this still the heat from the dryers?"

We had almost expired by the time we reached the boat from the heat and parching wind.

In contrast, on other days, there were cool refreshing walks down the dock and up onto blustery Muttonbird Island where the Shearwaters, or Muttonbirds, gathered to nest.

Two days later *Endymion* pulled in beside us and then *Onskan* arrived, having made her landfall in Brisbane. The local fishermen introduced us all to 'bugs', delicious crustaceans that looked like long armed crabs or short tailed lobsters, and gave us huge volutes, known as bailer shells.

The boys took the bus to town and for the first time did their Christmas shopping alone. It was very successful and they showed a creative use of their limited funds.

Meanwhile I worked on our Christmas mailing list, this year opting for a shorter newsletter but sending a photo. Taken of the family snorkelling by a tiny island of palms in the San Blas Islands, it symbolized our last twelve months. It was also perfect for the cover of *Just Cruising*!

One day a Tasmanian, Judy from *Mystery* came over.

"I wanted to warn you about the sun in Australia, as you have such fair-haired children," she said.

"I really appreciate that. As we have been in the tropics for a while they are used to using sun-block daily."

"It's just because you have been in the tropics that I wanted to warn you. The sun in Australia is twice as bad, and it gets worse as you go south. It's because there's a hole in the ozone layer here."

Only once did the children get burned. Colin was swimming for an hour after lunch, and that night to my horror blisters appeared on his shoulders.

As we waved goodbye to Coffs, Judy's husband, Noel, called out, "We'll be there to greet you as you arrive in Kettering in Tasi."

After a brief call into Port Stephens, close to Newcastle, we moved to Pittwater, just north of Sydney. Leisa, from *Mustang* had grown up in this area, and assured the children that they would like going to school here.

We stopped for the night in the Basin, a yachtsman's haven with white sands, picturesque pines mixed with palms, and parkland for a game of soccer. Behind lies a beautiful lagoon for swimming, with a shark's net across the entrance for one's peace of mind. To add to the setting are tame kookaburras, with their maniacal laughter, multi-coloured lorikeets, an amazing two metre long goanna (lizard) and on one occasion we saw a superb lyrebird with its striped tail, fascinating for its ability to mimic. It was to become a favourite of ours, a perfect 'Australian' day-trip for our visitors.

School was just out when I went to the grocery store the next afternoon and I was able to talk to several mothers and their children. Their reports were unanimous, Newport Primary was small and personal. It sounded just right for the boys.

It was confirmed the next morning when an older couple gave us a ride.

"Our children went to Newport. It's a wonderful school, you'll love it," they told the boys.

The principal was welcoming and agreed to take Colin and Jamie for the start of the school year in February, after the Tall Ships events. He felt Duncan should be starting at the High School.

"I must tell you though," he said as we were leaving. "If you move out of area, the children will no longer be eligible to attend."

"Out of area?"

"Yes, the borders are by the streets . . ." He looked up smiling with sudden realization.

I was smiling too.

"Never mind, just don't go sailing too far away!" he concluded. When I took Duncan up to Pittwater High School for an interview they wanted him to stay for an entrance exam. I knew a southerly buster, a bad weather system, was due. Andy wanted to leave as soon as possible, but school had to be organized. It was a quick test I was assured.

Duncan came out grinning.

"It wasn't hard at all and I finished it easily."

I was relieved, Duncan had been out of regular school for over two years.

We rushed back to the boat to find Andy relaxed.

"It's okay the front has slowed down. There should be plenty of time to make Sydney today with following northerly winds," he told us.

There was a definite line across the sky, brilliant blue to dark grey, marking the advance of the front. When it hit, with dramatic change in winds, *Bagheera* had already passed through the heads and entered huge Port Jackson. The boys were entranced. We had spoken little of Sydney to them but Colin called back,

"Look, there's the Opera House. It's so beautiful!"

"And the bridge is like the Lions Gate bridge in Vancouver," added Duncan.

Andy has been a member of the Royal Naval Sailing Association since his Navy days, and John, from *Time*, had arranged that we could tie up at the Australian Naval Association dock. Regular moorage was expensive. It was a convenient location in Rushcutters Bay and close to the Cruising Yacht Club, where all the Sydney-Hobart stripped-out racing machines were gathered. We felt so removed from the racing scene now, enjoying our creature comforts far too much.

One of Andy's concerns had been appropriate dress for some of the functions during the Tall Ships events, dinner with the Governor for example, as we didn't exactly carry a formal wardrobe on the boat. I had already phoned the Canadian Consulate and arranged an appointment to pick up some Canadiana to give out at the events, flags, pins etc., so at the same time Andy posed his questions.

The clerk went off to find out and came back looking flustered, the Consul General himself would like to see us. We liked Bob Birchell immediately and were amused when he stripped off his jacket to see if he and Andy were the same size. He also enquired as to our Christmas plans, and to our surprise we ended up at an extremely elegant, very entertaining Christmas dinner for nineteen at their lovely home. It not only overlooked the harbour, but also had a lighthouse in the garden. Jamie's memento from the evening is one of his favourites—a 'woopee' or 'poo poo' cushion which you place strategically before other guests sit down. Jamie and the visiting Canadian Ambassador for Pakistan mutually enjoyed the result!

The plan was to head for Tasmania on Boxing day, but we felt far too lazy. Instead Wayne and Ginney persuaded us to watch the start of the Sydney-Hobart race and it was a fantastic sight; the yachts gleaming in the brilliant sun as they beat out of the harbour. They were bordered by the wash of hundreds of spectator craft. Next morning it was our turn to head south, in lumpy seas and with hints of a hangover—not a commendable combination.

We arrived in Hobart on January 8th, 1988 after a staggered voyage down from Sydney. The weather along this eastern Australian coast is very changeable and was especially unpredictable this year (El Niño?). The prevailing winds are supposed to be north-easterlies and to be sure, they do occur (usually it seems when one has to go north!), but the frontal systems, known as Southerly Changes or Busters, come through with monotonous regularity, approximately once a week, when winds change from maybe NE 20 to SE 20/30/40 in minutes. After the front, one is left with an extraordinarily lumpy sea with a top wave often in conflict with

Jamie found a wombat

the swell, in fact both are noted in weather forecasts. Altogether it is most uncomfortable for the trade-wind sailor and we all retire to port whenever possible, ahead of these systems.

Eden was a place where several of us gathered. We were waiting for a favourable weather picture for crossing the infamous Bass Strait. We brought in the New Year on *Emily Jane* with Jack and Janine. Jack was convinced he would fall asleep—so we celebrated the Tongan New Year, then the Fijian, and easily saw in the Australian!

The next morning the boys were playing on the dock when a couple came over.

"We're Keith and Audrey Perry," Keith told us.

"We thought we recognised the boys," said Audrey, "and then we saw *Bagheera*. We were with you in Amorgos in Greece. We had chartered a boat."

"What memories you have!" I replied. "Why don't you come on board?" It was the beginning of a firm friendship.

We completed the first half of the 180 nautical mile trip to Tasmania in a flat calm and enjoyed the antics of the tiny, noisy fairy penguins at

Gabo Island. For the other half there was a full gale 'on the nose'. It was bitterly cold and I had to put on my thick padded suit, my 'duvet suit' as the boys call it, and heavy wet weather gear to stay warm. The shallow strait is notorious for its dangerous seas which quickly build up, and we had an uncomfortable trip until in the islands fringing the northeast coast of Tasmania gave us some shelter.

Soon we were admiring the spectacular rocky east Tasmanian coastline, topographically far closer to the South Island of New Zealand than the Australian mainland.

"Yes," it was subsequently stated with pride, "just as different as us Tasi characters." In fact they referred to the Australian mainland as 'The North Island'!

After a magical visit to the emerald waters of Wineglass Bay, watching the wallabies on the beach and tasting melt-in-your-mouth abalone given to us by local fishermen, we cruised down to Maria Island. Here we dug for clams, enjoying the change in fare from the tropical to the temperate.

Duncan dropped our coins into a bucket that was extended out on a pole by the attendant in the Denison Canal. As we motored away in a flat calm we saw the boats in front suddenly heeled over on their sides.

"There's an unbelievable wind ahead," said Andy looking through the binoculars. "Quickly, we must get a couple of reefs in the main."

He went forward and we had just enough time to finish the reefs, furl the genoa and complete a quick stow below, before we were hit. In contrast to the calm and cold of the previous days, this was a hot full gale. Temperatures were a wilting 42 degree celsius accompanied by gusts of wind up to 50 knots that left us choking and gasping.

"Can you get some damp towels?" called Andy to the boys. "We need them to breathe."

As we sailed across to Kettering, Eucalyptus forests went up in flames and the fires leapt over the inlets. *Bagheera* was in the middle of a two kilometre wide channel when the heat became intense.

"Quickly," urged Andy, "let's douse the sails, a spark could easily burn them."

It was still blowing hard when we arrived. The mooring buoys were full. We were wondering where to go when a voice boomed out,

"I told you we would be here to greet you!"

Our friends from Coffs harbour were right behind us.

22. The Australian Bicentennial Celebrations

With the Tall Ships in Hobart and Sydney

How was *Bagheera*, a 40 footer, a 'Tall Ship', you might ask. Interestingly the term 'Tall Ship' is quite loosely defined; you need not be large, nor be a square rigger. Firstly, 50% of the crew must be trainees, aged 16-25 years. Secondly, the yacht must have a minimum waterline length of 30 feet and, thirdly, she must be single hulled. Therefore, with a waterline length of 33 feet, we were eligible— a very small 'Tall Ship', but able to give the Canadian flag a showing.

The first Tall Ships Race, which was from Torbay in England to Lisbon in Portugal, dates back to 1956 and was the creation of Dennis Morgan. His idea was to organize a gathering of the last remaining Tall Ships to give young people of many nations an experience of deepwater sailing, sail training, seamanship, character building and competing in friendly rivalry. Traditionally, the host city provides entertainment, and the crew takes part in parades on the water, and through the city streets to show their appreciation for the hospitality.

Most of the gatherings have been in Europe or North America, so this Tall Ships' celebration, the first in the Southern hemisphere and requiring a huge commitment in time and mileage, was unique.

The Australian Tall Ships Committee stated: "It therefore behooves us all in Australia to provide additional services and hospitality to the vessels."

They certainly excelled, with an ambitious programme of celebrations starting in Perth, and continuing on to Adelaide, Melbourne, Hobart and Sydney. A feeder from Brisbane to Hobart was also included. At each port the numbers grew, with officially 69 vessels in Melbourne, 134 in Hobart and 190 in Sydney, representing 20 countries—Andorra, Canada, Cayman Islands, Ecuador, West Germany, France, India, Ireland, Italy, Japan, Netherlands, New Zealand, Oman, Poland, Russia, Spain, Switzerland, United Kingdom, United States and Uruguay.

We sailed to Constitution Dock in Hobart, Tasmania's capital city, with the Tall Ships, other participants, and Sydney/Hobart racers who had decided to stay down for the celebrations.

There was already a festive air.

"Can we put our flags up like everyone else?" the boys immediately asked.

"Of course, we must," replied Andy. "We have signal flags which should be tied together. Who's going to volunteer to check the knots?" he asked.

"We will," cried Colin and Duncan simultaneously.

"I'll help them too, if you like," said Lisa who, after touring New Zealand and Australia after leaving us in French Polynesia, had come down to Tasmania to meet us.

"Great," said Andy. "We also have the flags of the countries we have visited. There must be over thirty by now."

"And what about our 'Battle Flag' Mummy?" reminded Duncan.

I had spent most of Christmas Eve making this flag on a friend's sewing machine. Bob Birchell had given us a huge Canadian flag that was too big for an ensign, but I was able to use the material for a new Canadian style 'battle flag', with our logo of the black head, red slit eyes and paws of a cat (a symbolic panther after our boat's namesake *Bagheera*) in place of the Canadian maple leaf.

"Let's put it up on the spinnaker halyard and fly it at the forestay with these big green and yellow Tall Ships flags," I suggested.

"It's so exciting, Mummy," exclaimed Jamie, "but how can I get ashore?"

We were bow-to the dock and with our overhanging pulpit and the distance from the dock Jamie's small legs just couldn't bridge the gap.

"Don't worry I'll come and pull in the bow line for you," I said. "But let's get the flags up first."

Excitement was audibly rising at the spectacular sight of the Tall Ships arriving to dock. It's not hard to understand the charisma of these occasions with ships such as the Polish 354 foot, *Dar Mlodziezy*, built in 1981. Magnificent with her three masted square rig, she was funded through public subscription by the young people of Poland. Her name means the 'gift of youth'. The American 295 foot, three masted barque *Eagle*, was built in Germany in 1936. Her 175 cadets handle more than 20,000 square feet of sail and 20 miles of rigging.

The longest of the Tall Ships was *Juan Sebastian de Elcano*, built in Cadiz for the Royal Spanish Navy in 1927. A 371-foot, four masted sailing ship, square rigged on the foremast, she carried 83 cadets and 245 crew. Tied tallest with *Dar Mlodziezy*, was the four masted Japanese *Nippon Maru*, with a mast height of 162 feet above the waterline. Built in 1984 she is one of the most technologically advanced sailing ships in the world.

Other newer Tall Ships included the *Spirit of New Zealand*, just launched in 1986 and Britain's Bicentennial gift to Australia, the 145 foot, two masted brigantine *Young Endeavour*. She became a particular favourite of ours after Lisa won a bottle of wine at *Young Endeavour's* 6:00 AM run. Not only were we given an excellent breakfast after the run but we became well acquainted with the crew; thereafter the children frequently had the run of the ship, and their TV!

The rest of us were not quite as large but were all treated grandly. Poland had the strongest representation. Several yachts, such as *Aztec Lady*, *Adventure*, *Sabre*, and *Sir Thomas Sopwith*, represented Britain. *Galateia* was Swiss, *Abel Tasman* came from Holland, and there were several yachts from New Zealand and the United States, including our friends, Skip and Denise on *Endymion*. There was, of course, a fine Australian participation and to our surprise only *Bagheera* to represent Canada.

An attractive city, Hobart has a compact centre and sprawling suburbs up the slopes of Mount Wellington and along the Derwent Estuary. It is a city of rainbows which dance on the harbour with the hills behind, quite the photographer's challenge. It boasts Australia's oldest theatre and many old stone buildings. Its first suburb, Battery Point, is particularly attractive with tiny cottages competing in the narrow streets with Victorian terraces and Georgian mansions. It is also a city of 'English' gardens, with roses and rock plants, dahlias and hollyhocks. On the wharves are freighters of many nationalities, icebreakers gearing up for the Antarctic and deep sea trawlers delivering their catches.

Interested residents frequently stopped us on the street. One girl approached us in the supermarket. She just had to talk to a participant, as 'her' ship wasn't arriving for two days. She was but one of a bevy of enthusiastic, hardworking, welcoming liaison officers.

All the vessels had an assigned liaison officer. Ours was John Hartley and he, his wife Olwen, and daughter Kate, could not have been more hospitable.

"Where are you from originally?" Andy asked John, who had an obvious British accent.

"From the west country, in England," was the reply.

We subsequently discovered that his children and I had been born in the same nursing home! Another of the several coincidences that happened in our travels.

It was the liaison officer's job to see that those on their 'ship' arrived at the various functions on time, with the correct invitation, and suitably attired. No mean task as captains, crews, trainees and children disappeared in different directions each day. We were given a tour of the city by car and then a barbecue at the Hartley's home in Kingston, South Hobart. After two and a half years on the boat it was special for us to stretch out comfortably in a home with china, crystal and silver. With a dog for the children, the setting was complete.

It was our last day of relaxation for a while.

At 7:45 AM the next morning John and Kate arrived with our marching orders for the day.

They were earlier than we had expected and I was stranded in the head. I draped myself in a large towel and marched out. As John looked aghast I teased,

"Welcome to boat life. Sorry you caught me without clothes!"

After the relaxed life on tropical passages, it was a change to have to be dressed at all times, and respectably too!

What amazing hospitality we received. We were entertained by the Premier and Lord Mayor, and dined at the Governor's. Our trainees, Lisa and Mike, also from Vancouver, rushed off to 'Municipality Days of Hospitality', tours and entertainment every evening.

As per tradition, crews paraded en masse through the city, grouped behind brass bands, marching in time, and encouraged by the crowds. The city was throbbing, but the biggest cheer was for Andy. He had been delayed at the skipper's briefing, trying to establish our eligibility for the Tall Ships race, and was jogging to catch up to us.

"Just around the next corner," the crowds encouraged him on.

The Hobart Parade of Sail, and Tall Ships Race, were the next day. It was only when we had completed the entry form that the organizers had questioned the presence of our children aboard *Bagheera* during the race. There was, they told us, a minimum age limit of 16 years. So under the race instructions we applied for dispensation; we reasoned they were part of the boat, like the stove, the head and the budgerigar. As well, the children weren't exactly novices, having some 25,000 nautical miles under their belt by this time.

We were disappointed by the committee's negative decision, although realistically when comparing our laden vessel to the other Class C boats some of which were the stripped out Sydney/Hobart Race fleet, there was no chance of us being competitive. In fact, there were some distinct advantages. We could use the autohelm and motorsail if required. As well, we would be able to grab a good sleep the first night, by going back out through the canal thus cutting the corner, while the rest of the fleet were drifting in sloppy seas.

Parading out of Hobart, with the fleet, the boys chatted about our many new comrades and we waved out goodbyes to *HMAS Hobart*. On the bow the Premier recognized us and waved back exuberantly, calling bon voyage messages until well out of earshot. As we sailed eastwards towards the Denison Canal, I had a surge of sadness and regret that we could not have spent more time in this hospitable, dramatic, State of Tasmania.

The trip back to Sydney, logging 730 nautical miles, was varied. On the east Tasmanian coast we had dense fog and once again talked about radar. Alas, there was no point showing our trainees the delights of Wineglass Bay. After the fog had lifted it was flat calm, then suddenly the wind filled in and before long it was 40 knots from ahead. It was to be a beat again in gale force winds across Bass Strait.

Not long afterwards there was a Mayday call on the radio. *Evergreen*, one of the race participants, was taking on water. Andy responded to the call. We turned around and started heading back to their reported position.

"Do you think they were hit by a whale, Daddy?" Duncan asked.

"There are no confirmed reports of whales attacking boats that I know of," Andy replied, "except for whalers who have harpooned one, understandably provoking it. There have been stories of yachtsmen claiming such an attack but they are usually treated with scepticism by experts. However, whales do bask and sleep and a boat can run into them. Sadly, they are usually damaged far more than the boat. Often it is a container or other debris people hit, not whales, but a 'whale attack' story sounds much more exciting."

Young Endeavour and *Bagheera* sailing out of Hobart, Tasmania

We kept in radio contact with *Evergreen* for the next hour, then the Coastguard helicopter had them in sight. She subsequently was able to make it to port. One and a half years later Andy met one of the owners in the northern bauxite town of Gove. *Evergreen* had just been lost on a reef on the north coast during the Round Australia Race.

"Back to beating again," said Andy as *Bagheera* was put back on course for Sydney.

"I must say it was very pleasant going back down wind!" I replied.

"Actually the wind is backing," said Andy. "I think we'll be able to ease sheets soon."

Rapidly the wind clocked around to the west, and it was a fast reach with the wind on the beam instead. After one day of perfect conditions with the spinnaker flying, the wind became lighter; finally it was engine time.

Our last day was spent motoring into a strong north-easterly and we arrived at the famous Sydney Heads at 6:30 PM on January 19th. The distinctive Sydney Opera House came into view, impressing us yet again, then we moved into Darling Harbour to take our place with the rest of the Tall Ships fleet.

This time we were ready for the routine of events but unprepared for the thousands of visitors, all wanting a ship's stamp and autograph, particularly beside our picture in the official Tall Ships Publication.

"Have your books open at page 37," Jamie, with his wide freckled smile, would call out down the line.

In Hobart I was surprised when I had been asked for my autograph. In Sydney we signed our lives away, often fourteen hours a day, and we could not have survived without the children and a barrage of supportive friends from all around the world. In particular our Australian/Canadian friend Mary Light held the fort. Mary was in her element, had most of our travels down pat and was great at 'ad libbing' when she didn't. After a full day 'on duty' and playing with the children she would have a half hour 'power snooze' then come out of her cabin looking radiant, posing the question,

"And where is the party tonight?!"

How wonderful it will be if we all have her energy and 'joie de vivre' when we too are well past our three score and ten.

Again there was a wealth of entertainment both on the Tall Ships themselves, and at some spectacular settings ashore. We were impressed by the detailed decor of the Sydney Town Hall, and the Governor General's residence, with its immaculate gardens overlooking the harbour. It was here I introduced the Russian Ambassador to the Russian Captain, who was our neighbour on the dock. On our other side were our American friends on *Endymion*.

"Yes," quipped the Canadian Consul General, "Canada does it again, keeping you two countries apart!"

Meanwhile our trainees were given free 'plane tickets for hospitality visits around New South Wales, so they and the children went on tours, visiting a koala park, a surfing competition at Manly Beach and a day trip 4-wheel drive in the 'outback'.

On January 25th, the crews paraded through the streets of Sydney, stopped to watch Prince Charles and Lady Di flash by, then marched on into the Sydney Opera House, past all the ladies dressed in traditional clothing, for the Tall Ships' prizegiving. A ceremony of camaraderie, the sight of captains, crews and trainees waving vessel banners, national flags and battle flags, and all singing in full voice, will never be forgotten by those present.

As we rushed back to do more autographing and answer more questions, Duncan and his friends watched the official handover ceremonies of the *Young Endeavour*. It was a proud but traumatic occasion for this young British and Australian crew who had shared so many special times.

"We feel at a loss," Hilary, an English watch captain who had been so

Juan Sebastian de Elcano—the Spanish Tall Ship

good to the boys, told us. "We've all been together for months, now we have only two days left aboard."

Finally it was the big day, the Bicentenary of the arrival of Captain Arthur Philip and the First Fleet in Sydney. The Tall Ships left the dock in Darling Harbour and from pre-allocated positions watched the 'Re-enactment' vessels of the First Fleet, that had sailed from England, make their grand but somewhat poignant entrance through The Heads.

Then it was time, at about 4:30 PM, for the massive Tall Ships Parade of Sail. All carefully orchestrated, we had been given our exact positions, stationed behind the official representatives. There were seventeen units

in all, led by *Young Endeavour*. We were in Unit 2 with several of the
other overseas visitors but as we progressed under the Sydney Harbour
Bridge the expected channel free of spectator boats did not exist; there
were simply too many of them. There were moments of chaos but by
hook and by crook we all made it past Prince Charles and Lady Di,
although even the *Nippon Maru* had to back down twice to avoid
collisions with over eager watchers.

Despite the difficulties, the Parade of Sail was a magnificent sight and
Jackson Harbour, huge as it is, seemed hardly large enough to take the
tens of thousands of spectator craft. It was reported to be the largest
number of vessels ever assembled in one spot.

The day was also special because of our guests. We had Mary Light,
Bob and Betsy Baillie from *Belair* who had flown to join us from New
Zealand and Kate, our Tasmanian liaison officers daughter. Wayne and
Ginney, our South Pacific mates on *Velella* with whom we hoped to sail
in tandem to the Seychelles joined us as well with Lisa, our trainee and
crew from Panama to Tahiti. Amazingly, also on board was Joan Newman, the lady from Melbourne who had not only encouraged us but who
had organised our invitation for the participation in these Bicentennial
celebrations. That was back in Turkey, two thirds of the way around the
world, coming the 'long' way as we had done.

"How right you were," I told her. "The celebrations have been
enormous fun. What a way to enter Australia!"

How we will treasure all our mementos from the Tall Ships events in
Hobart and Sydney: books, shirts, medallions and our Tall Ships plaque.
Most of all, however, we will treasure memories of the great Australian
hospitality and the terrific comradeship from other Tall Ships captains,
crews and trainees.

"What an anticlimax it will be when it's all over," was a frequent
comment.

I have to admit that life came back to reality with a bang as I sped north
in a friend's car on January 27th to buy school uniforms. The children
were starting their new school in less than a week.

Epilogue

We lived at the south end of Pittwater, in 'The Puddle', some twenty nautical miles north of Sydney, for fourteen months. This southern arm of Broken Bay teems with boats and provides a cruising area far more comfortable than the open ocean. Around the shores the hills are rocky, steep and smothered with trees. With the wooden houses peeking through, it is reminiscent of British Columbia although on close scrutiny instead of conifers there are eucalyptus trees, or gums. Andy's gardener's fingers were soon itching. The climate is ideal for both tropical and temperate plants and all grow in profusion. At one time the hills are tinged with yellow wattle, then the jacarandas are in full violet bloom vying for vividness with the dense, cerise bougainvillaea.

A fifteen minute walk away is more of the famous Australian coastline, the sandy bays of the Baronjoey Peninsula, with great waves for surfing. It was the perfect spot to choose, "with plenty of yachts with winches," commented Andy grinning, as he planned to become 'The Winch Doctor'.

We took the boys to school by dinghy. Duncan went ashore near a trotter's training course and we often awoke to the sound of snorts as the horses took their morning exercise, several swimming or being towed behind a dinghy.

"Haven't you got that the wrong way round!?" called out Andy to a poor girl who was rowing hard with little progress.

"I wish!" she replied laughing.

The children all loved being back in regular school. Duncan was placed in a challenging Grade 7 class in Pittwater High School, on the basis of the entrance exam, and had a stimulating year. Being a typical 'groupy' he had a perfect Aussie twang inside three weeks. Colin was apprehensive, but had an encouraging teacher. On his second day he gave a thirty-five minute talk on the Galapagos Islands, fortunately we had bought a myriad of posters. He was subsequently voted class captain.

"It was the pins that were the clincher with the girls," confided his teacher, referring to the maple leaf pins left over from the Tall Ships events, which Colin had distributed at the end of his talk. Colin entered Year 4, again age appropriate. Although this in effect meant he went back a term, it further boosted his confidence and performance.

Jamie couldn't wait to go to school. We arrived only just in time for his first day, as the harbour police had stopped us for speeding in our dinghy! Kindergarten was a full day programme and reading the goal. Jamie loved it from the first minute, and spent hours at home spontaneously writing and boisterously singing an array of new songs.

In the next few months we became entrenched in suburban living again: the routine of school (great to have a uniform until the socks blew overboard and there were no spares), community soccer and baseball games (back to car pooling around the countryside), birthday parties (what are 'in' presents?), having to look respectable (learning how to wield an iron again), and a twelve year old who became fashionable (I have to have 'boardies' for swimming, Mummy). Hardest of all was having to become programmed, whether with the children, one's work or in one's social life. Somehow we coped!

You may recall that one of the perks of being a participant in the Tall Ships was a one year unrestricted working visa. Living a regular lifestyle was expensive and the kitty needed to be replenished. Andy operated as the Winch Doctor with some success, worked some boat shows for Beneteau, and became the painter for a couple of houses. I obtained a job with the Department of Health as a Psychologist, working with a community programme for disabled adolescents and young adults. It was an interesting new area for me and challenging being back in the work force again.

It was readjustment for us all but we loved our time in Australia and the boys were soon talking 'Strayan'—g'day, bonza ocker, g'd on yer, fair dinkum, no worries mate, and how yer going?

We also became land travellers in a borrowed campervan. Having missed Expo '86 in Vancouver it enabled us to visit Expo '88 in Brisbane. We camped at Lamington Park up in the hills, went on bushwalks and explored old aboriginal caves. Another trip was to Melbourne, and visiting Wilson's Promontory overlooking Bass Strait (very calm as we were on land!) and the temperate rain forest in the Tara valley on our way back through Canberra. We found the capital city spacious and gracious with its wide boulevards. Each suburb has a lake at its focal point with the Parliament buildings on a central knoll.

The boys threw some snowballs, their first since the Menorca. They saw duckbilled platypuses, 'talked' with kangaroos and their joeys, petted a wombat who was conveniently dawdling at the side of the road, and caught emus trying to steal a delicate morsel from the barbecue. We identified a varied collection of birds: monstrous pelicans, vibrantly coloured lorikeets, the magnificent (if somewhat noisy) sulphur crested cockatoos, pink and grey galahs, crimson rosellas. Although we all have seen parrots in captivity, they are twice as stunning in the wild.

All the while, however, we were planning our future travels. *Bagheera* had now completed over 26,000 nautical miles, more than all the way around the world at the equator; but by our route we were only two thirds of the way around—so of course she had to complete the circuit!

We had already planned to take part in the Darwin Ambon Yacht Race. It promised to be a fun event and made simple one's entry visa into Indonesia. A major decision was to extend our cruising for an extra year in the Indian Ocean, rather than hurrying to South Africa or to the Mediterranean in the usual five months. This meant acquiring and organizing several hundred charts, and writing many letters regarding visas and cruising regulations. We also added new equipment: a freezer section in the 'fridge, solar panels, radar, a weather fax, and had a new mainsail made by Dave Bonner, a fellow cruiser on *Windborn*.

On Easter weekend, March 1989, we were ready to leave. We bade farewell to many new and several old friends at our dockside party in 'The Puddle' before heading north. We all felt a vacuum. Pittwater had become home and we were used to the regular life of school and work. However, as we moved up the coast and met more longterm sailors, our spirits rose. Before long we were fully into the cruising mode and exhilarated by our imminent voyage to discover the mysteries of the

Indian Ocean—South-East Asia, Sri Lanka, India, The Maldives, Seychelles and Africa.

What a stimulating time it was. Without doubt we had some of our richest experiences in cultural diversity and scenic beauty; and it was certainly full of challenges.

You will hear about them all in **Still Cruising**.

Pre-Cruising Decisions Related to Cruising Experiences

Job, Finances, Home, Health, Family and Children, the Route, Skills Required, Anxieties and Concerns

Will we call our new boat *Bagheera*?" inquired an excited Duncan.

It was but one of a torrent of questions from both Duncan and Colin after we had shared with them our plan for the family to go cruising. "Where would we go, what kind of boat, what about school, would there be any other kids...?" followed in quick succession. Andy and I answered the questions as best we could, but there was no hesitation in our minds about the name.

"Well what do you think?" we answered.

"*Bagheera*, of course," they both cried out in unison.

It was our seventh yacht of the same name. *Bagheera* was the black panther in the Rudyard Kipling's Jungle Book. Not only were the stories our childhood favourites but we felt the sleek, fast *Bagheera* was symbolically perfect for our first racing yacht. It was also ideal for our new boat, a Beneteau First 38s.

A simpatico name is an important concern for your offshore vessel, as this becomes part of your identity. Whilst travelling only officials and banks will be interested in your usual surname. As far as the yachting community was concerned we were Andy and Liza Bagheera, the Bagheeras or the Bagheeras' parents. A name warrants careful selection. For example we once sailed on a boat in the Caribbean called *Golly Gee*. I am sure this name aptly expressed its new owners' sentiments about their recent purchase, but being referred to as the 'Golly Gees' wouldn't have been our choice!

The ability to adapt to a very different lifestyle is fundamental to the decision of going cruising longterm. The fact that increasing numbers are heading off on the high seas is inspiring and stimulating, but there are generally many difficult decisions to be made.

Concrete issues such as one's job and finances, the house, the boat and the route are easier to tackle than the less tangible, more emotional, concerns. These include the risks: giving up a comfortable lifestyle for one where modern appliances barely exist, the loss of support systems of extended family, friends and community, leaving the familiar and coping with the unknown (new places, languages, food and customs), feeling inadequate regarding boat handling, which may be heightened by the fear of battling storms, and being alone on a vast ocean.

Involving children creates a new set of issues such as the timing in their lives, safety, potential health problems and the major challenge of the family being able to live with each other compatibly twenty four hours a day in confined, isolated quarters.

Then, after passing the hurdle of one's own indecision, one has to cope with everyone else's reactions. These can be hugely varied, from the 'Wow' of speechless wonder to a torrent of horror, with many who are completely mystified as to why you would want to do it at all. When children are involved 'advice' is often given that implies total irresponsibility, particularly if the children are being taken out of school or are very small.

An unexpected reaction was hostility, either because we had shattered people's excuses or somehow, in their eyes, had let them down. In Andy's case several men said to him "Of course I would be going off too but I have my own business." Andy soon learnt not to say "But I just sold mine!" In my case many women made it quite clear that I had let the side of women down by actually agreeing to go. They totally ignored the fact that I had spent a good deal of my life on boats and had always competed as one of the 'guys' on the race course. We soon learnt it was best to nod in agreement or look sympathetic and say nothing! Fortunately most reactions are somewhere in between the extremes and somewhat easier to deal with objectively.

However much one dreams of sailing into the sunset, stimulated of course by an ever increasing pile of colourful yachting and travel magazines in the bathroom, concrete plans do require leaving or re-organising one's job, and an in-depth consideration of finances.

It was actually Andy's business situation that helped us in the timing of our decision. Andy was a Yacht Broker in Vancouver and his office was on the future EXPO site. He and his partner were offered premises on the picturesque Granville Island. Unfortunately the crowds who came to the market to buy fresh baguettes and cappuccinos showed slim interest in boats, but took up all the parking spaces. Andy was disgruntled and depressed, and cheered himself up by making PLANS.

Fortunately he was able to sell his partnership. The proceeds could pay for the boat. As we had decided to keep our house, our cruising income was to be from the rent. Although we could live on this, it was horrifying how many expenses we still had back home, a point I think often forgotten in the planning stages. Insurance policies, house and income taxes, medical plans, university policies for the children all added up to a substantial amount.

One major expense was boat insurance. We found that quotes from England through Lloyds were the cheapest. In the crowded Mediterranean, rates were less than 1.0% of the yacht's value. There was a surcharge for crossing the Atlantic but the Caribbean was hardly more expensive. You will recall that whilst in Antigua we had to renew our policy to take us through the Panama Canal and across the Pacific to Australia. It was at this point that the complications began. Far fewer boats crossed the Pacific compared to the Atlantic, even fewer are insured and in the eyes of the insurance companies the risks are vastly increased. The Indian ocean is even further off the beaten track, and rates were 2.5%. Only about 10% of international yachts in South Africa were covered; the rate for us was up to 3%. Apparently most insurance companies require three adults for passages. We were fortunate that after Australia the boys were considered to be experienced enough to qualify as our 'third'.

The reason we persisted with the expense of insurance was as much because of the psychological reassurance as from the financial. As we had bought the boat from the proceeds of Andy's business, the boat represented the ability to get re-established into the business world on our return. We found that people without insurance had either come to terms with the possible financial loss, or felt that with their boat handling skills the odds were against any major damage occurring.

Unfortunately it is frequently a second party that causes the accident, or an unpredictable weather disaster. For example in Australia we were hit by a 14-foot tin boat going about 30 knots whilst we were at anchor, causing nearly $10,000 worth of damage. I might add we were the only boat within miles and the 13-year-old hit us right amidships penetrating the hull from the deck to the waterline. Fortunately no-one was on board *Bagheera*. The boy was catapulted into the netting around our lifelines, and amazingly was unhurt. In South Africa, having monitored weather pictures and forecasts for days we were hit by front, which had supposedly dissipated, and were struck by lightning. Almost all our electrics and electronics were fried. Several days later just as one friend was commenting "Well if there is any justice in this world at least the lightning hit a boat with insurance," the telephone beside him was also struck. He went off to enquire about insurance rates for his boat the next morning!

Like prices for airline flights we found insurance is often cheaper when purchased in the area that the insurance coverage is for. With insurance from England we were given a huge surcharge for entering Australian waters, for example, only to find Australian rates very reasonable. Having informed Lloyds of local examples we were given a refund.

Another worthwhile expense is being members of a yacht club. Firstly it provides a group of people who can offer invaluable help and information about your intended cruise, and, in particular, people who are generally steadfastly supportive. Secondly, it is extremely helpful whilst travelling to have reciprocal privileges at other sailing clubs around the world. Incidentally many like to see a current membership card, or letter of good standing from the Commodore, before offering you the use of their facilities.

We met interesting and helpful people at yacht clubs, and were toured around by not a few. In turn they were thrilled to come on board and become part of the group of international yachts. We also enjoyed the facilities—hot showers, telephone access, a comfortable place in which to relax, a mailing address and staff who were generally happy to give information and take messages.

It is impossible to project a monthly figure for cruising except to suggest that it will probably be considerably less than your regular budget, and to point out that you can't live on 'peanuts'. Countless people have remarked how wonderful it must be to live on $500 a month. They seem to have forgotten what they are spending a month at home on food and sundries—just because you are away from shops in the middle of the ocean doesn't mean that those mouths still aren't forever open—and food is just the beginning.

Because we picked up our boat in France we were straight into an offshore budget. I find that those who leave from their home port, particularly for short periods, always claim considerably lower cruising costs. Not only do they have the boat organized just how they want it, and gear in tip-top condition before they leave, (part of the cruising ritual in itself) they have unbelievable quantities of those essential staples— cans galore, dried goods and paper products including copious spare parts—that have 'inexplicably' made their way to the boat during the previous months. None of these supplies, however, are counted in the cruising budget as the cost had been absorbed into the regular super- market or chandlery shop.

On the same vein of advanced purchasing we were the recipients of many a leg of lamb and roasts of beef or pork from friends with large freezers on board. When entering both Australia and New Zealand any meat has to be handed over to the authorities to be destroyed. In Tonga and Fiji many friends realized that even if they indulged in meat morning, noon and night they could never consume the quantities they had left.

Although having some familiar staples and reserve food supplies on board is desirable, it is not necessary to leave with one's vessel loaded to the gunwales. Shopping in every new country is part of the excitement of a new culture for us. There was almost nowhere in our travels, and we enjoy going off the beaten track, where we could buy almost every- thing—even down to peanut butter and maple syrup for the boys! It took some adaptation, often foods were presented differently, but the pro- ducts were mostly comparable, sometimes superior, to those at home. Frequently prices were lower, especially in the markets.

About half the budget went on boat-related items. This included fuel, water, moorage where necessary, as well as maintenance, repairs and spares. Prices around the world vary greatly, even for identical items. However you never completely win because where food is cheap, marine equipment is generally outrageously expensive or inadequate, then parts have to be flown in. Incidentally it is imperative to label parcels with "For yacht in transit" to hope to avoid duty, a concession most countries have provided providing you are on a cruising permit.

I am fortunate in having a very practical husband who follows a philosophy of preventative maintenance. We carried a wide variety of spares and tools, and he was able to repair almost anything on the boat that went wrong. This is an important factor when deciding to cruise 'off the beaten track'. Those who have to call in professional help for every mechanical or electrical problem will find their budgets soaring.

Most long distance cruisers appeared to have similar budget constraints as ourselves. We enjoyed eating and drinking the local fare where cheap, but restaurants were given a miss where uneconomical and even entertaining on board was reduced. In French Polynesia, for example, you will remember a case of 24 cans of beer cost $37, a particular shock after $2.95 a case in Venezuela!

Most cruisers also maintain an excellent yacht and leave a good impression. In the past we have known boats that were run-down, and owners who left without paying their bills. This creates a negative reaction to boaters and sometimes an unwelcome reception, even additional charges, for those travelling in their wake.

Again, most could afford to take advantage of travel opportunities in the lands they visited. As we found in Europe, when anchoring in ports or tourist towns, one often misses the true flavour of the culture. Travelling inland is a must. What a crime it would be to anchor in Mombassa, in Kenya, and not be able to afford to go on safari, or visit Phuket in Thailand and not see the Grand Palace in Bangkok, let alone miss Patphong Road, home of the infamous go-go bars!

Andy had always been keen on the idea of selling our house when we went offshore. It would eradicate the problems of maintenance and tenants and, of course, would help with the finances. I wasn't so sure for a number of reasons. Firstly, we only planned to travel for two years. We had invested considerable energy into renovating our home, its size suited us well and it was in a convenient location, close to the yacht club and downtown. If any crisis occurred whilst we were cruising necessitating the family to return early, I felt the trauma would be compounded by having to first find rental accommodation and then set out house hunting again. A further concern was the trend of sudden soars and declines in house prices. What if we sold at the bottom of the cycle and had to rebuy at the top; would we ever be able to afford to live again in the area we wanted?

We finally decided to keep the house and were extremely lucky in having Alison, my eldest step-daughter, to manage the house and indeed all our affairs. In the six years we only had two sets of tenants. The first lasted four and a half years. When I returned to Vancouver from Phuket, Thailand, to re-rent there were some interesting gibes from those in the fleet who had been convinced that to be foot loose and fancy free one should definitely abandon home ownership.

Keeping our home in fact worked to our advantage as house prices rose considerably during our absence. We were also fortunate with our tenants, and returned to a house that had only received the normal wear and tear of a six year period, although the garden was a jungle.

It is important to consider the experiences and expectations of everyone concerned, when planning the route. Nothing turns people off boating more quickly than being cold, frightened, feeling totally inadequate and being yelled at by their easy going partner who has suddenly become 'Captain Bligh'. To build in success for a compatible life afloat it is often necessary to ease into the cruising mode gradually.

Of the areas we have sailed, the Caribbean, including Central and South America, and the Mediterranean are ideal areas to cruise for the more or less experienced, whether for one year or two, as distances are short and navigation generally not complicated. The Caribbean provides year round tropical bliss, although one does have to be in certain areas or monitor the weather carefully during the hurricane season. The Mediterranean has a variety of seasons, and wonderful ancient cultures. Although very different, both provide many varied experiences and excellent cuisines.

Of course the route that is chosen is often dictated by the location of the boat. If the boat is in British Columbia, for example, this builds in complications. Whether heading down the coast to San Francisco or across to Hawaii the route can be cold, rough and long, by no means ideal for anyone who is reticent about going away cruising in the first place. If visiting the South Pacific islands is the plan then an option for this person is to fly to Tahiti. There never seems to be a shortage of people who are keen to have the experience of helping take a boat offshore.

What about the less tangible concerns; the anxieties and the feeling of inadequacy? For the most part these are common, natural emotional reactions which can be remedied with a little time, planning, experience and knowledge.

Any courses that are locally available, such as on basic sailing skills, navigation, radio operation, seamanship, first aid, engine repairs, refrigeration, provisioning etc., will not only be useful but will boost confidence, allay fears and put you into a cruising mentality.

Time spent on boat handling, route planning and the running of the vessel will in particular build courage and enthusiasm. Thus when adverse conditions occur instead of panic, the situation can be assessed objectively and mutual decisions calmly made.

Although Andy and I were fortunate in that we had both grown up sailing and racing, cruising offshore does not require the sophisticated techniques that are used on the race course. Basic knowledge of the rudiments of sail trim are quite sufficient for cruising the oceans. The important aspect is competence with operations such as hoisting and reefing the mainsail, furling the genoa, and gybing the spinnaker pole to wing out the genoa. Using the spinnaker itself should probably only be considered when confidence in these basic skills has been achieved.

Often modifications need to be made. For example, I frequently have to use a winch when Andy can use brute strength, so leads may have to be altered. Differences between people's abilities have to be acknowledged and accepted.

Practice with docking and anchoring is never wasted time. Nothing is more frustrating or demoralizing than the verbal interchange that can ensue between the bow and helm, with the volume of course at an ever escalating pitch. Afterwards you just want to slink below, to dissipate your fury at the injustice of it all and hope, impossibly, that all you other cruising pals are currently ashore. Developing your own set of hand signals can work wonders, eradicating the need for this interchange— well most of the time!

Knowing how to work the radio, and the important information frequencies, is necessary to access weather information, finding out relevant details about the next port of entry, and to cope with crisis situations, as well as for regular social contact. I was horrified, for example, by a couple on a small boat with two young children. We had talked to the husband frequently. On arrival in port emergency mail was waiting requesting he fly home immediately. The wife felt rather lost having just arrived in a new country so I suggested we keep in radio contact.

"Oh, I can't do that," she replied.

"Is the time inconvenient?" I inquired. "I can make it any time that suits you."

"It isn't that," she said. "I haven't a clue how to work the radio."

How would she have coped if her husband had been sick, or fallen overboard? What a crime to have a radio and not be able to access information that could help enormously in these situations, such as calling for medical advice, and learning about imminent weather systems, besides the psychological benefit of being given ongoing support.

Taking a Ham radio licence before leaving is popular, particularly since the changes in the morse code requirements. We joined several radio 'scheds' whilst offshore. Those on the marine bands worked well between a group of yachts in close proximity, however as soon as the distances between them increased, and particularly if reception was poor, they would lose contact. After a few days without response most people become lax in making the effort to keep to schedule and the 'sched' peters out. The Ham nets have the advantage of frequently being run by shore-based operators who have strong signals due to their high sophisticated antennae. (The subject of hours of conversation on the air, be warned!) These people are generally extremely committed and have a daily schedule with weather reports, messages, take yachts' positions, and often make arrangements for yacht equipment or other necessities required.

Phone patching is another advantage of having a Ham licence. A call from the yacht radio to a shore based Ham operator who can then patch you through to your friends, relatives etc. is very convenient and free of charge in several countries if a local phone call is made. We have some friends who talk to their families every night. No business is allowed, that includes ordering spares. This system saves considerable time, frustration, not to say money compared to using the regular phone system. Travelling into an unfamiliar town, locating the international phones, lining up for them, waiting around to phone back hoping the party will be home sooner rather than later, getting this co-ordinated with the time difference, and sometimes having to organise quantities of the right change, can take a whole day.

A previous trip with ocean experience is very useful. Many bare-boat charters are available these days. Those in the Caribbean or Pacific, where one sails the ocean between islands are excellent for offshore practice, and inexpensive, especially out of season. Who would argue with a legitimate reason to visit those warm seas and blue skies? Better still take your own boat or crew on an excursion into the ocean for a few days.

Monitor your reactions to seasickness, tiredness and areas of concern or incompetence. Work on these upon your return. It is important to know one's limitations, accept them and plan to work around them. It's amazing how many people fight seasickness for example, regarding it as a weakness, particularly men! My attitude is that there is nothing to be lost by taking medication, (except pride, and you don't have to tell anyone!) but a huge amount to be gained. It not only makes life far more pleasant, it is much safer, being the difference between a fully functioning seaman compared to a marginally coping person.

For short trips I use seasick pills. There are many types on the market these days, trying out different brands is really worthwhile. The most popular brand in Europe appeared to be Stugeron; I have not found them available in North America. As being alert on watch is of paramount importance one needs to find a brand that controls nausea but does not cause drowsiness. When you find a brand that works for you, buy plenty. You may not find them in the next country or even the next port.

For long trips I have found the Transderm Scop earpatch very successful in not only preventing seasickness but reducing the irritability produced by a constantly moving hot, humid environment; although I do have to put it on twelve hours in advance, rather than the instructed five/six hours. Scop helps reduce the activity of the nerve cells in the inner ear. Motion increases the activity of these cells in many people, leading to dizziness and nausea, and ending in vomiting. A problem can arise if a decision is made to leave without this required advance warning time. What is disastrous, I have found, is to put on an earpatch then take a seasick pill to cover the acclimatization period. Mixing the drugs seems to guarantee a severe case of malaise. Although an ear patch can give side effects to some people, such as dryness in the mouth and temporary blurring of vision, most people seem to find them very successful when used correctly. Ear patches last for three days and a second is approved if needed. Almost all people have adjusted to the motion in that period, most seem to take forty eight to seventy two hours. I find it frustrating that once in harbour I lose my immunity very quickly. I might get away with one night but not two. I can also have my sea legs for a downwind motion but can feel queasy again with the winds on the beam or ahead, as the boat lurches in a very different manner.

Some people find the Dea pressure point wrist bands, developed from Chinese acupuncture principles, very successful. They didn't work for me so I gave them to a friend whose daughter suffered from severe car sickness. She never worried about going in a car again.

As we had both made several offshore passages previously, and cruised extensively, Andy and I were realistic about the lifestyle and it appealed to both of us. For many, like ourselves, it is a mutual decision to go blue-water cruising but in my experience frequently women are more reticent. Besides concerns regarding the sailing they know that, despite those promises of exotic countries and endless romantic sundowners, the chores do continue; like preparing the nibbles to go with the sundowers for a beginning! The fact that they have in effect chucked all the handy helpers overboard—such as the dishwasher, washing machine, dryer, vacuum cleaner, mixers, toaster, microwave etc. not to mention the car—has not contributed too generously to the 'pro' column. Nor has the fact that they have to give up privacy, space, a large wardrobe and unlimited hot water showers.

A trip on a yacht in tropical climes will also show that the chores are not quite so formidable as anticipated. A boat is considerably smaller than a home, and once you have learnt to remember to secure the ketchup, coffee and soy sauce . . . before heading out, (shock-cord or fiddles across the inside of lockers works wonders), the time needed for clean-up is not such a burden. Even laundry takes on a different light when completed in the cockpit and hung out in the sun to dry, with the wind being a natural iron. (Maybe it's a good idea not to have a full length mirror around.) If water is limited on board, showers are frequently available ashore, and water makers are coming down in price and size, and up in reliability.

It was particularly special for us that we were able to cruise with our children, but what did they feel about our proposed new lifestyle? When we actually made our decision to 'blue water' cruise, you will remember that Duncan was eight, Colin just six and Jamie not yet two years old. As far as the elder two were concerned, going away on the boat was an exciting proposition. They had cruised most long weekends and all their summer holidays, and they loved being on board. When we mentioned that it would at times be rougher than the benign waters of the Pacific North West, they cheered, "Better bouncing in the forward cabin." They had never had a problem with sea sickness or living in confined quarters, so we had no qualms about their adaptability on a full time basis—so long as we could take them ashore regularly to run off their energy.

We had received several comments like "Won't the boys be bored out of their minds? How will you be able to entertain them all day long?" While we were cruising the boys never once said "I'm bored", although they've said it frequently since we've been back. We never had to entertain them but did provide quantities of materials for them to amuse themselves, and took an active interest in any of their projects. Toys such as Lego, Playmobil and farm animals were used separately or in combination, and frequently 'set-ups' covered the entire main cabin table. Duncan was a great motivater in getting these started, Colin creative with the role playing to go with them. With the fiddles at the edges of the table in place and with the help of non-slip mats these creations grew in the roughest of seas, although entire battalions of horses were likely to keel over in unison.

Art supplies—coloured paper, glue, scissors, pens, crayons and paints (in harbour!) were a great favourite with Colin, and latterly he spent hours making most detailed models in multi-coloured Fimo clay. I thoroughly recommend this clay; it stays malleable, the dyes do not stain and it only takes ten minutes to bake, although keeping the necessary low temperature in our oven was quite a challenge.

We had many board games. They were played in the evenings when we were cruising alone and occasionally on trips, but card games were played morning, noon and night. I wonder how many thousands of games of UNO I have played . . . !

Reading was a number one activity and the boys never hankered after TV although I have to admit they made a beeline for the closest television set when on shore. When crossing the Indian Ocean I calculated we had about five hundred books on board, a major portion being for the children. We often swapped books and ended up with interesting literature, and some that we would never purchase ourselves!

The boys also started collections. They all had bags of foreign coins, we started an album for stamps with underwater life, they had their own boxes of shells and carvings, and Colin became interested in gems and fossils.

With all these activities, together with the excitements of the sea, the changing routine of the daily watches, the special attention on preparing enticing culinary creations, and the chit-chat on the radio, far from boredom, the problem was finding time to fit everything in.

I am frequently asked the best age for children to cruise. I strongly believe that if the opportunity to sail offshore presents itself you should take advantage of it. It is too wonderful an experience to be missed. However, now that I have known many 'boat kids', I have concluded that the optimum ages for children to sail extendedly are between six and twelve. If a child is under six there is no problem having them aboard, with certain safety requirements, but they themselves do not remember very much. The isolated incidents they can recall might have happened anywhere and the special flavours of different cultures and scenery is lost to them. Over thirteen, children are getting into those rather daunting teenage years—daunting for the parents anyway. One minute they are full of enthusiasm to rush off diving, to the beach, or just to come ashore with their parents to wander the wondrous sights. The next moment it seems they are much too old to build dams or look for shells, and going ashore to see yet another ruin is plain boring, particularly with their parents—sound familiar? The mood and character changes associated with puberty put a particular strain on child and adults when confined together.

Travelling in itself is a wonderful education but being committed to the regular curriculum I never considered that the children's formal schooling could be abandoned. As far as Andy and I were concerned although we were opting out of a regular lifestyle we did not want to compromise our children's future in it, and I was delighted with the existence and quality of the British Columbia Correspondence Education Programme. The reactions to our taking the boys out of regular school were varied, most felt the travels in themselves would compensate, whilst others were quite critical (although being a qualified teacher did help allay their fears.) Ironically, while we were away home schooling became an acceptable popular alternative and I was rebuked by one lady on our return for then putting the boys back into the regular system!

Although having a Teaching Certificate gave me the confidence to take them out of school and familiarity with the texts, goals and realistic expectations, it wasn't necessary for the boys to complete the programme itself. Except for the younger grades each level was presented so the children could complete the work themselves. My involvement was in supervision, extra explanation, inspiration or materials— and generally encouraging them along. School often involved the family and friends. As one of the disadvantages of working independently is the lost stimulation from the rest of the class we had to substitute with family brainstorming, friends also became interviewees and audiences.

There were many different educational programmes being completed by the children afloat. Some were completing Canadian programmes from other Provinces while most American families subscribed to the Calvert system, with University of Nebraska courses for the later years of High School. The Australian States, with many children in the Outback, also have their own well developed programmes. Our boys took the correspondence programme from New South Wales between leaving their Australian schools and the beginning of the next Canadian school year. (The Australian school year runs with the calender year).

All these programmes appeared to work successfully particularly because they were structured, setting out a daily routine to be followed, with supervision by parents. The systems themselves used different teaching and marking methods. The Calvert system appeared to be run on traditional lines, was not as child oriented in instruction as the Canadian and Australian, and there were complaints about the cost of the exams which assessed the individual's performance. The Canadian and Australian systems followed modern educational philosophies and were both experiential and creative. Both programmes charged minimal costs for supplies. They required papers to be sent off at regular intervals for assessment which were marked and returned. This system works well in a regular postal area. However the nature of yachting, going off the beaten track and having to take advantage of favourable weather conditions, produces erratic itineraries. Feedback is often several months away, and the educational impact substantially reduced. I tried to overcome this by marking the boys work at the time and explaining their errors. However this involved many hours of extra work, particularly when I had to figure out all the math problems myself!

The New South Wales system emphasised the verbal and the personal. Colin in particular enjoyed completing many of his lessons into the tape recorder. Feedback was also given verbally by tape. The problem with this method was that it took hours to listen to every aspect of their work and corrections suggested, compared to speed reading the written and focusing on the pertinent comments for the subject at hand. The lessons involved several separate sheets which provided variety but were easily mislaid and made school in the cockpit impossible, as they could be whisked up by the wind and into the water in an instant.

A popular British course is the World-wide Education Service which sets out programmes for a year. Texts have to be ordered and work sent off at the end of each semester with an evaluation of teacher and pupil. Most parents seemed to feel that this offered a flexibility that suited the lifestyle but that they were very much the teacher, rather than a supervisor.

An alternative to following a regular system is for the parents to set school schedules daily. We met very few people who did this because of the work involved and the resentment from their children, who resisted a timetable imposed by their parents. When this route was followed it was generally short term, filling in the gap between two systems, returning home, or following math and reading texts, and writing a dairy, if only out for a year.

Time spent on school varied from about two to five hours a day. In our case it was generally three to four and a half hours depending on the type of assignments required. Story writing, research, science experiments and art projects often took longer but were the most fulfilling. The Canadian programme included all regular subjects including four language arts, maths, science, social studies and art, and suggested games and drama activities as well. Those completing only the academic basics took a shorter period of time to complete their courses but often, we noticed, these children complained they were bored with school. We met no-one who adhered to a Monday to Friday routine. School fitted in around visits ashore and weather conditions on trips.

Although the correspondence programmes work well for elementary school the high school programmes were often restricted in scope, particularly in science, and much more demanding. After a year of enjoying school in Australia, Duncan found the Grade 8 B.C. programme somewhat tedious and very time consuming. He was approaching thirteen and although he still enjoyed the travel, he greatly missed the challenge of the classroom, team sports and general socialization with his mates. We met a number of teenage 'boat kids' around the world who were obviously happy with their alternate lifestyle; however, like Duncan, almost all were equally looking forward to returning back home and becoming 'regular' adolescents at the local high school.

Having been a regular programmed Mum with Duncan and Colin, planning, paying for, and helping organise their pre-school, I was fascinated to find that Jamie did ninety percent of the fine and gross motor activities spontaneously. Mind you I did by this time know what equipment to have around. Not surprisingly water play was his favourite activity and he spent hours in 'his' swimming pool, dripping also in suntan lotion and decked in a large hat. Swinging from the rigging, or even climbing up the chart table was great fun when no playgrounds were around and how many little boys have been able to 'help' Daddy with their own set of tools on a daily basis?

Children on board also raises the question of safety. When the boys were small we tied the car seat to the stern pulpit. They were safe, secure and on the leeward side they were entertained by the wake gurgling by. It's the one to three year old stage that is hectic and we have always put netting all around our boats during this period. It makes the boat safe, (stops toys going overboard too) and psychologically takes a whole load off one's mind. At sea the boys were not allowed out of the cockpit except on specific supervised occasions. Andy and I also had the rule that if one went on deck, the other was in the cockpit watching. Our cockpit is very roomy, feels secure and we never felt confined. Andy and I were diligent in wearing life harnesses when we went forward or on night watches. Jamie wore his comfortable lifejacket, (some you can't sit down in), daily until Australia. Duncan and Colin wore life-harnesses when on watch alone or when it was rough. If rough and we wanted to make a trickly manoeuvre, or sail adjustment the boys generally stayed below. Flogging lines, a swinging boom and not being able to work the cockpit freely, were the particular hazards of having them on deck.

As we planned to cruise the Mediterranean I wasn't concerned about medical issues. I knew that with a basic understanding of French and Spanish as well as English being the world-wide language we were unlikely to have any communication problems, and that European countries practise first rate medicine. The Caribbean is less sophisticated but having lived in the area for many years we knew that it was satisfactory and improving all the time. As we continued our travels west we found most areas of the world had more than adequate medical facilities and that third world countries were helped with supplies and personnel from Europe and the United States.

I was also reassured because my family rarely gets sick. Andy suffers the most, mainly because bugs love to bite him. If he is around, I can relax, no mosquito will come near me, although a few will attack Duncan. We found the local repellents the most effective. Andy's worse bite was from a spider in Indonesia. It took several treatments of antibiotics to clear.

It wasn't until the Indian Ocean that we had to have shots such as yellow fever, gammaglobulin, typhoid and cholera. We first took malaria pills in Venezuela. I gave them to the children in strawberry jam and they have never eaten strawberry jam again! In the Indian Ocean we took malaria pills for one and a half years. At times we were in chloroquine resistant areas so had to change to different medication. A relatively new drug mefloquine, taken just once weekly, is now readily available. During our travels many doctors advised us not to take malaria pills for an extended period because of side effects; Andy for example, developed eye troubles. They recommended that a three day treatment of fansidar should be taken as a treatment, and contact made with a doctor as soon as possible. The problem, of course, was confidence in oneself in being able to diagnose the symptoms, especially worrying when one was in the middle of the ocean.

People who have recurrent health problems should plan their supplies and route with these in mind, to avoid their own distress and the inconvenience of others. We were surprised, for example, to hear how many had been taken from Chagos (an idyllic atoll isolated in the middle of the Indian ocean with no resident population) to Diego Garcia, (an American military base some 200 kilometres away) to be flown out for specialised treatment of previously existing conditions. As they could not be flown back to the military base, their partners were left behind to complete the long passages to the Maldives or the Seychelles alone.

Our medical friends had helped us to compile supplies for the spectrum of health hazards with dressings, ointments, lotions, powders and medications for every aspect and function of the body! We also carried medical books, oriented both for general family health and boat travel. There are many of these volumes on the market. It's worth taking time when choosing one. I found some difficult to read, others hard to access information from whilst others just weren't geared to practical treatment.

We always washed fruit and vegetables carefully in case of poor hygiene and the world-wide use of insecticides, and had medication handy for upset stomachs when eating ashore. We were seldom smitten, our antibodies must have been varied and powerful by the end of our trip, but Imodium always sorted us out quickly. I once suffered from dysentery. It was just after we had left Madagascar. Bactrim was suggested in our backpackers handbook. This is a general purpose antibiotic that we had been recommended in Singapore and we had it on board.

In the tropics one has to be particularly careful with skin and sun.

For those of us reared with the maxim 'salt water heals' it is a shock to find that in tropical waters it does quite the reverse. The tiniest of cuts can fester and grow to a sore, ugly wound in days. The most effective remedy is to keep it dry, (a great out for washing-up!), but particularly away from the vibrios bacteria that are found in sea water. Band-aids must also be used sparingly and those that breathe are much better than the water proof variety, they stay on better too. Once the bleeding has stopped the wound must be exposed to the open air (although in dusty areas cover with a light gauze to prevent infection); enclosed in the heat it will soon fester.

I was horrified on our trip to India. Jamie had scratched a mosquito bite, so I put on an Elastoplast. During the trip I was busy, as Andy was suffering from heat exhaustion. It was two days before Jamie brought to my attention that his leg was hurting. The bite had ulcerated and was now twice the size, angry red and oozing. It took three weeks to heal, he still has the scar.

You've heard the saying 'only mad dogs and Englishmen go out in the mid-day sun' and its quite true. We do tend to have set ideas of what we will accomplish in a day regardless of the climate. Many of the towns in the tropics are stifling, as they are built in sheltered areas in case of storms. St.Johns in Antigua is one; we all used to gather in the Banks as they were air-conditioned, and few places were at that time.

Andy, Colin and Jamie went shopping in Galle, in Sri Lanka for my birthday. I was in England, as tragically my sister had died of cancer, so they wanted it to be a special celebration. It was during the pre-monsoon, unbelievably hot and humid, but they persevered. Colin was very sick the whole of my birthday, and the other two not feeling well but with plenty of liquids they recovered quickly. Heat exhaustion, and particularly heat stroke can be very debilitating and dangerous, especially for children.

In the past salt tablets were prescribed. Now salt reduced diets are recommended. Today we have the knowledge that it is best not to work, and sweat, in the heat of the sun and we can drink gatorade for electrolyte replacement. If this is not available one should drink anything soft, even tea with lemon (potassium) and sugar. Incidentally 'drowning your sorrows' in Caribbean rum will only create more sorrows. Alcohol is also very dehydrating.

I can't emphasize enough the dangers from the sun. When we first lived in the tropics in the sixties no-one realised the long term effects of being sunburnt. Both Andy and I are fair-skinned and freckled, although both ultimately tan, and we did immeasurable harm to our skin. In Australia Andy had to have 56 liquid nitrogen treatments to his face and hands for pre-cancerous tissue. I had a small mole that bled and distorted on my arm. A biopsy showed it to be malignant, only a pinprick of a melanoma but a centimetre all round had to be removed. I had the surgery completed in Panama. It was our only expensive medical bill, $500 of which I recouped only $90 on a medical plan. Sun blocks are excellent these days, choose those that filter out all the harmful rays and use them. My skin specialist says one should never use less that a protective level of 15, as it lulls one into a false sense of security. Use as high as is available on one's face. Wind, salt and sun together are dynamite for damage as well as horrendous for wrinkles.

Maybe some of these issues are relevant to you and I hope the suggestions have helped. Although one might feel uncertainty and confusion over the many decisions and bogged down with the chores, whether before or during travelling, it is important to remember that irritations occur with any major change and in every lifestyle. By keeping the positive aspects of the travel—visits to exotic lands, the joys of being free from the routines and stresses of society, the wonders of the sea and the closeness with one's family—in the fore-front of one's thoughts, the rest generally seems to sort itself out.

Initially it may also be helpful to visit the local library for books with full-page glossy colour pictures of the countries on your proposed route.

Make sure no pictures are included of luxurious hotels, however! Face-tiousness aside, these books can both stimulate enthusiasm and give valuable information. We always try to have a backpackers handbook, such as the Lonely Planet series, as well as a cruising guide, if available, for every area, as they are so useful for visits ashore. Incidentally often these books are not available in the country itself so have to be purchased ahead. They always became my reading material on a long trip, after I had caught up on sleep.

To anyone planning to go offshore or travelling overland, good luck with all your decisions. We know how busy your last few weeks will be and some of the frustrations you might endure. One last suggestion. I'll guarantee that once away the time will fly. You won't want to come back when you planned, so work on stretching those finances further than expected!

Our Boat and Equipment: Some Technical Decisions

One of the particular joys of the sailing lifestyle is meeting up with other cruisers, and it's fascinating to find how their ideas regarding the perfect yacht are as different as their personalities. Even if you do happen to come across two boats of the same design, a rare event, the similarities frequently stop at the factory. Those enticing boat catalogues are not for naught and, particularly in the first stages of their travels, yachtsmen have widely varying equipment and ideas of installation. This was dramatically demonstrated at the marinas in Gibraltar. Its amazing how boats can be disguised, when solar panels, wind generator, instruments, dinghy, outboards, life-raft, fishing gear, windsurfer, jerry cans, washing bowls and bicycles are creatively attached around the deck. In Antigua we even saw a 45 footer with a light aircraft complete with floats cunningly segmented round the hull.

As one progresses inefficient equipment is discarded, better systems are installed and modifications are made to improve reliability, comfort and safety. By the time we reached South Africa where international yachts were commonly on their last leg of a circumnavigation, most boats had similar equipment, mounted or stowed in like fashion. Also most were production boats constructed of fibreglass, (rather than of wood, steel, aluminium or cement) and were of relatively similar hull and keel design. In contrast to the traditional full keeled, heavy displacement designs, lighter displacement, modern performance cruisers were favoured for their sailing ability, speed and comfort. Somewhere between 37 and 45 feet appeared to be most popular. This size gave ease of handling and ample interior space and stowage, but was also large enough for a sea kindly motion.

As we frequently observed on the docks around the world, the hours spent in discussing the pros and cons of different types of vessels and their equipment can be infinite. Here, I just touch on some specific areas—from our perspective naturally!

Thankfully designs have changed radically over the last twenty five years, and it is no longer mandatory to live in total discomfort to prove one can belong to the yachting fraternity. I remember well my first experiences of 'big boat' cruising. In my small clinker built (lapstrake) wooden dinghy I had sailed over to the Isle of Wight to watch Cowes Week, the well known international racing event on the south coast of England. Some friends, moored on the 'trots', hailed us to join them on their 40 footer. Later, as we made our way across several other yachts to get ashore, I thought how uncomfortable so many looked below with narrow berths, tiny stoves and minute inoperable heads. So often there was that odour—an indescribable mix of fuel, bilge and mould—which guaranteed waves of nausea before even hoisting the sails.

Fortunately the age of comfort has invaded even this diehard group. Modern designs permit large, comfortable, dry beds with regular duvets, gimballed stoves with big ovens, walk around bathrooms with separate shower stalls and plenty of water to use in them. In addition, one still has a boat that is strongly built, performs well and whose size is easy to handle for two people.

We looked at several boats but always came back to the Beneteau First 38s for our travels. Beneteau is a French company which builds a wide range of yachts. Andy had been the Beneteau dealer in Vancouver, we had inspected their factories in France, and trusted the company's integrity. The 38 is an excellent design for our family of five. With a hull length of 40 feet 2 inches and a beam of 12 feet 9 inches, it is roomy, airy and has excellent storage below. On deck the aft cockpit is large and comfortable. Termed a cruiser- racer its speed satisfied our racing instincts and it was rare in the tradewinds for us to cover less that 150 nautical miles a day. Being of fibreglass it was easy to maintain, with just enough varnished wooden trim to look like a yacht. Unlike older designs with shallow long keels and attached rudder, we have an under-water configuration of fin keel and spade rudder. We drew 7 feet initially but with six years of school textbooks and accumulating souvenirs, the water line was forever getting higher! Our deep draft gave us a good upwind performance, little leeway when the wind was on the beam and stable downwind tracking. It is one of the best behaved boats we have owned.

With the large berth forward and two double cabins aft, we all had our own areas of 'retreat' and the boys were able to have quantities of toys, books and tapes at hand. The galley was not large but the designer had cleverly thought to have the upper locker doors open downwards and stop at the horizontal. This becomes another counter and is very useful for getting rid of everything that always seems to have accumulated on top of the fridge when the family is desperate for a cold drink. We started our travels with a 12-volt fridge run off the batteries which did a sterling job of cooling. After the long trips in the Pacific, however, I thought it would be an advantage to have a freezer. As we had no available space for a separate unit we converted the back of our existing fridge compartment, dividing it with plexi-glass. For the new system we installed hold-over plates and drove the compressor from the main engine. The freezer section suited our needs perfectly. It could hold about one month's supply of meat and allowed us to freeze some fish. As we had found, however creative we were with cans and dried goods, it really all became mush in the end. Using frozen meat gives a good chewable base, and it is easy to fill in the rest. We never completed a trip without some fresh foods still at hand.

The galley had a gimballed yacht stove, with two burners and oven. Although the oven looks small it could hold a 7 kilogram turkey or three large bread pans front to back.

The chart table held a British Admiralty chart perfectly. American charts come in varying shapes and sizes and technically are not our preferred choice. Although we traded and sold charts whenever possible, as they are a major expense, we still ended up with huge number on board—Andy estimated we had over 800 aboard when we left Sydney, Australia, to take us across the Indian Ocean. The current portfolio is always stored in the chart table and the rest under Colin's mattress. We catalogued first by area and then within area by number. As we ended up with charts of many nationalities this meant numbers didn't necessarily follow the sequence of our route. We overcame this hurdle by drawing in the area and marking the number on a master Admiralty catalogue to which we could easily refer.

Our main cabin can seat eight comfortably and behind the seats are large storage areas used for books, clothing, spare parts, boat manuals and 'paperwork'. This we had adapted from the original pilot berth design. Further I had asked Andy to put in shelf dividers so I could arrange double rows of books which facilitated having a years worth of school books at hand. The teak table has hinged flaps for all round seating, large locker for wine, and convenient shelves facing the galley which hold twelve stacked glasses. The cotton slip covers, attached by velcro, which I had made for all the cushions works well. Not only do they make the interior lighter and more attractive but the cotton is cooler and more comfortable in the tropics than the normal hard-wearing, but scratchy, tweed. They can be easily laundered, quite significant with the wear and tear of three small children, and the salt that inevitably comes below. We carry flexible water tanks under the seats, which hold over 500 litres. On long trips we carried a further 60 litres in jerry cans on deck, and about 120 litres in auxiliary tanks fore and aft that were originally installed as holding tanks for the heads (but not used!).

We had two 'heads', or bathrooms. The forward one was the larger, with shower and good storage, which we had also increased with extra cupboards and shelves. Aft, behind the companionway, the designer had cleverly fitted another head with access from both aft cabins. Initially we kept it this way but later it became a wonderful storage area for all those items that just wouldn't fit anywhere else. Thus the portable generator kept company with Long Life milk, wine and beer, fenders, paper towel, sail cover, etc. In fact it was my saviour many a time when my enthusiasm for provisioning had exceeded my regular storage capacity.

Our main engine is a 50 horsepower, Perkins 4108. We can carry 125 litres of diesel in the main tank and another 100 litres in jerry cans on deck for long trips. The Perkins suits the boat well, pushing us along at 7 1/2 knots if needed and is extremely economical at 4 knots. We had no difficulties obtaining service around the world and the cost of spares was reasonable. A small portable 110/220 volt generator is useful for emergency charging of the main batteries and running electric tools; particularly because our Canadian power tools are 110 volt while most places we visited used a 220-volt system.

We started with the minimum electronic and extra boat equipment we considered essential: self steering, VHF radio, depth sounder, hand anchor windlass, genoa furling gear, log and wind instruments.

Having to care for three little ones it was important to have reliable self-steering system. We chose an Autohelm 6000 automatic pilot which could cope with all wind and sea conditions for our displacement. We were pleased we had decided on a powerful unit (the manual claimed it was fit for a vessel up to 70 feet) when several friends had problems with lighter makes and models. The advantage of our electrical self steering-system is that we can be assured of an exact compass course. Before crossing the Pacific we added an Aries windvane as a back-up, but Felicity was never as easy to operate or as reliable—guess who gave it a female name? In particular we found that our sun awning over the cockpit interrupted or deflected the required wind flow. As a mechanical back-up, we purchased a small tiller steering Autohelm 800 which attached to the vane mechanism on the Aries, after seeing this system on an Australian boat. This worked well, although in heavy weather we had to reduce sail earlier.

An electrical steering system requires considerable battery power, particularly in rough conditions. We started our trip with two batteries, each of 160 amp hours, but gradually added more. We now have two banks of three batteries each, with a total of 660 amp hours. We charge an hour a day with the main engine which is fitted with a high output alternator and three-stage quick charge regulator.

From the beginning Andy had been interested in a wind generator and you will recall we were fortunate in finding a fellow yachtsman who had a Rutland for sale in Menorca. The power it makes depends on wind strength, for example, it generates about 4 amps in 20 knots of breeze. In Australia we also added two solar panels, which were even more efficient, and we've had no further problems with having enough 'juice' to run all the gadgets we managed to acquire.

We felt a short range (up to 30 miles) VHF radio would be adequate for communicating with port authorities, listening to weather forecasts, and keeping in touch with friends, as we day hopped around the Mediter-ranean. Part of making the decision to cross the Pacific Ocean was the purchase of a 'ham' high frequency radio, so we had a means of com-munication during the long trips between islands. This radio has a several thousand mile range depending on the frequency used and conditions. We have never regretted the expenditure. Besides being important for safety and weather reports, we enjoyed being able to have the contact with other yachtsmen. We all looked forward to the daily chitchats on long passages and frequently were able to meet friends we might never have seen again.

Modern day navigation systems are remarkable, not only giving your position, but the course to steer and distance to your destination, besides a mass of other information. I have to admit the sextant rarely came out of its box. Our Satnav saved a huge amount of time, energy and plain anxiety when, without sun or stars, no position could have otherwise been determined. We found satellite fixes frequent in the Mediterranean and Caribbean, fewer in the South Pacific and sporadic in the Indian Ocean. Going up the Tanzania and Kenyan coastlines we were without a fix for seven hours, frustrating as we were curious to see if we were getting the 4 knot current boost that was reputed in this area. The 'transit' Satnav programme is now being faded out in favour of the Global Positioning System(GPS). With these new satellites, one knows one's position within metres (100 metres with the US military desensitising) every second of the day, reducing the anxiety of trying to find those elusive reefs—providing the charts are correct . . .

As we continued in our travels, we accumulated more and more equipment, generally when a good deal came along. It's a strange phenomenon about all these 'toys'; as soon as you acquire one you just can't imagine life without it. Then, of course, you begin rationalizing about the next 'necessity'. We purchased an SMR hand held VHF radio which became a great baby sitter. The Apelco 8-mile radar transformed navigation particularly in fog and at night, and also allowed flexibility with arrival and departure plans. A weather-fax machine was useful in the Indian Ocean when we could receive few voice weather forecasts by radio. We bought a Nillsen Maxwell electric anchor windlass cheaply from a chandler who was anxious to leave Fiji after the second coup. It replaced the Simpson Lawrence manual windlass. As we had decided on an all chain rode, instead of the chain and rope we had used previously, to anchor in the coral of the Pacific, it saved Andy's back and time in the intense sun on the foredeck. Our anchor inventory includes a 15 kilogram Bruce with 90 metres of 8 millimetre high tensile chain, a 24 kilogram French fluked FOB with 25 metres 10 millimetre chain and 90 metres 2.5 centimetre diameter nylon octoplait, and an 8 kilogram Danforth kedge. The anchor in use was stowed in one of the two bow rollers. Spare anchors, rope and chain fitted in the anchor locker forward. If there had been extra space we would also have carried an Admiralty pattern anchor as an additional storm anchor.

An inflatable dinghy is the ideal tender for a 40 foot yacht. It is easy to stow, soft on the topsides, good to tow, stable in the waves and surf, easy to carry up the beach, and planes well for distant sightseeing. Ours was 10 feet 6 inches in length and was a dry and stable design. Unfortunately, we chose the wrong make as neither the material nor bonding stood up to the tropical heat, and we seemed to spend our lives gluing seams. To give the manufacturers their due they have stood behind us and we are now on our fourth dinghy under warranty. In Thailand a sailmaker friend made us, and many others, a white dinghy cover that has been a great success. It shields the dark grey tubes from the intense sun, prevents wear and tear at docks and is much cooler to sit on.

We set off with a 8 horsepower Yamaha outboard which could just get us up on the plane with the whole family when the boys were small. In Singapore outboard prices were cheap, in fact half the cost of American prices even for an American built engine. By this time our Yamaha was getting quite elderly with four and a half years of everyday use, so we exchanged it for an 3.2 horsepower Mercury and some cash; then splurged on a new 9.9 horsepower Mariner. This was an excellent combination. When we wanted to go far afield exploring or diving, the big engine was ideal as it could easily get the whole family up on the plane. Meanwhile, when we were in port, and the main use was commuter runs backwards and forwards to shore, the small Mercury pushed us along remarkably well, had minimal fuel consumption and wasn't as attractive to 'borrow'. We stored both on the aft pulpit and used a simple tackle system on the windmill post to hoist them up.

Our six man Beaufort liferaft lives in a stainless steel cradle which was built to sit on the upper supports of the Aries windvane, over the reverse transom. Here it is out of the way and ready for instant use. It lives in a metal container and I made a canvas cover as we were informed this greatly increases the liferaft's life. Inside it is packed with parachute flares, smoke flares, handflares and sea dye; space blankets, heliograph and solar still; fishing gear and basic tools; water packs and emergency rations; sunscreen and seasick tablets; repair kit, pump and paddles for the liferaft itself; and an Emergency Position Indicating Radio Beacon (EPIRB).

When activated EPIRBS transmit emergency signals. Ours sends out signals on 121.5 MHZ and 243 MHZ frequencies which are primarily listened to by aircraft and satellites. Batteries last about forty eight hours. Now there are new 406 MHZ EPIRBS whose signal is picked up by the SARSAT satellites which store the information until they are over a ground station. The signal is then transmitted to a receiver which in turn notifies the rescue service of the country. Your personal code is also transmitted along with your position within a one mile radius. The disadvantage is their cost—about $1,000—although they are coming down in price. They were about $4,000 when it was suggested we buy one in Australia.

A must, in our opinion, is roller furling gear on the genoa. The advantages are ease of handling as the furling line is operated from the cockpit and safety as no-one has to clamber up to the foredeck and wrestle with a flogging sail in pounding seas. A reduction in sail inventory is another advantage, as with a foam luff the sail keeps its shape even when partially furled. Another benefit is that we seldom have to disturb the person off watch because of wind increases. Generally it was possible to furl the genoa and delay the decision of reefing the mainsail until the next watch change. Furling equipment is now very reliable and it is hard to think of an offshore cruiser without it. Even our friends on the Swedish *Orkestern*, who steadfastly sailed around the world with regular hanks on the forestay, succumbed for their trip home across the Atlantic, after having completed their circumnavigation. They are now firm believers and will never cruise without it again. Many yachts now also carry a furling system for the mainsail. Again techniques have been perfected and all seem very happy with the reduced toil and added safety.

We carried five foresails but used the big 155% number one genoa nearly all of the time, only changing to the 130% (320 square feet) number two genoa when we knew we would be going to windward in a stiff breeze. This was rare as we were generally headed west thus mostly downwind. Other foresails included a short hoist No. 3 Genoa and two storm jibs. These last two were tiny bulletproof sails, with one for use with the headfoil, while the smaller one was for use in extreme conditions and was hanked on the jack stay which could be moved forward to a mid-foredeck pad-eye to become an inner forestay. Our original mainsail was of a racing design, drooping at the end of the boom, and for safety we kept in a permanent flattening reef so that the boom cleared our heads when gybing. In Australia we had a new mainsail made, designed so that the outer end of the boom was slightly higher than the gooseneck. This was safer for gybing and the boom was less likely to touch the water on a roll. It also gave more height for the bimini cover over the cockpit and facilitated collecting rain from the mainsail into a bag and tube at the gooseneck. In a tropical storm our tanks filled in fifteen minutes. We also changed the reefing positions, with the three points dividing the sail into quarters. Our experience was that if a reef was needed at all, a significant reduction in mainsail size was generally required for the changing conditions. Our mainsail had conventional slides and battens and we decided against a full-battened main as there can be major chafe problems with these when sailing downwind offshore.

We had both cruising and racing spinnakers. As a cruising spinnaker requires an angle of at least 20 degrees off downwind we mostly flew the racing spinnaker, and used this frequently in 10-15 knot winds. We hoisted it at dawn and lowered it again at dusk. We found winds were often more fluky, and line squalls harder to detect, at night and after one collapse, on a particularly black evening, when the spinnaker tightly wrapped and 'glued' itself to the sun strip on the genoa, we vowed never again to leave it up after dark.

It is significant that virtually all boats which have been in the Tropics for a while have a bimini sun cover over the cockpit. With the depleting ozone layer, in our opinion it is not cyclones, pirates or mosquitoes that are your greatest enemies, it is the sun. As mentioned both Andy and I have had scares with skin cancer. Besides protection from the ultra violet rays a bimini also makes being on watch far cooler and thus more pleasant. After adding ours in Panama we noticed the children were up in the cockpit all the time. In Singapore we added side curtains on the lifelines around the cockpit which also displayed the boat's name. We found these considerably reduced burning from the reflection off the water and made a far dryer cockpit in rough conditions.

To help cool the boat below we rigged nylon wind scoops on both the forward and main hatches. Andy installed hatches at the end of the aft cabins to create a through draught throughout the boat. It also made the cabins much lighter. He also added several 12-volt fans, as they only draw 0.2 amp they do not drain battery resources. As mentioned we first enjoyed them in the heat of the Mediterranean summer, and have steadily added more. We now have fans over every berth, over school work areas, the galley and the chart table. We frequently have them running twenty four hours a day in hot, humid conditions. The correlation between fan running and family harmony is remarkable.

APPENDIX C

Equipment List

SAILS
- mainsail with 3 reefs—321 sq.ft.
- medium air 150% Hood furling genoa—533 sq.ft.
- No. 2 130% genoa—320 sq.ft.
- No. 3 100% short hoist Genoa 210 sq. ft.
- No. 1 storm jib—83 sq.ft.
- No. 2 storm jib—36 sq. ft.
- spinnakers—asymmetric cruising and tri-radial racing

RIGGING
- anodized aluminium 55' keel-stepped mast with double spreaders and internal halyards
- anodized aluminium boom with 3 internal reefing lines and topping lift
- 1 x 19 stainless steel shrouds and stays: lowers, uppers, intermediates, baby stay, forestay, split adjustable backstay and running backstays
- aluminum and stainless steel blocks, chromed bronze turnbuckles

DECK FITTINGS
- genoa tracks and cars
- cabin top main traveller and car
- boomvang (5-1 purchase)
- preventers (rope with light weight shackles (see chapter 10)
- 2 genoa halyards and 2 spinnaker halyards—all lines (except genoa halyard and reefing) come back to the cockpit
- teak handrails
- teak covered cockpit seats
- teak grating in self-bailing cockpit
- wheel steering and binnacle compass
- emergency tiller
- 2 lazarette lockers and one cockpit locker
- opening transom for propane and spare fuel
- 2 Goiot (500MM x 500MM) opening hatches with vents (main and forward cabins)
- 1 Goiot (185 MM x 320 MM) opening hatch with vent in main head
- 5 Goiot portholes for aft cabins and aft head ventilation
- 2 opening hatches added aft in stern cabins for through ventilation
- 2 life rings and man overboard pole
- Beaufort 6-man liferaft in offshore pack—with food, water, fishing gear, anchor, EPIRB, solar blankets and solar still
- 2xSolarex 50 watt solar panels
- Rutland wind generator

- Rope and block tackle to hoist the outboard engine from wind generator support
- Manual bilge pump
- salt water deck wash/emergency pump
- Beaufort 6 man liferaft
- 10 Lewmar 2 speed winches (various sizes)

ANCHORS AND EQUIPMENT

- 2 anchor rollers
- 33lb (15 kilo) Bruce anchor
    —with 120' CHAIN AND 200' octoplait rope in the Mediterranean
    —with 300' high tensile chain for the remainder of the voyage
- 24 kilo (53lb) FOB anchor
- 18lb (8 kilo) Danforth Kedge anchor
- anchor windlass—first a Simpson Lawrence manual 555 replaced by an electric Nillsen Maxwell V700
- self-bailing anchor locker

SELF-STEERING

- Autohelm 6000, Series 2 linear drive
- Autohelm 800
- Aries windvane

ENGINE and BATTERIES

- PERKINS 4-108M diesel engine in sound insulated engine compartment
- s/s fuel tank 35 Imp. gals
- 2 x 120 amp hr batteries at the beginning, 6 x 110 amp hr deep cycle at finish
- Charging system—90 amp hr alternator with high output, multistage regulator
- 40 litre hot water tank

ELECTRICS AND ELECTRONICS

(Changes due to a lightning strike off South Africa)
- Navigation—Navstar Transit Satnav A 300s then GPS Navstar XR4
- Log: Brooks and Gatehouse then Autohelm
- Wind instruments: Plastimo then Autohelm
- Depth Sounder: initially Seafarer with alarms then Autohelm
- Weather fax: FAX MATE, then SEA with a Kodak Dikonix Printer linked to HF radio
- Radios:
    —VHF Demek RS 1000   —VHF SMR Handheld
    —HF Icom 735   —Panasonic shortwave receiver
- Radar: Apelco LDR 9910, 8 mile range
- Radio Direction Finder (RDF): Brooks and Gatehouse
- Refrigeration: initially a 12 volt electric refrigerator, in Australia changed to deepfreeze/ refrigerator engine driven with hold-over plates
- EPIRB x 2 (Emergency Position Indicating Radio Beacons)

Glossary of Terms

(Definitions Specific to **Just Cruising**)

BEAM Off one side of the boat

AFT At the back of the boat; behind

ANTIFOULING Bottom paint, to deter growth of weed, barnacles etc.

ASTERN To go backwards; behind the boat

AUTOPILOT Electro/mechanical steering device for automatic course keeping

BACKS, BACKING When the wind changes in an anti- clockwise direction

BACKSTAY Wire supporting the mast which attaches to back of boat

BAGGYWRINKLE Material on the shrouds, to stop chafe damage to sails, traditionally made out of old rope

BEAM Width of a boat at its widest point; 'On the beam'—at right angles to the length of the boat

BEAM REACH Sailing at about 90° to the wind direction

BEAR AWAY To alter course away from the wind

BEATING To sail into wind by zig-zagging (TACKING) towards it

BEAUFORT SCALE International scale of wind strength, Forces 0-12

BELOW Inside the boat

BERTH A bed; To berth—to come into the dock; A berth—the place in which a boat lies at the dock

BILGE Space under the floor boards

BINNACLE A stand in the cockpit on which the compass in supported. On Bagheera it also supports the steering and engine controls

BLOCK A pulley

BOOM Horizontal spar supporting the bottom of the mainsail

BOOM VANG Tackle from the boom to the deck to keep the boom from lifting (also called a kicking strap)

BOSUN'S CHAIR A chair for going up the mast generally made from wood and canvas and hooked onto a halyard

BOW The front of the boat

BROACH Heading up into wind uncontrollably

BULKHEAD An interior divider like a wall in a house

BUOY A floating device anchored to the sea's bottom. Used as markers for navigation, automatic weather reporting, to enable vessels to tie up, as fishing net markers etc.

CAST OFF Undo a mooring or towing line

CATAMARAN Boat with two hulls

CHAIN PLATE Place on the hull where rigging supporting the mast is secured

CHART Nautical map showing navigational aids, depths, hazards and land forms

'CHUTE Spinnaker

CLEAT Fitting on which to secure a line

CLEW Aft bottom corner of a sail

CLOSE-HAULED (on the wind) Sailing the boat as close to the wind as possible, sails are hauled in and boat may heel

COCKPIT A recessed part of the deck in which to sit and steer (in the stern in *Bagheera*)

COMPANIONWAY Entry and stairway to get below

DEAD RECKONING (DR) Estimate of the boat's position based on course and speed

DECKHEAD Underside of the deck (ceiling in a house)

DEPTH SOUNDER An electronic instrument that measures the depth of the water below the boat

DEATH ROLL Side-to-side uncontrollable motion when going downwind

DINGHY A small boat or tender

DRAFT Depth of the boat below the waterline

DRAGGING When an anchor slips along the bottom

DROGUE A device trailed behind a boat to create drag

EPIRB Emergency Position Indicating Radio Beacon

FATHOM A measurement of depth still used but being superseded by metres. 1 fathom = 6 feet

FENDERS (bumpers) Inflated cylinders used to protect the sides of the boat when berthed

FEND OFF To push the boat away from an object so no damage occurs

FIDDLES Strips of metal or wood to stop objects from sliding off e.g. the stove or table

FLOOD TIDE A rising tide

FOOT Bottom edge of a sail

FOREDECK Deck at the front of a boat

FOREGUY (downhaul) Line to pull down the spinnaker pole

FORESTAY Wire supporting the mast which is attached to the front of the boat

FORWARD Towards the front or bow

FREEBOARD The height of the hull between the water and the deck

FRONT Leading edge of a moving mass of cold or warm air. Cold fronts are usually associated with rain, lightning and squalls. Warm fronts are associated with heavy clouds and rain.

FURL Mainsail—To drop and lash to the boom. Genoa—To roll round a vertical aluminum extrusion which rotates around the forestay

FURLING GEAR Equipment used to enable furling of the genoa

GALLEY Boat kitchen

GENOA Large foresail (overlaps the mainsail)

GIMBALS A device to enable an object, such as a compass or galley stove, to remain horizontal regardless of the boat's motion

GOOSENECK Hinged fitting which attach the boom to the mast

GPS (GLOBAL POSITIONING SYSTEM) Position indicating electronic navigational aid

GO ABOUT (to tack) To turn the bow through the wind when sailing

GUST Sudden increase in wind

GYBE (jibe) To change course downwind so that the sails change sides (can be dangerous when unplanned)

HALYARD Line for hoisting sails

HANKS Clips for attaching foresail to the forestay

HATCH An opening through the deck

HEAD(S) Boat toilet

HEAD OF SAIL Top corner of the sail

HEADSAILS Sails that attach forward of the mast

HEAD-TO-WIND When the front of the boat, or bow, points into wind

HEEL When boat leans over at an angle (most severe when beating in a strong wind)

HELM To steer; steering device (*Bagheera* has a wheel)

HOIST Pull up

HULL Main body of the boat

JIB Small foresail (in front of the mast)

KEEL Appendage under the hull running fore and aft, needed for vertical stability and to prevent leeway. (*Bagheera* has a cast iron keel encased in epoxy and bolted onto the hull

KNOT One nautical mile per hour; method of fastening a line

LAZARETTE Storage lockers on deck aft of the steering wheel

LEE CLOTH Length of Canvas secured at the side of a berth to keep occupant in when boat heels or rolls

LEECH The trailing edge of a sail (back edge)

LEE SHORE Coast onto which the wind is blowing

LEE SIDE, (LEEWARD SIDE) Side of the boat away from the direction of the wind

LEEWAY Sideways drift

LIFELINE Lines around the boat to stop people falling overboard (*Bagheera* has double lines)

LIFERAFT Specially designed inflatable raft with food, water and an EPIRB for use when the yacht has to be abandoned

LIFERING Floating ring to throw to a person who has fallen overboard

LOG Measures distance through the water (ours also gives boat speed and water temperature)

LOGBOOK, OR THE LOG Regular record of boats progress with position, speed, weather etc.

LUFF Front edge of a sail

MAINSAIL Sail attached to the main mast (on Bagheera it is smaller than the No. 1 genoa)

MAKE FAST Tie securely

MAST Vertical spar which supports the sails

MASTHEAD Top of the mast

MOORED Boat is tied to a permanent object e.g. a mooring buoy

NAVIGATION LIGHTS Lights used at night. Red faces port (left side) and green faces starboard (right), white faces aft. (*Bagheera* had 2 sets, one at deck level and the other at the top of the mast)

NEAP TIDES Smaller changes in the height of the tide, occur twice monthly at the half moon (alternate with spring tides)

OARLOCK, OR ROWLOCK Fitting which acts as a pivot point for an oar

OFF THE WIND Sailing on a reach or run

ON THE WIND See close-hauled

OUTBOARD Outside the perimeter of the deck; portable engine for a dinghy

PADEYE A fitting on deck used for attaching lines or blocks

PAINTER Dinghy tie-up or towing line

PORT SIDE Left side of the boat when looking forward

PORT TACK When the wind comes on the port side, (sails will be to starboard)

PREVENTER Line leading forward which holds the boom at right angles to the boat when going downwind, to prevent a gybe

PULPIT Metal railing at bow and stern to which the lifelines are attached

QUARTER Between astern and abeam (back and middle) of the boat

RADAR Electronic instrument for detecting and tracking other vessels, land and storms

RADIO, HF High frequency for long distance

VHF Very high frequency for short range

RAFT UP Tie alongside another vessel

REACHING Sailing when the wind is on the beam, the sail is approximately halfway out.

REEF A ridge of rocks which is at or near the surface; a portion of sail furled and tied down to reduce the area exposed to the wind

RIG To prepare a boat for sailing; the mast and its supports

RIGGING The equipment required to use sails, i.e. spars, sheets, shrouds, stays and halyards

RUNNING To sail with the wind from behind the boat

RUNNING BACKSTAYS Adjustable lines supporting the back of the mast

SAILS Shaped dacron, or other strong material, used to catch the wind and propel the boat through the water

SAIL TIES Webbing strips used to tie the sails when furled

SATELLITE NAVIGATION, OR SAT NAV Electronic device that aids navigation

SET Trimming a sail for the wind direction; course error due to current

SEXTANT An instrument used to aid navigation by measuring altitudes of celestial bodies and hence determining position of the boat

SHEET A line attached to the sail used to adjust its position

SHROUDS Wire supports on either side of the mast

SOLE Floor of the interior of the boat

SPAR A mast or boom

SPINNAKER Lightweight, parachute-like sail (usually colourful) used when the wind is aft of the beam

SPINNAKER POLE A boom attached to the mast at one end and the spinnaker at the other, used to support and control the spinnaker

SPREADERS Short struts between the mast and the shrouds to add support to the rig

SPRING TIDES Greatest change in the height of the tide, occurs twice monthly at the new and full moons (alternates with neap tides)

STANCHIONS Metal supports for lifelines around the boat

STARBOARD Right side of the vessel when looking forward

STARBOARD TACK Sailing with wind on the starboard (right) side of the boat, (sails will be to port)

STAY Wire supporting the mast fore and aft

STERN The back of the boat

STOWING Securing or putting away

TACK Act of passing the bow through the wind when sailing; the front corner of the sail

TIDE The rise and fall of the sea level due to the gravitational pull of the moon and sun

TOPPING LIFT (uphaul) Lines supporting main boom and spinnaker pole

TOPSIDES Area of hull above the water line

TRANSOM Flat part across the back of boat

TRIM Fine tune a sail

TRIMARAN Boat with three hulls

VEER When the wind changes in a clockwise direction

WATERLINE Demarkation between portion of hull above water and below

WEATHER FAX Instrument for receiving graphic weather charts

WINCH Round metal drum with detachable handle for winding in lines

WIND GENERATOR Wind driven electricity-producing device

WIND INSTRUMENTS Devices that measure wind speed and determine its direction

WINDLASS Mechanical or electrical device to lift anchor and chain

WINDSHIFT Change in wind direction

WINDVANE steering A device which automatically steers a boat at a pre-set angle to the wind

WINDWARD Direction from which the wind is blowing

WING ON WING Sailing downwind with the genoa and mainsails on opposite sides to catch more wind

About the Copeland Family

LIZA—Born in 1946 Liza grew up in Twickenham, England and studied Medical Social Work at Trinity College, Dublin. She emigrated to Canada in 1967 and completed an Hons BA in Psychology at Queens University in Kingston, Ontario, and a Teaching Certificate and Masters Degree in Special Education from the University of British Columbia in Vancouver. Her working career includes Vocational Rehabilitation, Medical Social Work and Educational Psychology, mostly in hospital settings.

Liza grew up racing on the Thames River, the Solent, on University teams and in several RORC events offshore. She and Andy met in a sailing championship in the Caribbean. They ran charter boats together for two years and were married aboard the yacht *Ticonderoga*. They came to live in Vancouver in 1973 where they continued to race, and cruise in the local waters with the family.

Since returning from the voyage Liza has been busy with several slide shows, working on a multi-grade education programme related to the family's world travels, writing articles and **Just Cruising**, and helping the family get re-adjusted to regular life—she has succeeded with every-one but her husband!

ANDY—Born in 1934 Andy grew up in Portugal and in Seaview, Isle of Wight, England. An officer in the Royal Navy, he was a fighter-pilot for ten years, obtaining both Naval and Airforce Instructor qualifications. He spent seven years in the Caribbean, in the charter and marine business, before coming to Vancouver and becoming a yacht broker. Since returning he has formed a new yacht brokerage company.

DUNCAN, COLIN AND JAMIE are now aged 17, 15 and 10 years and are in grades 12, 10, and 6 respectively. Duncan and Colin are very content to be regular social teenagers. Duncan is also involved in team sports, and plays Rugby for the Province, while Colin has followed artistic pursuits—ceramics, art, drama, and is a knowledgeable gardener. Jamie also enjoys a regular lifestyle, but is still happy to spend time cruising in *Bagheera*. He has become an keen Optimist dinghy sailor.